*image* COMICS PRESENTS

# INVINCIBLE
## FAMILY MATTERS

D1318223

**CREATED BY**
# ROBERT KIRKMAN
# & CORY WALKER

*image*

**Writer, Letterer**

# Robert Kirkman

**Penciler, Inker**

# Cory Walker

**Colorist**

# Bill Crabtree

WWW.IMAGECOMICS.COM

**FOR IMAGE:**
**JIM VALENTINO**
PUBLISHER
**ERIC STEPHENSON**
DIR. OF MARKETING
**BRENT BRAUN**
DIR. OF PRODUCTION
**TRACI HALE**
CONTROLLER/FOREIGN LIC.
**BRETT EVANS**
ART DIRECTOR
**ALLEN HUI**
WEB DEVELOPER
**CINDIE ESPINOZA**
ACCOUNTING ASSISTANT
**TIM HEGARTY**
BOOK TRADE COORDINATOR

INVINCIBLE
VOL. I: FAMILY MATTERS
AUGUST 2003. FIRST PRINTING.
Published by Image Comics, Inc. Office of publica-
tion: 1071 N. Batavia St. Suite A, Orange, CA 92867.
Image and its logos are ® and © 2003 Image
Comics, Inc. All rights reserved. Originally published
in single magazine form as Invincible #1-4. INVINCI-
BLE and all related characters are ™ and © 2003
Robert Kirkman and Cory Walker. All rights
reserved.The story presented in this publication is
fictional. Any similarities to events or persons living
or dead is purely coincidental. With the exception of
artwork used for review purposes, no portion of this
publication may be reproduced by any means without the expressed written permission of the copy-
right holder.
PRINTED IN USA

# THE EVIL THAT IS ROBERT KIRKMAN

*Run.  Run, and whatever you do, don't look back.*
*-- Erik Larsen*

*Listen to me.  For the love of God, listen to me.  Don't try to understand it.*
*Just go.  And go quickly.*
*-- Eric Stephenson*

*It's too late – too late for us.  Leave us -- just save yourself.*
*-- Jim Valentino*

If only I'd listened.

Understand something.  I don't know Robert Kirkman.  I've never met Robert Kirkman, at least not that I'm aware of.  He could be six foot two, with a full head of wavy blond hair, a cleft in his chin and the build of a champion surfer.  But that's not how I think of him.  I think of him as about four foot eight and hydrocephalic, with a head like a pumpkin.  Lank thin hair, beady little eyes, and a shriveled body that you'd barely think could hold that enormous head up.  And his voice.  One of those voices like nails on a blackboard, that suddenly shrills out behind you when you were thinking of something else, and you're halfway to the ceiling, nerves on fire, before you even realize what you've heard.

If only I'd listened.

*

But no, here I am.

Like the vast majority of smart-thinking Americans, I passed up Invincible #1 at least twice.  Heard about the new Image "superhero line," saw the books in the catalog, and breezed right by Invincible.  Just another superhero book, I thought.  I've got a complete run of *Nova*.  Of *Firestorm*.  Of *Speedball*, for Pete's sake.  This isn't anything I need.  Firebreather, that's what I went for.  *Firebreather* and *Dominion*.

Smart man.

And then the books came out, and there I was in the comics shop, and there was Invincible, and I passed it up again.  Didn't even pick it up and flip through it.  Just another superhero cover, nothing special, don't bother.

Ah, for the days of freedom.  Were they really only months ago?

*

So here I am, writing introductions, suggesting cover copy, even coming up with cover concepts (like the one for the cover to the volume you currently hold in your hot little imperiled hands).  And all for free. All for that pumpkin-headed freak with the chalkboard voice, who cackles – I just know it, I know he cackles – as I slave away for his benefit.

I'm an Eisner Award-winning writer, for the love of heaven. A Harvey Award-winner! Multiple times over! I have interview requests to disdain, characters to abuse, fan hopes to dash. I have artists to torment, editors who still cling to faint hopes of getting me to do something on time! I'm a busy man!

And yet here I am, working for Kirkman when I could be getting *Astro City* out monthly. When *Avengers/JLA* could already be out. When I could be reading classic Little Lulu issues to my daughters. But no.

Kirkman. Goddamn Kirkman.

*

I ignored the warning signs. I saw people talking about Invincible on Erik Larsen's message board, but I missed that hysterical, compulsive undertone. I saw someone point out that the entire first issue was available to be read for free at the Image website. I figured what the hell, it's free, right?

Nothing's free. I should have listened to Larsen.

I went over to the Image site and I read it. Went back to the Larsen site to comment. Mostly just to rag on that first cover, which I thought was a big mistake, if you must know. And now look at me.

*

The thing is – and this is the dark secret they don't want you to know until it's too late – Kirkman's good. Really good.

Invincible is fun, fresh, energetic. It's not one of those superhero books that doesn't want to admit to liking superheroes, so it tries to put a different spin on it and winds up being an uncomfortable mélange of nothing. No, Invincible embraces its genre. It's a superhero book that loves being a superhero book, one that isn't out to deconstruct or expose or undermine or scathingly satirize. It just wants to be a good superhero book. And yet, it still manages to put a different spin on things, and winds up being distinctive and clever and alive, all the while standing foursquare at the heart of a longstanding, well-worked genre that many would say has nothing more to offer.

If only.

I think my favorite character is Mark's mom. Her casual acceptance of her family life, her tension when her "boys" are out of touch even by the reach of CNN, her matter-of-factness about the fantastic, that's the glue that makes this book work. I want to see an annual, *Invincible's Mom, Debbie Grayson*. It's that aspect – not contrast, but melding – of Mark's two worlds that makes Invincible so compelling.

It'd be okay if that was all there was to it. A new good comic? Fine, bring it on.

But Kirkman is relentless. Invincible led me to *Tech Jacket*. To the *Superpatriot* series he and Cory Walker did. To *Battle Pope*. And now there's *Brit* coming up. And *Capes*. And *Masters of the Universe*.

*Masters of the Universe*, for cryin' out loud!

And then there are the artists. Cory Walker is the one we're concerned about here, and his clean, clear storytelling, his deadpan characterization, his sleek designs, his distinctive, stylized rendering … it all brings the book to life in a way that'll make you feel you know these people. That you could sit down and have a conversation with them, at least while you weren't surreptitiously checking out Atom Eve's butt.

But there's E.J. Su on *Tech Jacket*. Tony Moore on *Battle Pope* and *Brit*. And they're all good. All distinctive, clear, solid, compelling. Where does he find these guys?

It's not natural, I tell you.

\*

So here you are. You may still have a choice. Maybe you're someone who's already been reading *Invincible*, and those proliferating other books. If so, never mind. You're as gone as I am, one of the chittering wrecks on the message board, unable resist trying to pass on your addiction, share it with the unwary. But maybe you just heard the buzz, or picked this up in the store because of that cool cover concept, or something. If so, then there's still time.

You're standing on the precipice, like I was. You can put this back on the shelf, back away slowly, and get on with your life. Or if you've already purchased the book, but you're just reading the intro before you get into the stories, well … you probably have a furnace, don't you?

Because otherwise, you'll take that step. You'll take it, and there'll be no turning back. You'll get swept up into Kirkman's world, one more helpless victim unable to break free, hopelessly drawn to each new release, to each new character, caught on tenterhooks between episodes, as you wait to see what'll happen next. Just one more Funk-O-Drone. You'll be recommending the book to friends, spreading the word online. You might even end up working for that hellish fiend for free.

He'll have you, then. And Kirkman doesn't let go.

\*

So listen to me. Listen carefully. Like I should have listened, when I was where you are now. But no, I was cocky. Confident. Foolish. *Doomed*.

It's too late for me. But you -- you can still get away. Can warn others.

Put the book down. Back away. For God's sake, don't turn that page.

And if you do, then remember this, in those still small hours:

*I warned you.*

-- Kurt Busiek

May 2003

**KURT BUSIEK has enough awards plaques to tile his bathroom, and enough damn statuettes to play chess on the result. He writes, in theory, for Marvel, DC, Wildstorm, Dark Horse and more. In fact, he should be doing paying work right now.**

**Think of the children, won't you? The children.**

# CHAPTER ONE

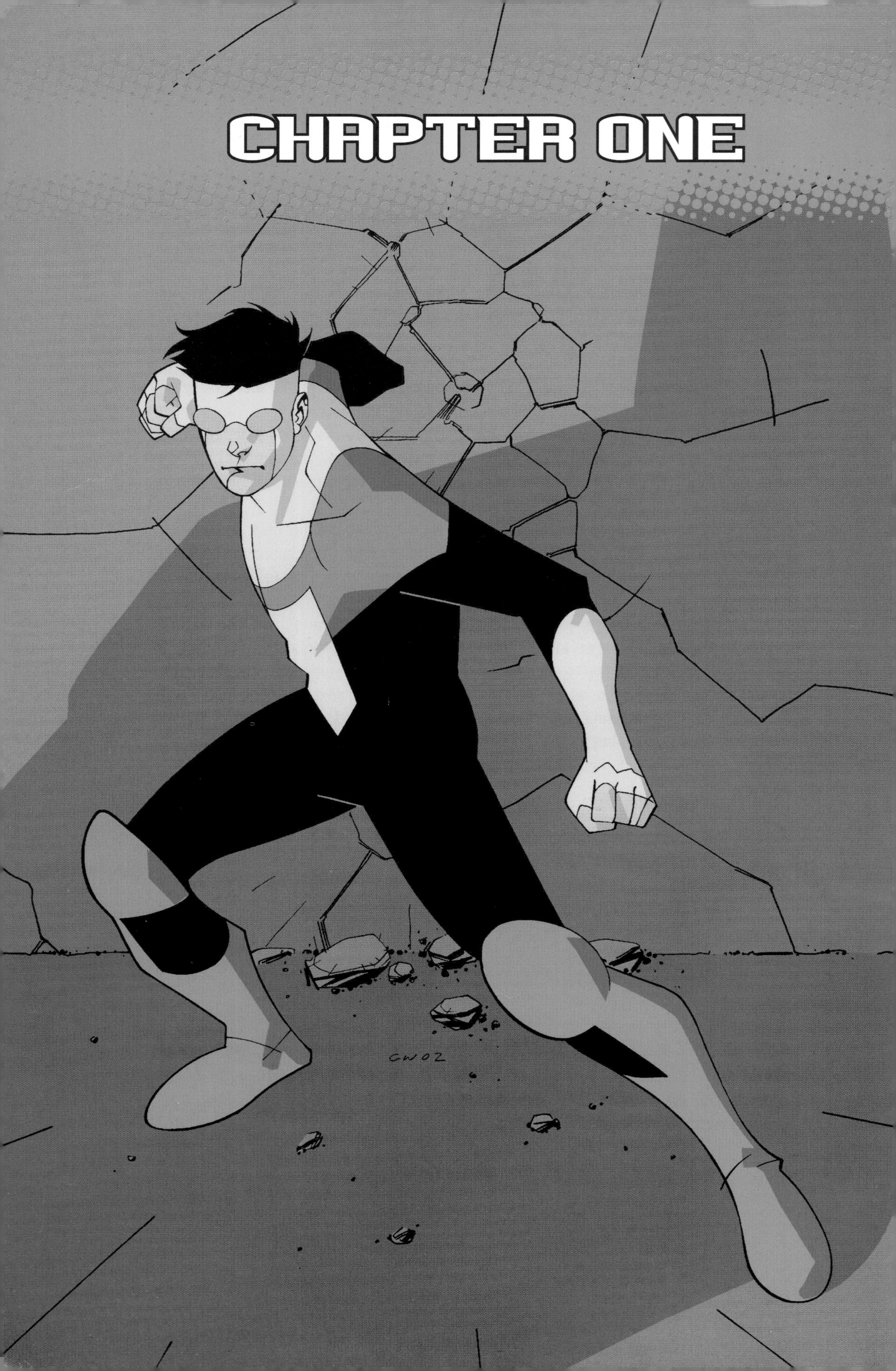

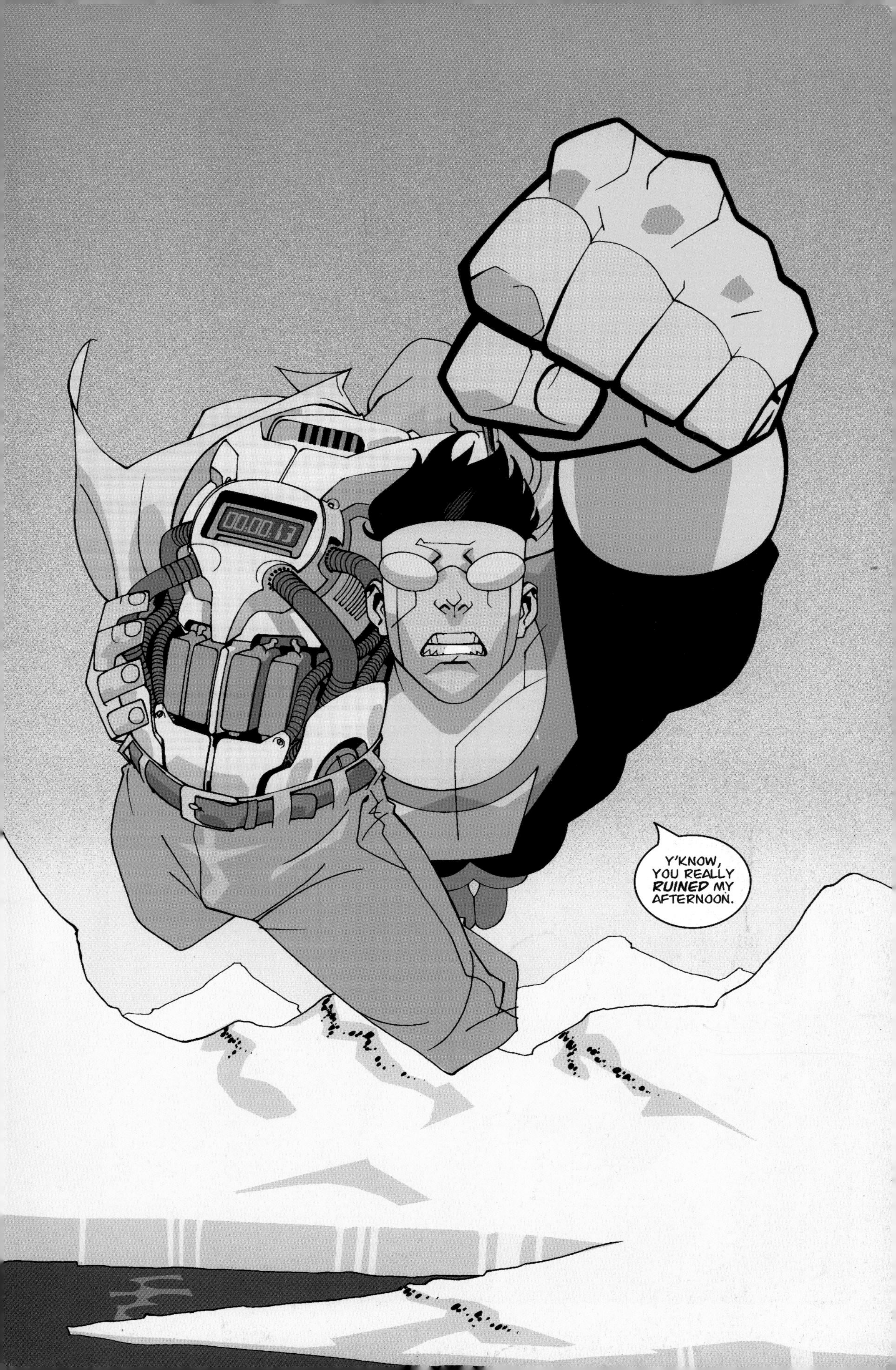
00:00:13
Y'KNOW, YOU REALLY **RUINED** MY AFTERNOON.

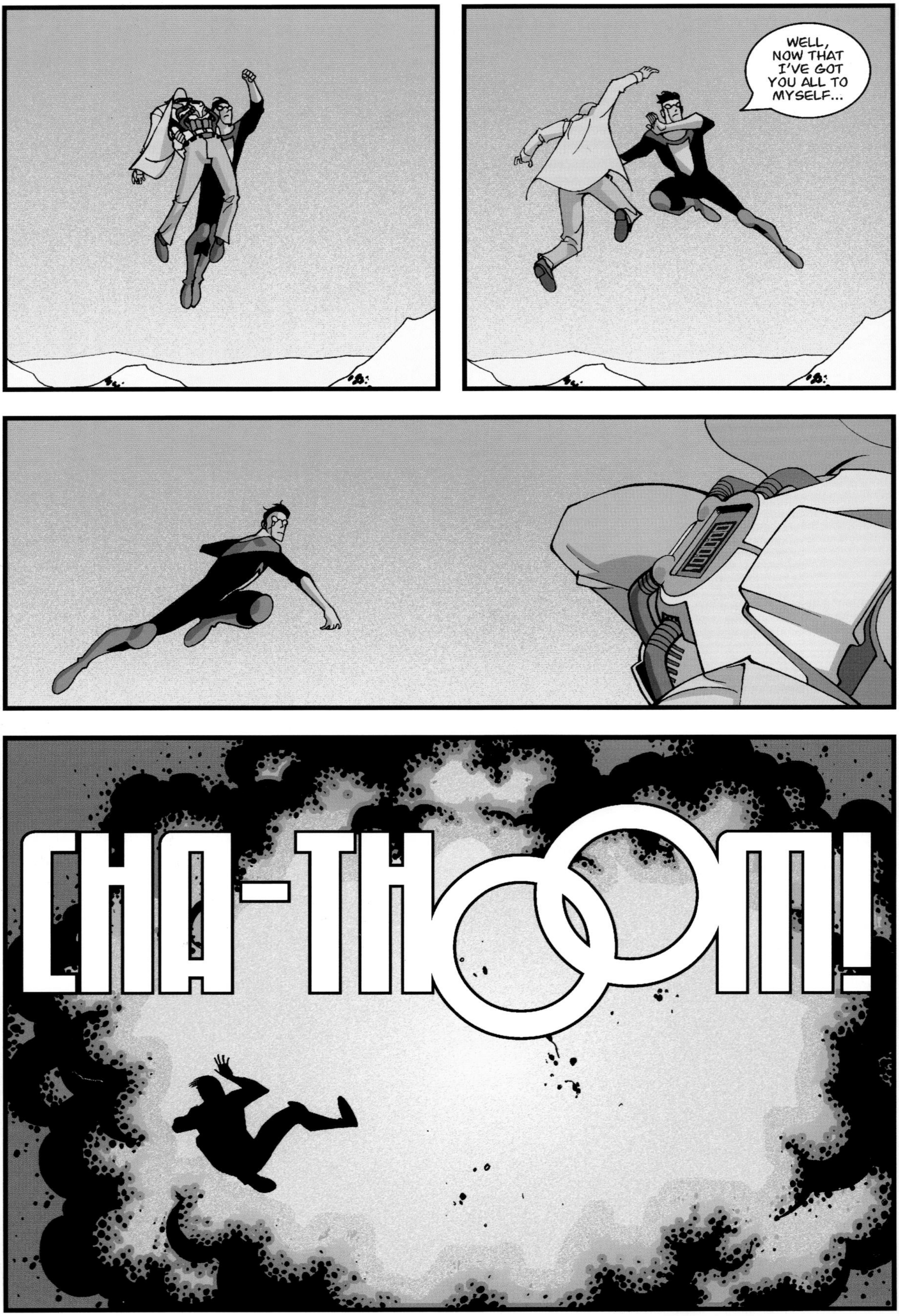
WELL, NOW THAT I'VE GOT YOU ALL TO MYSELF...
CHA-THOOM!

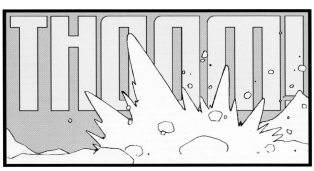

=SIGH=

IF I KEEP THIS UP I'M GOING TO GIVE MYSELF A HEART ATTACK!

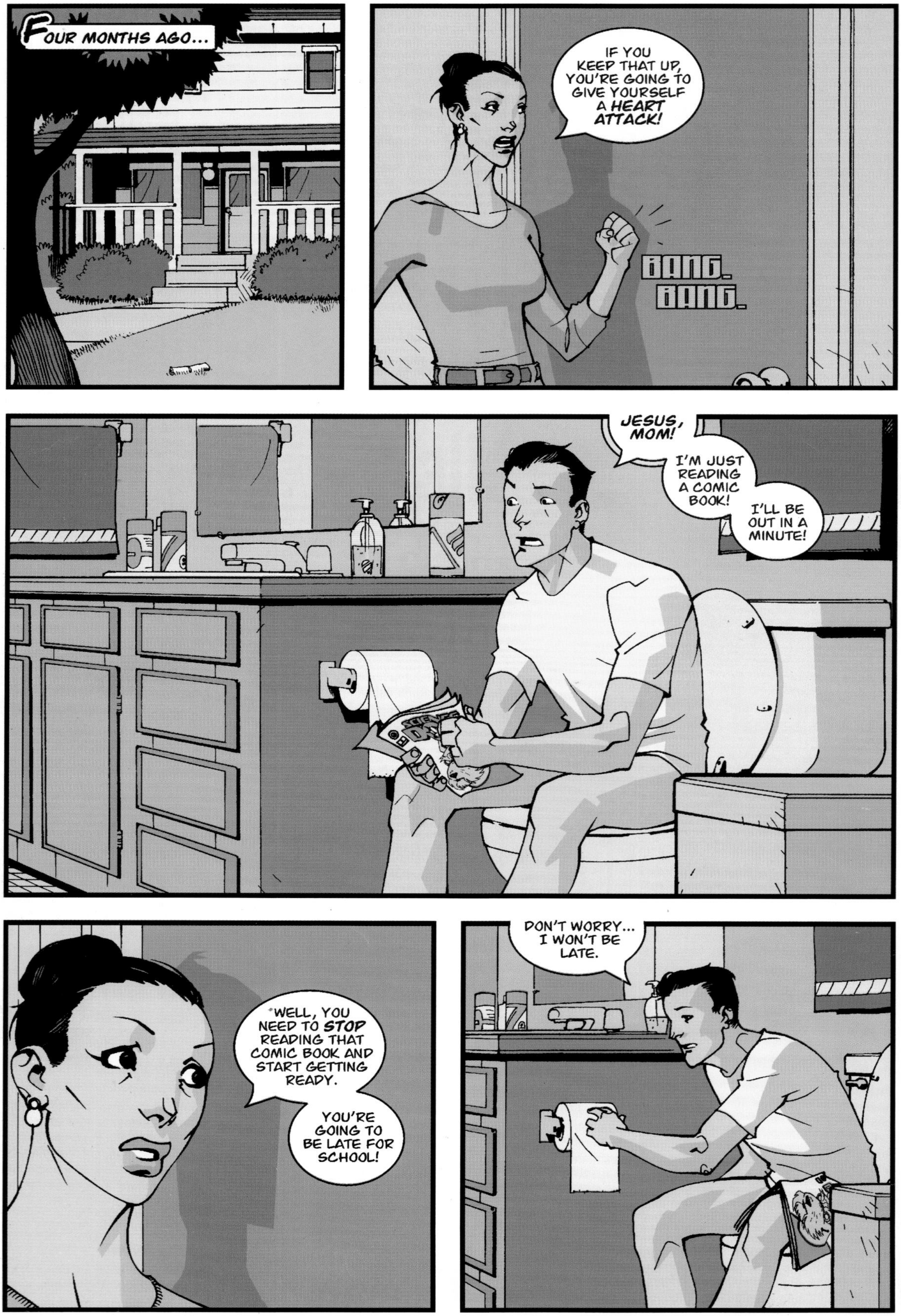
FOUR MONTHS AGO...
IF YOU KEEP THAT UP, YOU'RE GOING TO GIVE YOURSELF A HEART ATTACK!
BANG. BANG.
JESUS, MOM!
I'M JUST READING A COMIC BOOK!
I'LL BE OUT IN A MINUTE!
WELL, YOU NEED TO STOP READING THAT COMIC BOOK AND START GETTING READY.
YOU'RE GOING TO BE LATE FOR SCHOOL!
DON'T WORRY... I WON'T BE LATE.

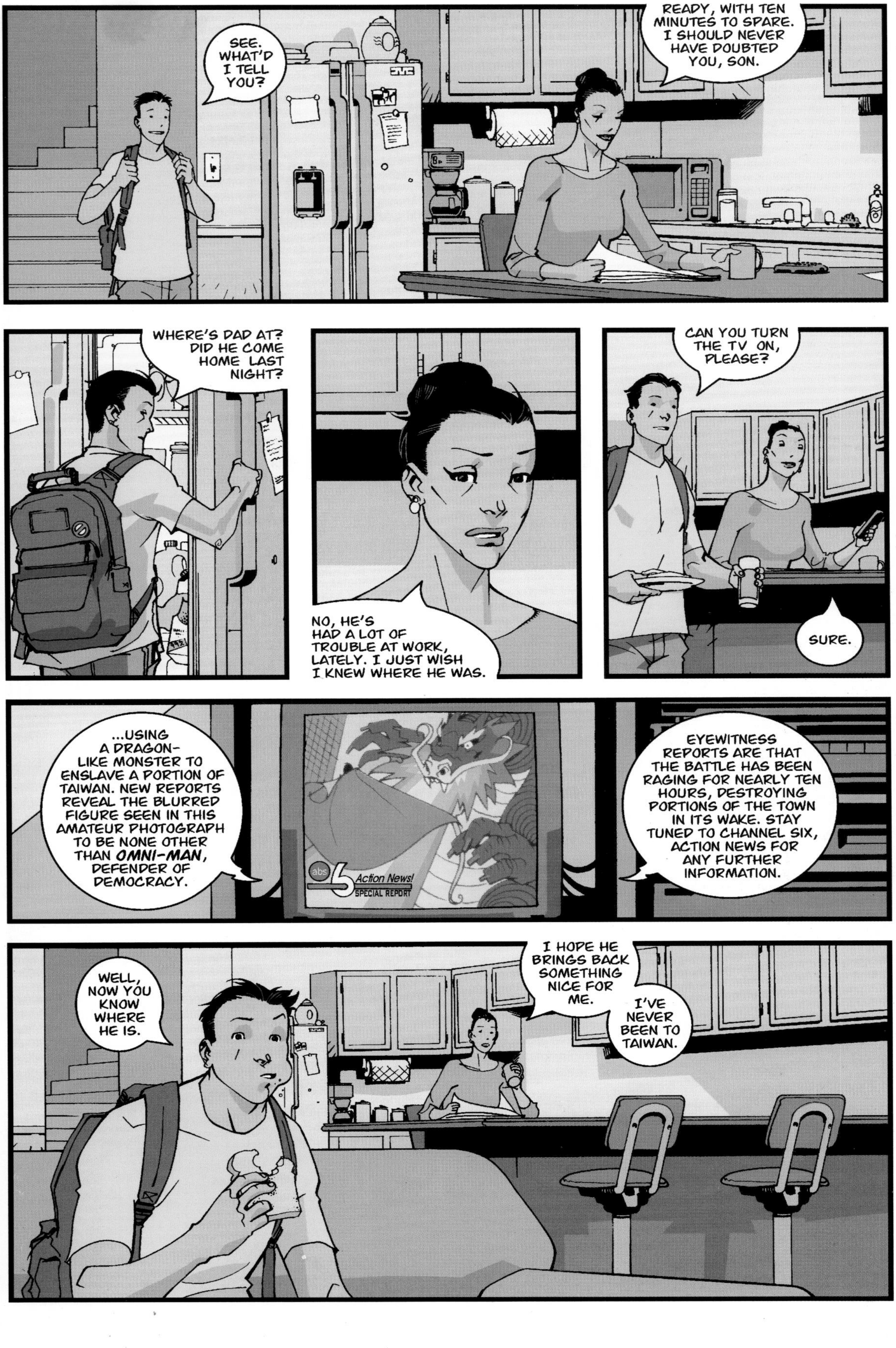
SEE. WHAT'D I TELL YOU?
READY, WITH TEN MINUTES TO SPARE. I SHOULD NEVER HAVE DOUBTED YOU, SON.
WHERE'S DAD AT? DID HE COME HOME LAST NIGHT?
NO, HE'S HAD A LOT OF TROUBLE AT WORK, LATELY. I JUST WISH I KNEW WHERE HE WAS.
CAN YOU TURN THE TV ON, PLEASE?
SURE.
...USING A DRAGON-LIKE MONSTER TO ENSLAVE A PORTION OF TAIWAN. NEW REPORTS REVEAL THE BLURRED FIGURE SEEN IN THIS AMATEUR PHOTOGRAPH TO BE NONE OTHER THAN OMNI-MAN, DEFENDER OF DEMOCRACY.
abs 6 Action News! SPECIAL REPORT
EYEWITNESS REPORTS ARE THAT THE BATTLE HAS BEEN RAGING FOR NEARLY TEN HOURS, DESTROYING PORTIONS OF THE TOWN IN ITS WAKE. STAY TUNED TO CHANNEL SIX, ACTION NEWS FOR ANY FURTHER INFORMATION.
WELL, NOW YOU KNOW WHERE HE IS.
I HOPE HE BRINGS BACK SOMETHING NICE FOR ME.
I'VE NEVER BEEN TO TAIWAN.

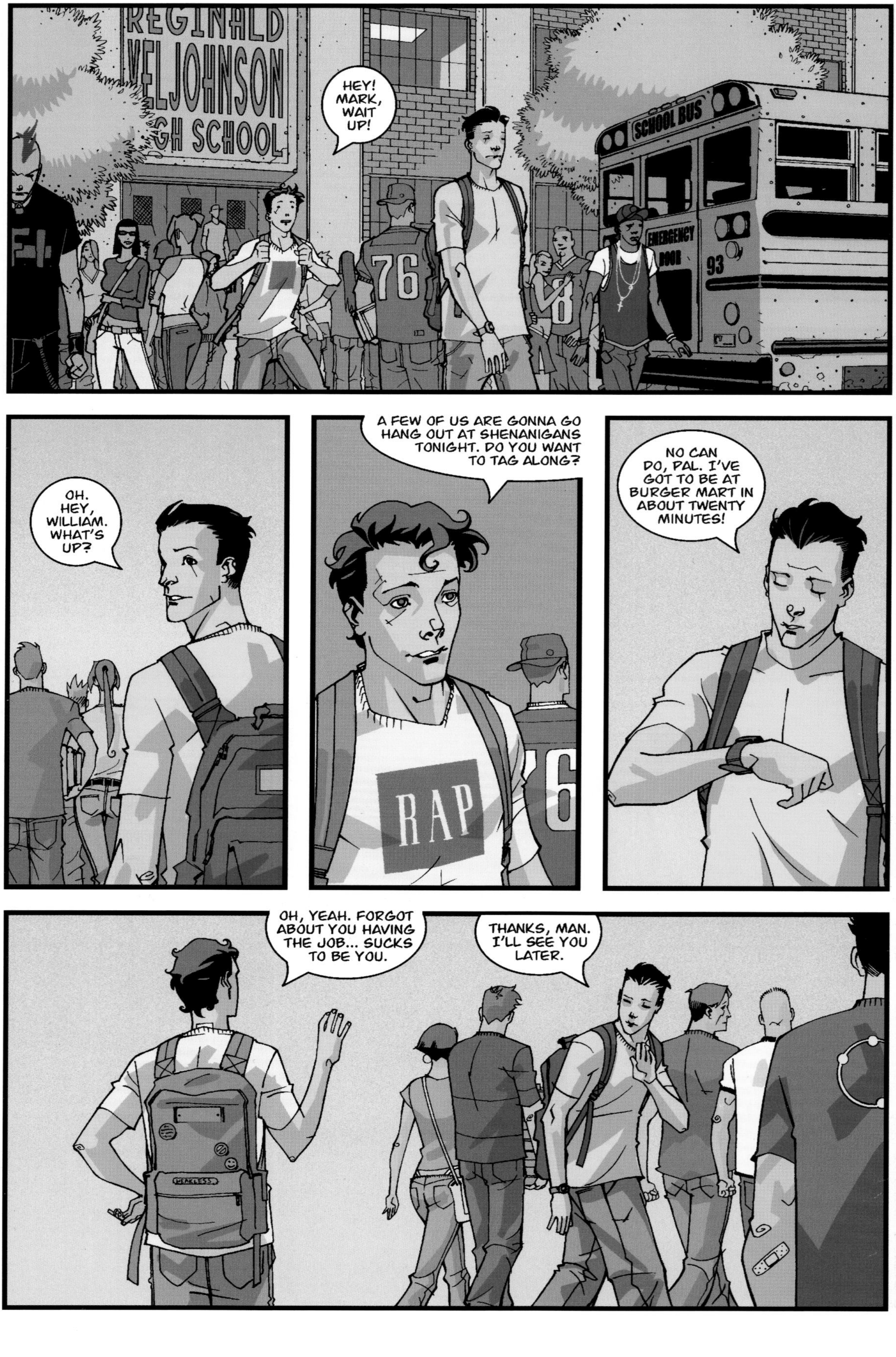
REGINALD VELJOHNSON GH SCHOOL
HEY! MARK, WAIT UP!
SCHOOL BUS
EMERGENCY DOOR
93
OH. HEY, WILLIAM. WHAT'S UP?
A FEW OF US ARE GONNA GO HANG OUT AT SHENANIGANS TONIGHT. DO YOU WANT TO TAG ALONG?
NO CAN DO, PAL. I'VE GOT TO BE AT BURGER MART IN ABOUT TWENTY MINUTES!
OH, YEAH. FORGOT ABOUT YOU HAVING THE JOB... SUCKS TO BE YOU.
THANKS, MAN. I'LL SEE YOU LATER.

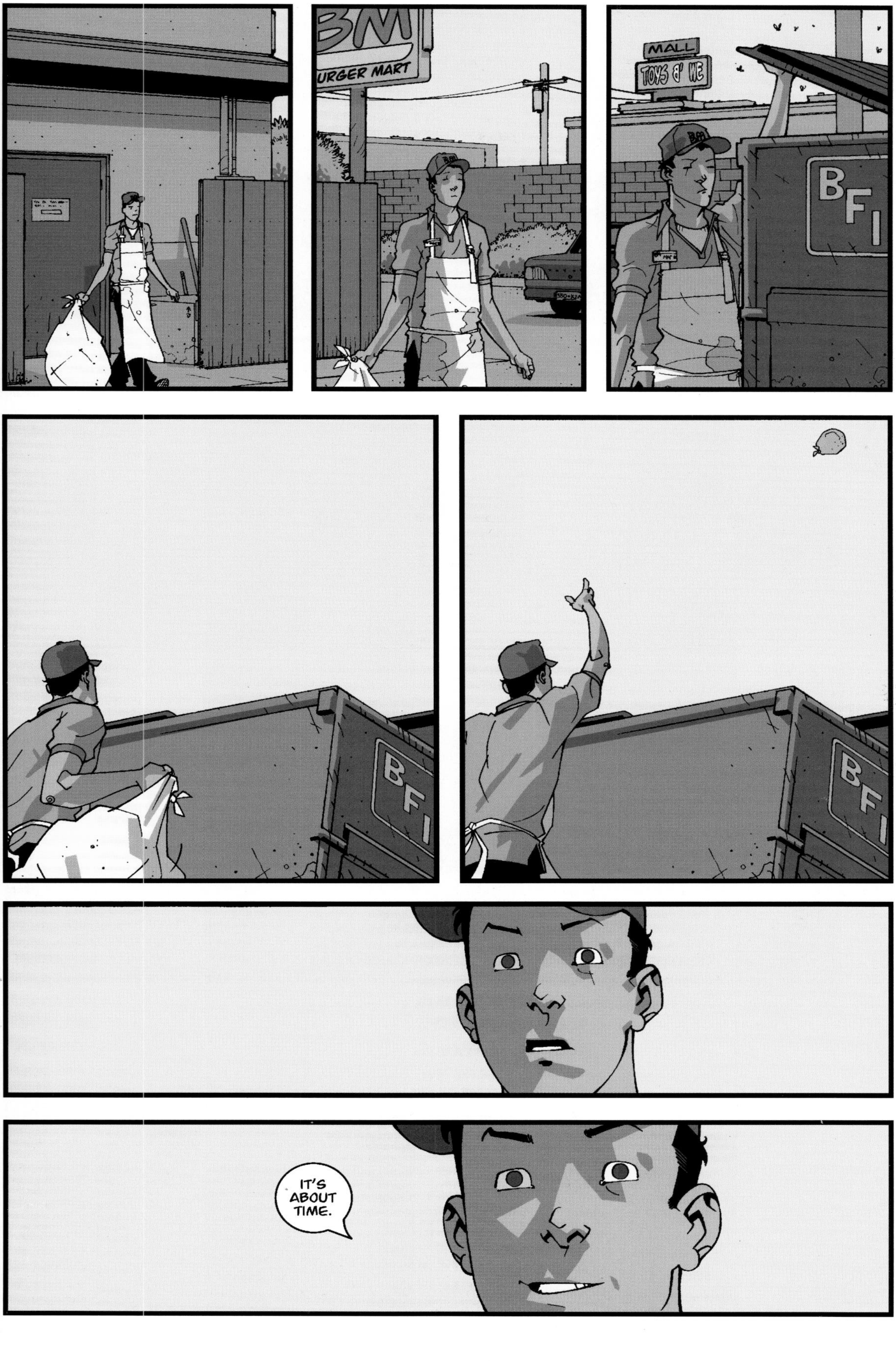
BM
URGER MART
MALL
TOYS 8' WE
BFI
BFI
BFI
IT'S ABOUT TIME.

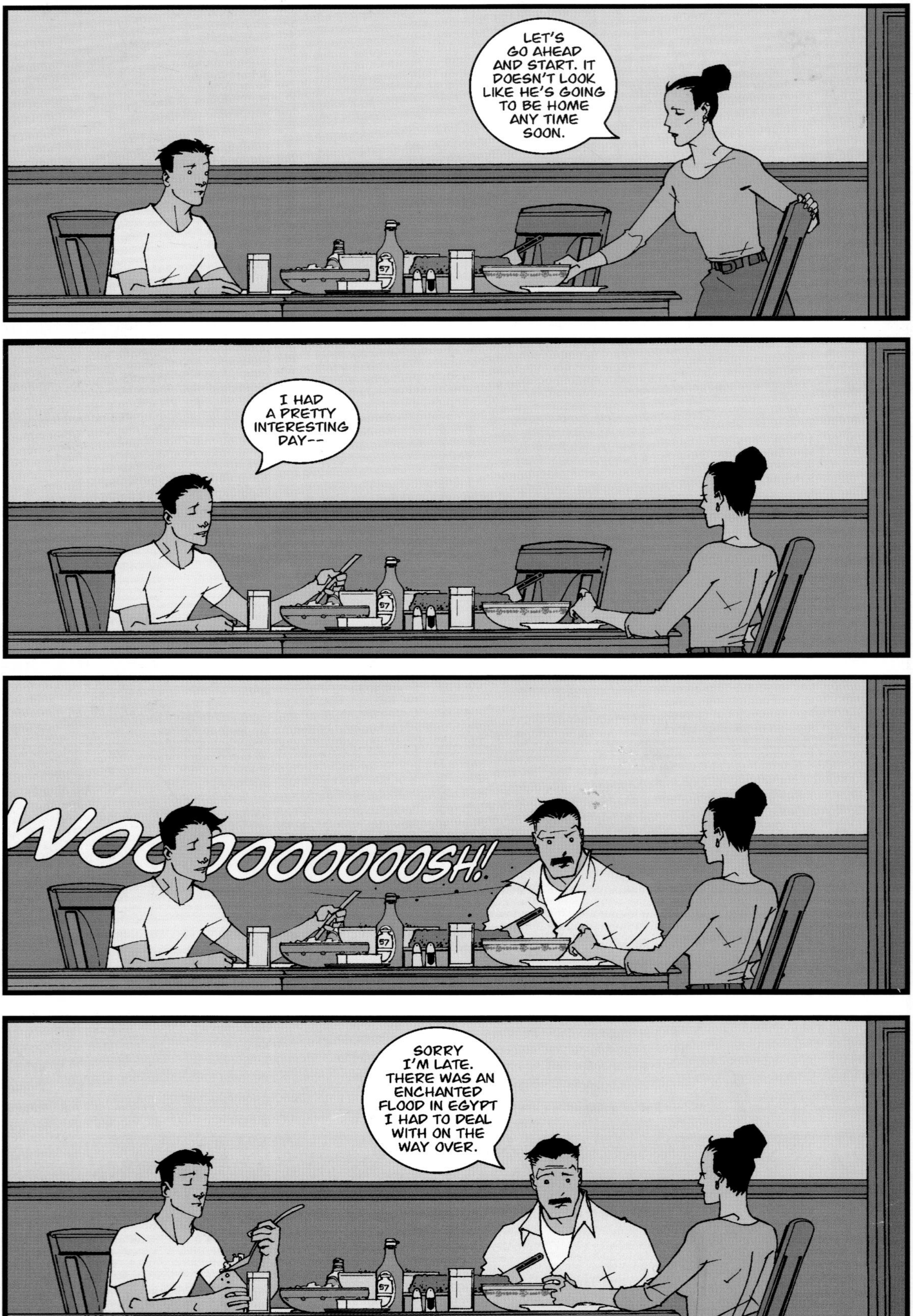
LET'S GO AHEAD AND START. IT DOESN'T LOOK LIKE HE'S GOING TO BE HOME ANY TIME SOON.
I HAD A PRETTY INTERESTING DAY--
WOOOOOOOOOOSH!
SORRY I'M LATE. THERE WAS AN ENCHANTED FLOOD IN EGYPT I HAD TO DEAL WITH ON THE WAY OVER.

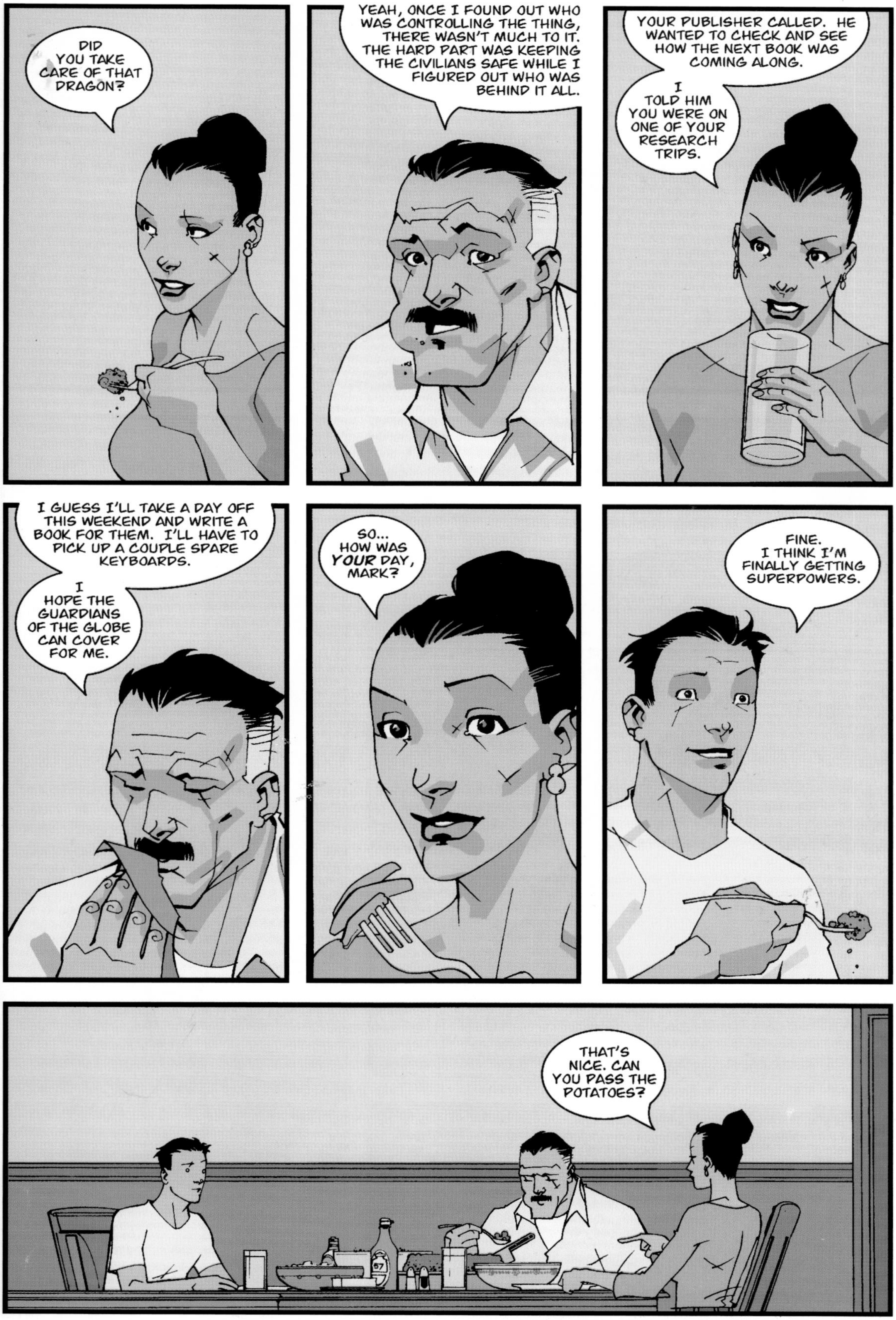
DID YOU TAKE CARE OF THAT DRAGON?
YEAH, ONCE I FOUND OUT WHO WAS CONTROLLING THE THING, THERE WASN'T MUCH TO IT. THE HARD PART WAS KEEPING THE CIVILIANS SAFE WHILE I FIGURED OUT WHO WAS BEHIND IT ALL.
YOUR PUBLISHER CALLED. HE WANTED TO CHECK AND SEE HOW THE NEXT BOOK WAS COMING ALONG.
I TOLD HIM YOU WERE ON ONE OF YOUR RESEARCH TRIPS.
I GUESS I'LL TAKE A DAY OFF THIS WEEKEND AND WRITE A BOOK FOR THEM. I'LL HAVE TO PICK UP A COUPLE SPARE KEYBOARDS.
I HOPE THE GUARDIANS OF THE GLOBE CAN COVER FOR ME.
SO... HOW WAS *YOUR* DAY, MARK?
FINE. I THINK I'M FINALLY GETTING SUPERPOWERS.
THAT'S NICE. CAN YOU PASS THE POTATOES?

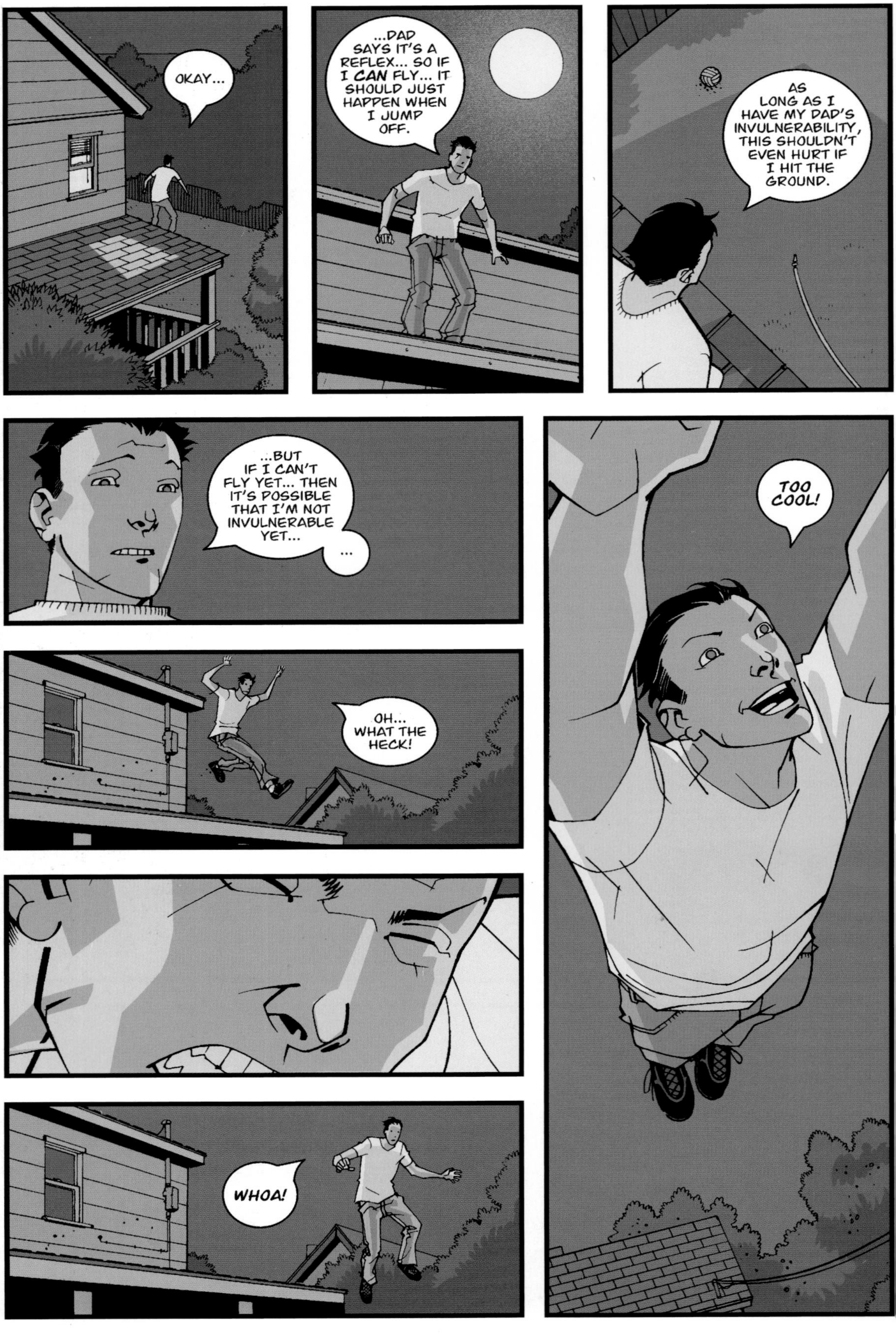
OKAY...
...DAD SAYS IT'S A REFLEX... SO IF I **CAN** FLY... IT SHOULD JUST HAPPEN WHEN I JUMP OFF.
AS LONG AS I HAVE MY DAD'S INVULNERABILITY, THIS SHOULDN'T EVEN HURT IF I HIT THE GROUND.
...BUT IF I CAN'T FLY YET... THEN IT'S POSSIBLE THAT I'M NOT INVULNERABLE YET...
...
OH... WHAT THE HECK!
WHOA!
TOO COOL!

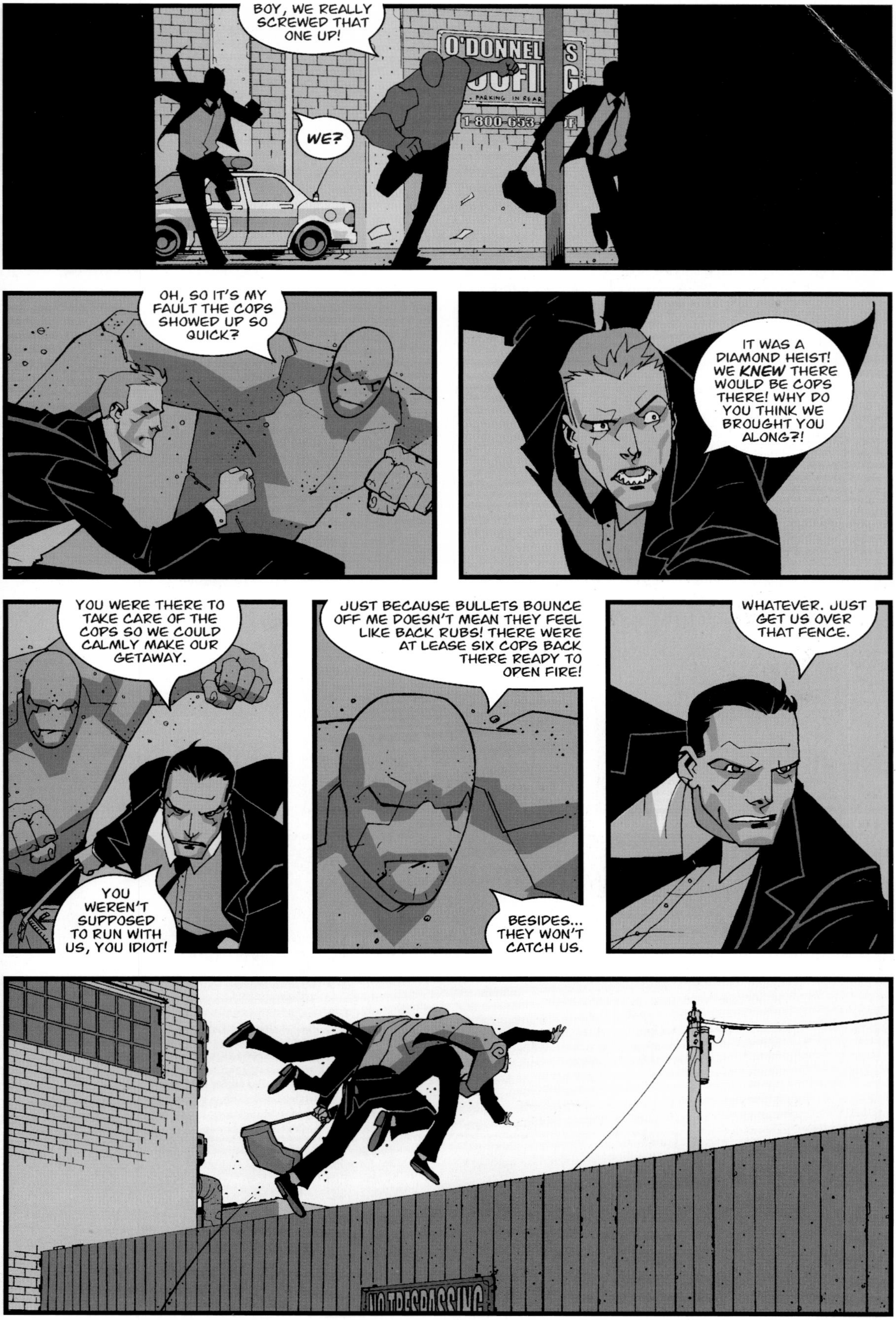
BOY, WE REALLY SCREWED THAT ONE UP!
WE?
O'DONNELL'S ROOFING
PARKING IN REAR
OH, SO IT'S MY FAULT THE COPS SHOWED UP SO QUICK?
IT WAS A DIAMOND HEIST! WE KNEW THERE WOULD BE COPS THERE! WHY DO YOU THINK WE BROUGHT YOU ALONG?!
YOU WERE THERE TO TAKE CARE OF THE COPS SO WE COULD CALMLY MAKE OUR GETAWAY.
YOU WEREN'T SUPPOSED TO RUN WITH US, YOU IDIOT!
JUST BECAUSE BULLETS BOUNCE OFF ME DOESN'T MEAN THEY FEEL LIKE BACK RUBS! THERE WERE AT LEASE SIX COPS BACK THERE READY TO OPEN FIRE!
BESIDES... THEY WON'T CATCH US.
WHATEVER. JUST GET US OVER THAT FENCE.
NO TRESPASSING

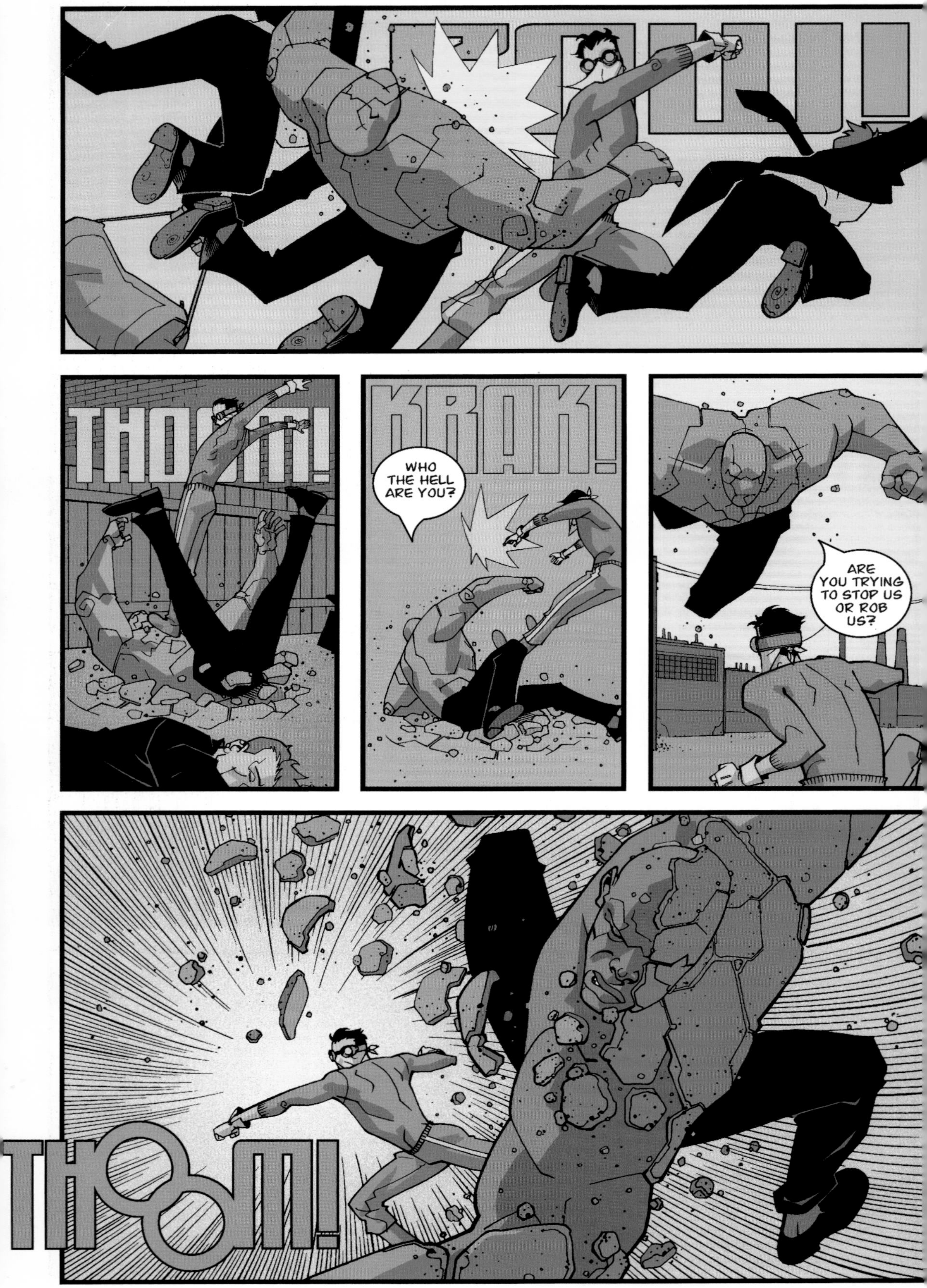
THOOM!
KRAK!
WHO THE HELL ARE YOU?
ARE YOU TRYING TO STOP US OR ROB US?
THOOM!

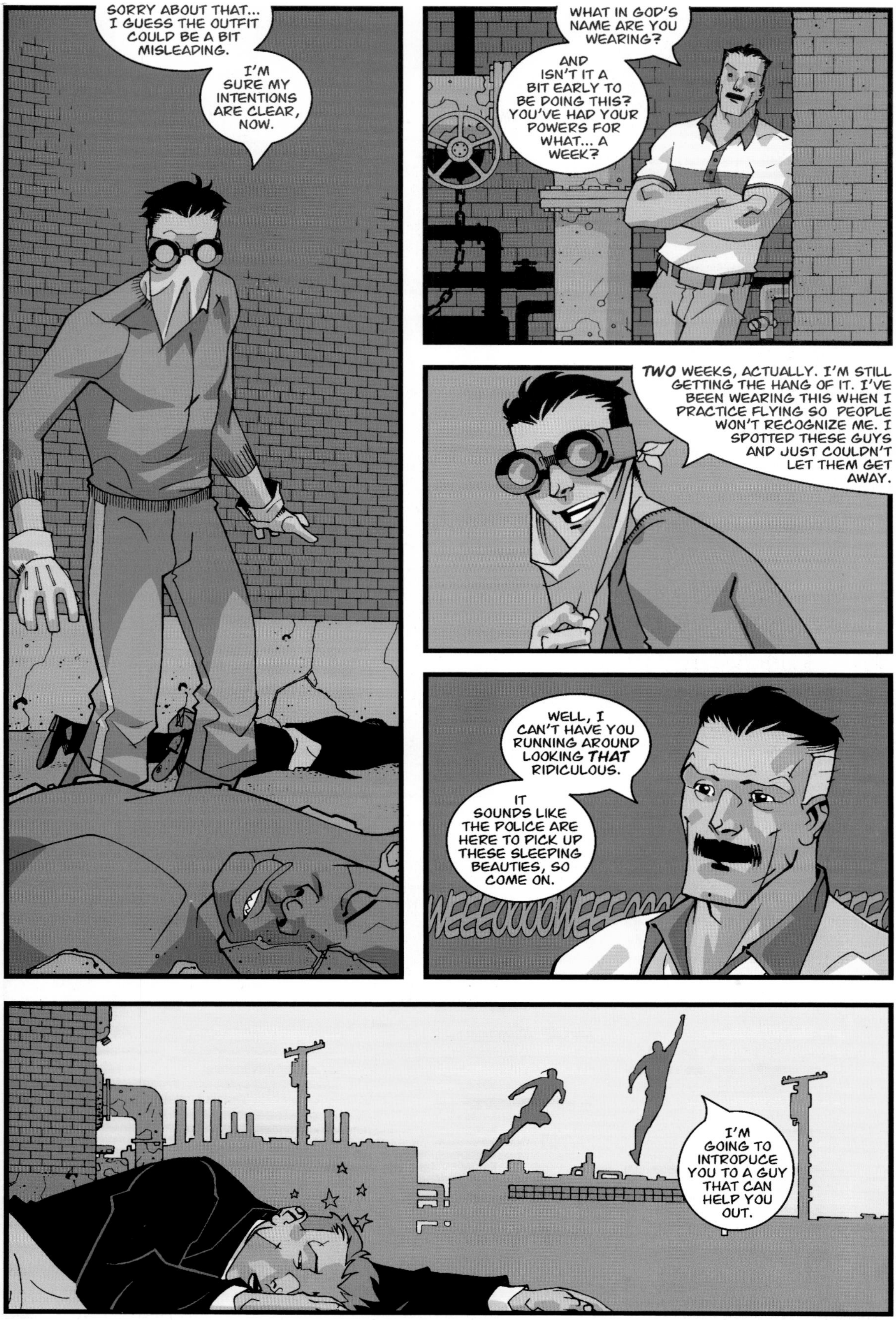
SORRY ABOUT THAT... I GUESS THE OUTFIT COULD BE A BIT MISLEADING.
I'M SURE MY INTENTIONS ARE CLEAR, NOW.
WHAT IN GOD'S NAME ARE YOU WEARING?
AND ISN'T IT A BIT EARLY TO BE DOING THIS? YOU'VE HAD YOUR POWERS FOR WHAT... A WEEK?
TWO WEEKS, ACTUALLY. I'M STILL GETTING THE HANG OF IT. I'VE BEEN WEARING THIS WHEN I PRACTICE FLYING SO PEOPLE WON'T RECOGNIZE ME. I SPOTTED THESE GUYS AND JUST COULDN'T LET THEM GET AWAY.
WELL, I CAN'T HAVE YOU RUNNING AROUND LOOKING THAT RIDICULOUS.
IT SOUNDS LIKE THE POLICE ARE HERE TO PICK UP THESE SLEEPING BEAUTIES, SO COME ON.
I'M GOING TO INTRODUCE YOU TO A GUY THAT CAN HELP YOU OUT.

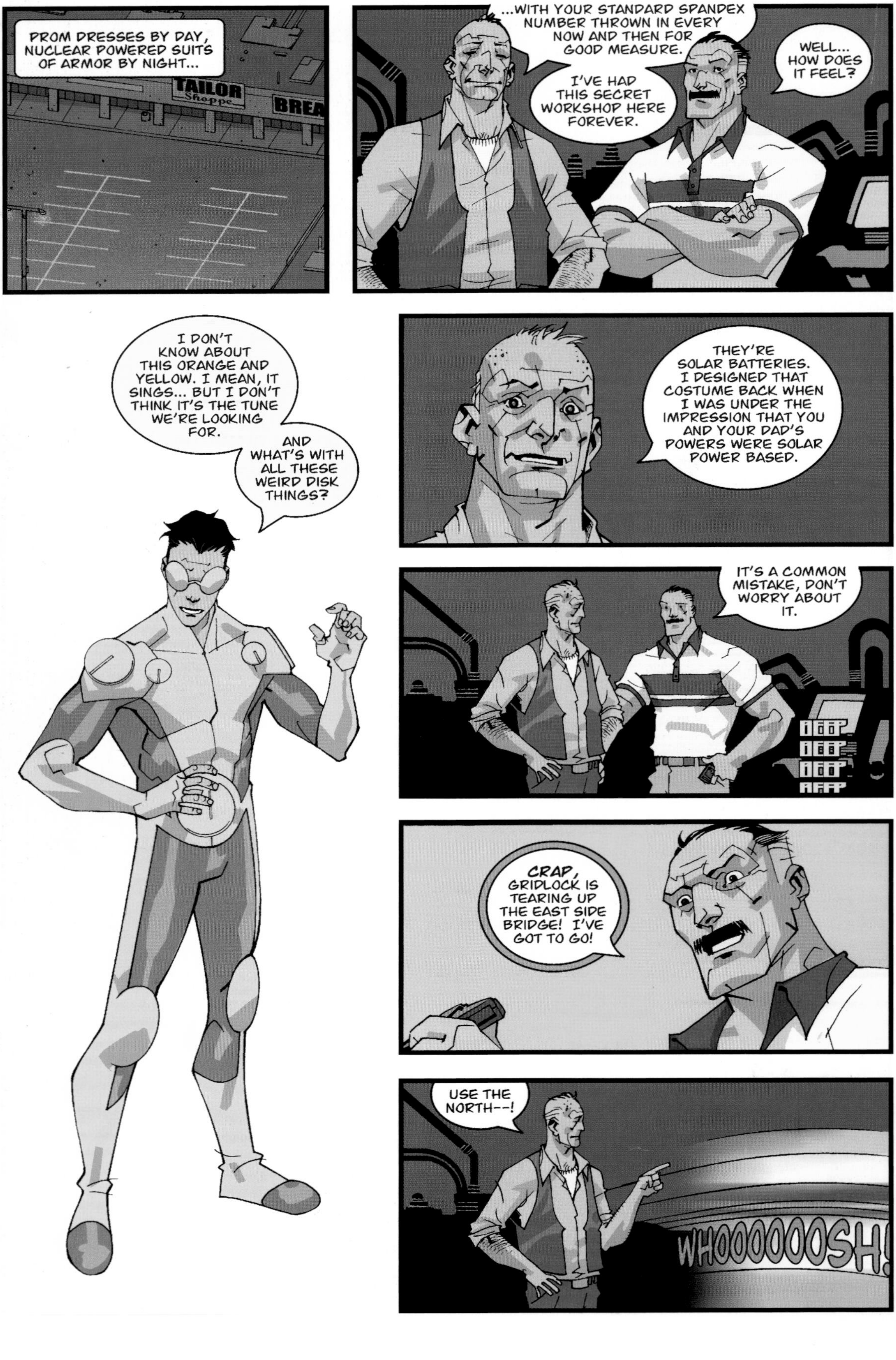
PROM DRESSES BY DAY, NUCLEAR POWERED SUITS OF ARMOR BY NIGHT...
TAILOR Shoppe
BREA
...WITH YOUR STANDARD SPANDEX NUMBER THROWN IN EVERY NOW AND THEN FOR GOOD MEASURE.
I'VE HAD THIS SECRET WORKSHOP HERE FOREVER.
WELL... HOW DOES IT FEEL?
I DON'T KNOW ABOUT THIS ORANGE AND YELLOW. I MEAN, IT SINGS... BUT I DON'T THINK IT'S THE TUNE WE'RE LOOKING FOR.
AND WHAT'S WITH ALL THESE WEIRD DISK THINGS?
THEY'RE SOLAR BATTERIES. I DESIGNED THAT COSTUME BACK WHEN I WAS UNDER THE IMPRESSION THAT YOU AND YOUR DAD'S POWERS WERE SOLAR POWER BASED.
IT'S A COMMON MISTAKE, DON'T WORRY ABOUT IT.
BEEP
BEEP
BEEP
BEEP
CRAP, GRIDLOCK IS TEARING UP THE EAST SIDE BRIDGE! I'VE GOT TO GO!
USE THE NORTH--!
WHOOOOOOOSH!

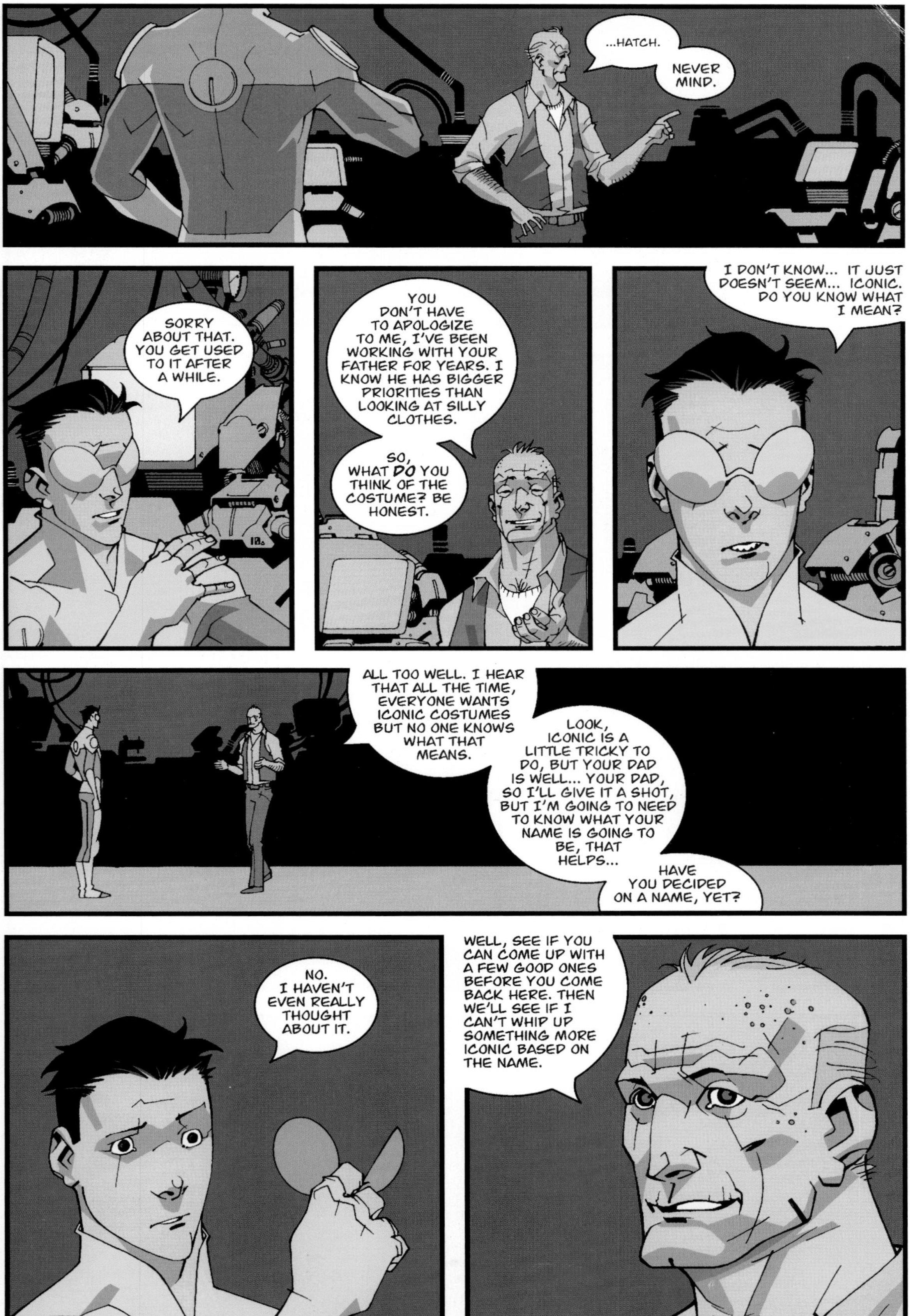
...HATCH.
NEVER MIND.
SORRY ABOUT THAT. YOU GET USED TO IT AFTER A WHILE.
YOU DON'T HAVE TO APOLOGIZE TO ME, I'VE BEEN WORKING WITH YOUR FATHER FOR YEARS. I KNOW HE HAS BIGGER PRIORITIES THAN LOOKING AT SILLY CLOTHES.
SO, WHAT DO YOU THINK OF THE COSTUME? BE HONEST.
I DON'T KNOW... IT JUST DOESN'T SEEM... ICONIC. DO YOU KNOW WHAT I MEAN?
ALL TOO WELL. I HEAR THAT ALL THE TIME, EVERYONE WANTS ICONIC COSTUMES BUT NO ONE KNOWS WHAT THAT MEANS.
LOOK, ICONIC IS A LITTLE TRICKY TO DO, BUT YOUR DAD IS WELL... YOUR DAD, SO I'LL GIVE IT A SHOT, BUT I'M GOING TO NEED TO KNOW WHAT YOUR NAME IS GOING TO BE, THAT HELPS...
HAVE YOU DECIDED ON A NAME, YET?
NO. I HAVEN'T EVEN REALLY THOUGHT ABOUT IT.
WELL, SEE IF YOU CAN COME UP WITH A FEW GOOD ONES BEFORE YOU COME BACK HERE. THEN WE'LL SEE IF I CAN'T WHIP UP SOMETHING MORE ICONIC BASED ON THE NAME.

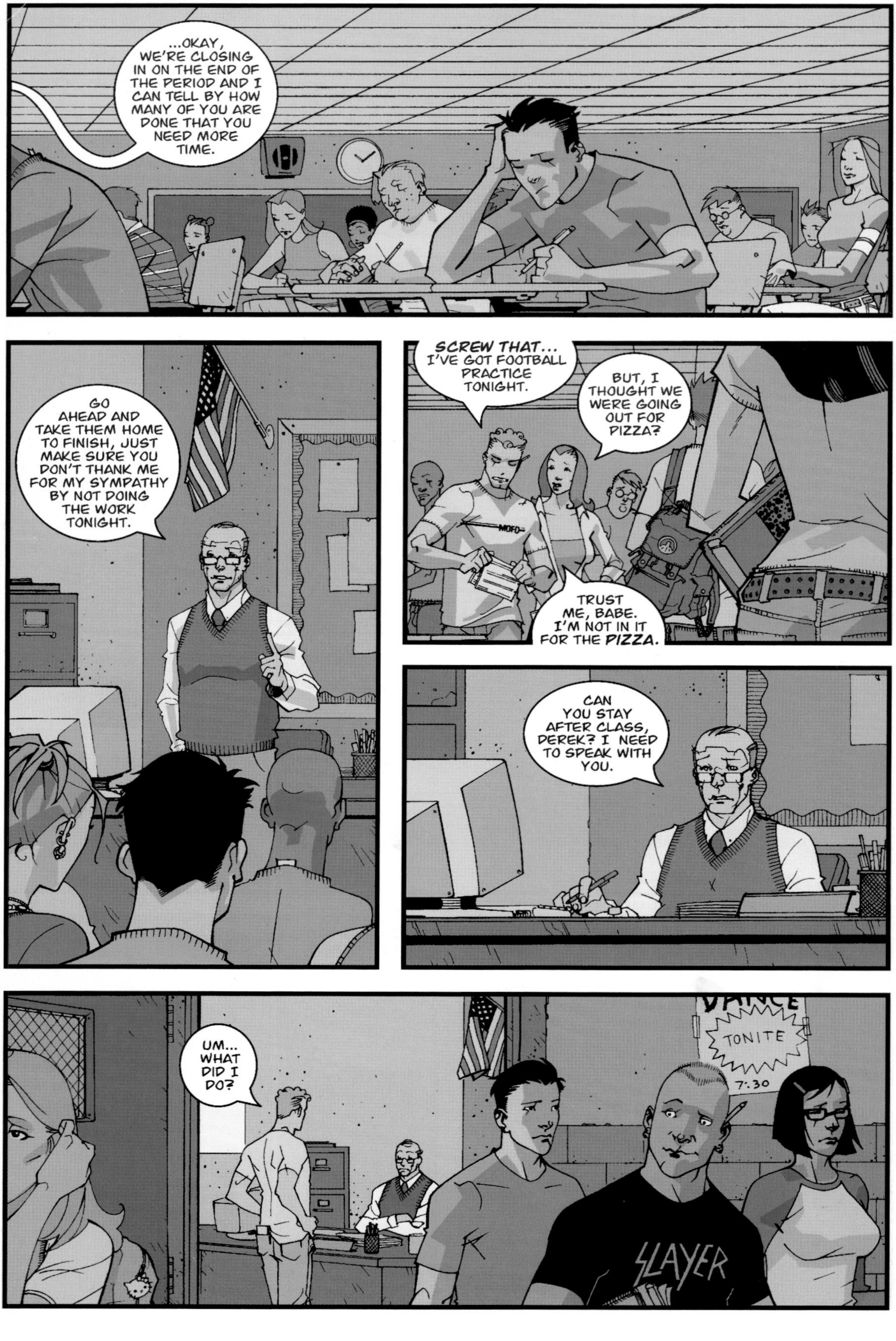
...OKAY, WE'RE CLOSING IN ON THE END OF THE PERIOD AND I CAN TELL BY HOW MANY OF YOU ARE DONE THAT YOU NEED MORE TIME.
GO AHEAD AND TAKE THEM HOME TO FINISH, JUST MAKE SURE YOU DON'T THANK ME FOR MY SYMPATHY BY NOT DOING THE WORK TONIGHT.
SCREW THAT... I'VE GOT FOOTBALL PRACTICE TONIGHT.
BUT, I THOUGHT WE WERE GOING OUT FOR PIZZA?
TRUST ME, BABE. I'M NOT IN IT FOR THE PIZZA.
CAN YOU STAY AFTER CLASS, DEREK? I NEED TO SPEAK WITH YOU.
UM... WHAT DID I DO?
DANCE
TONITE
7:30
SLAYER

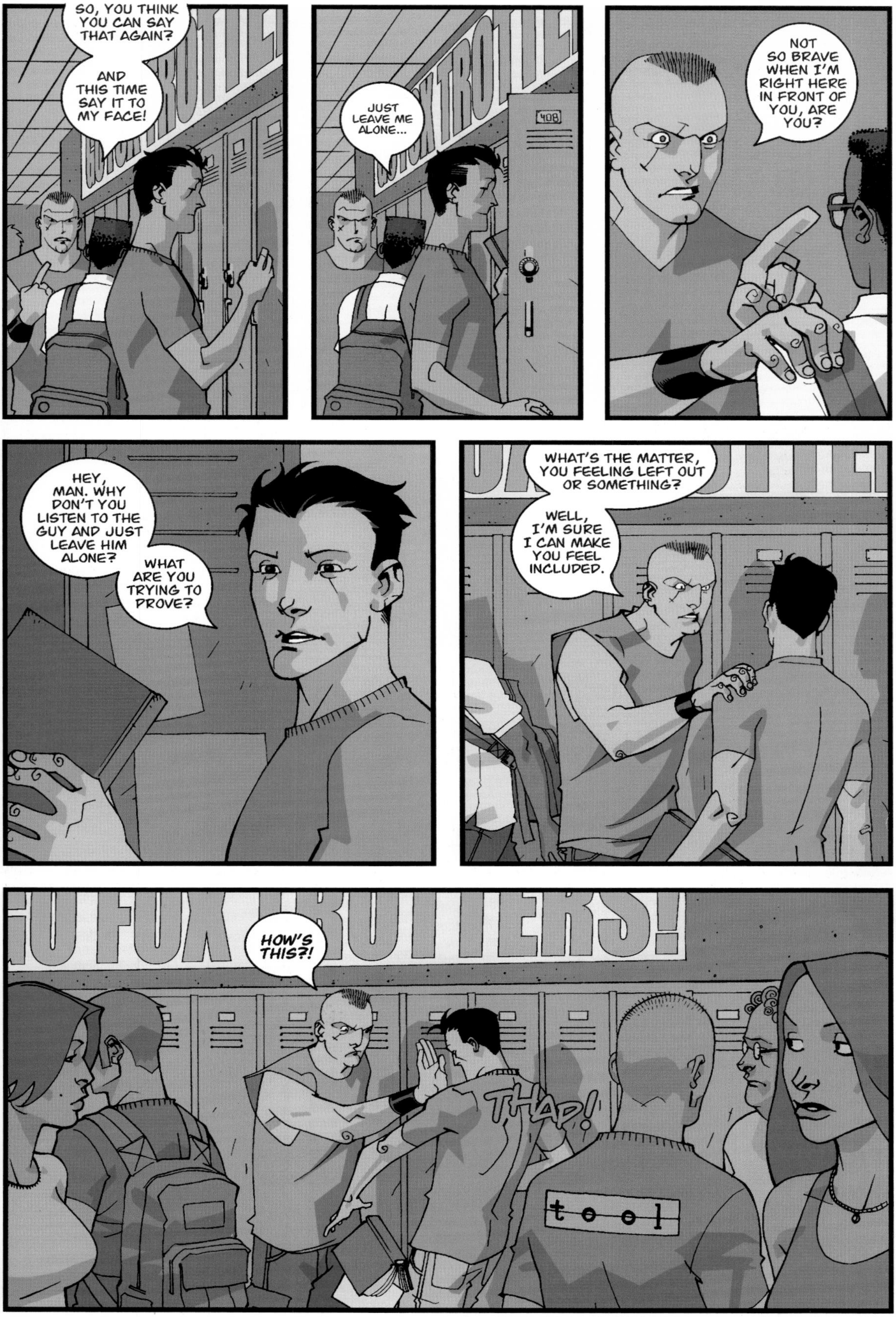

SO, YOU THINK YOU CAN SAY THAT AGAIN?
AND THIS TIME SAY IT TO MY FACE!
GO FOX TROTTE
JUST LEAVE ME ALONE...
408
NOT SO BRAVE WHEN I'M RIGHT HERE IN FRONT OF YOU, ARE YOU?
HEY, MAN. WHY DON'T YOU LISTEN TO THE GUY AND JUST LEAVE HIM ALONE?
WHAT ARE YOU TRYING TO PROVE?
WHAT'S THE MATTER, YOU FEELING LEFT OUT OR SOMETHING?
WELL, I'M SURE I CAN MAKE YOU FEEL INCLUDED.
GO FOX TROTTERS!
HOW'S THIS?!
THAP!
tool

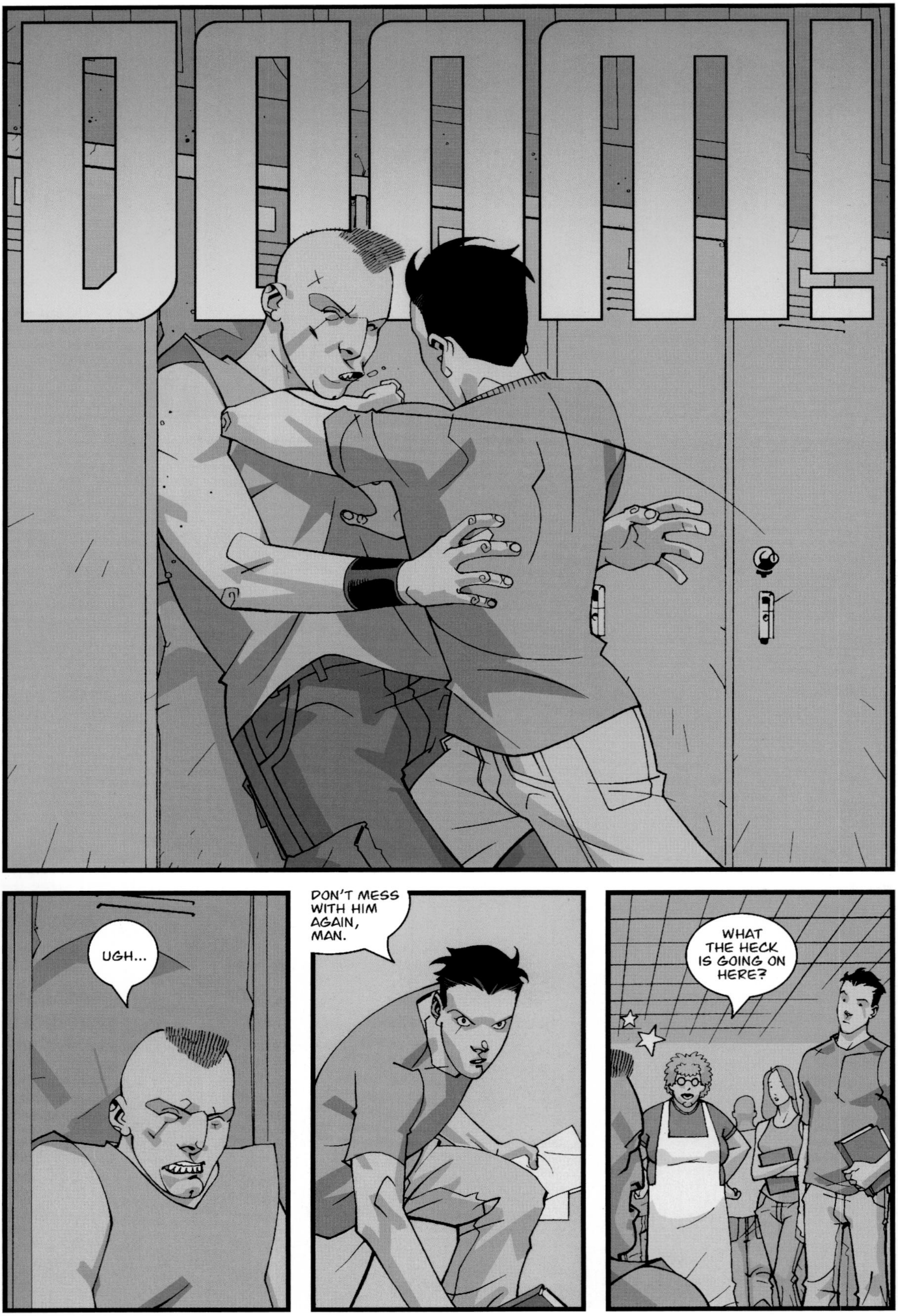
DOOM!
UGH...
DON'T MESS WITH HIM AGAIN, MAN.
WHAT THE HECK IS GOING ON HERE?

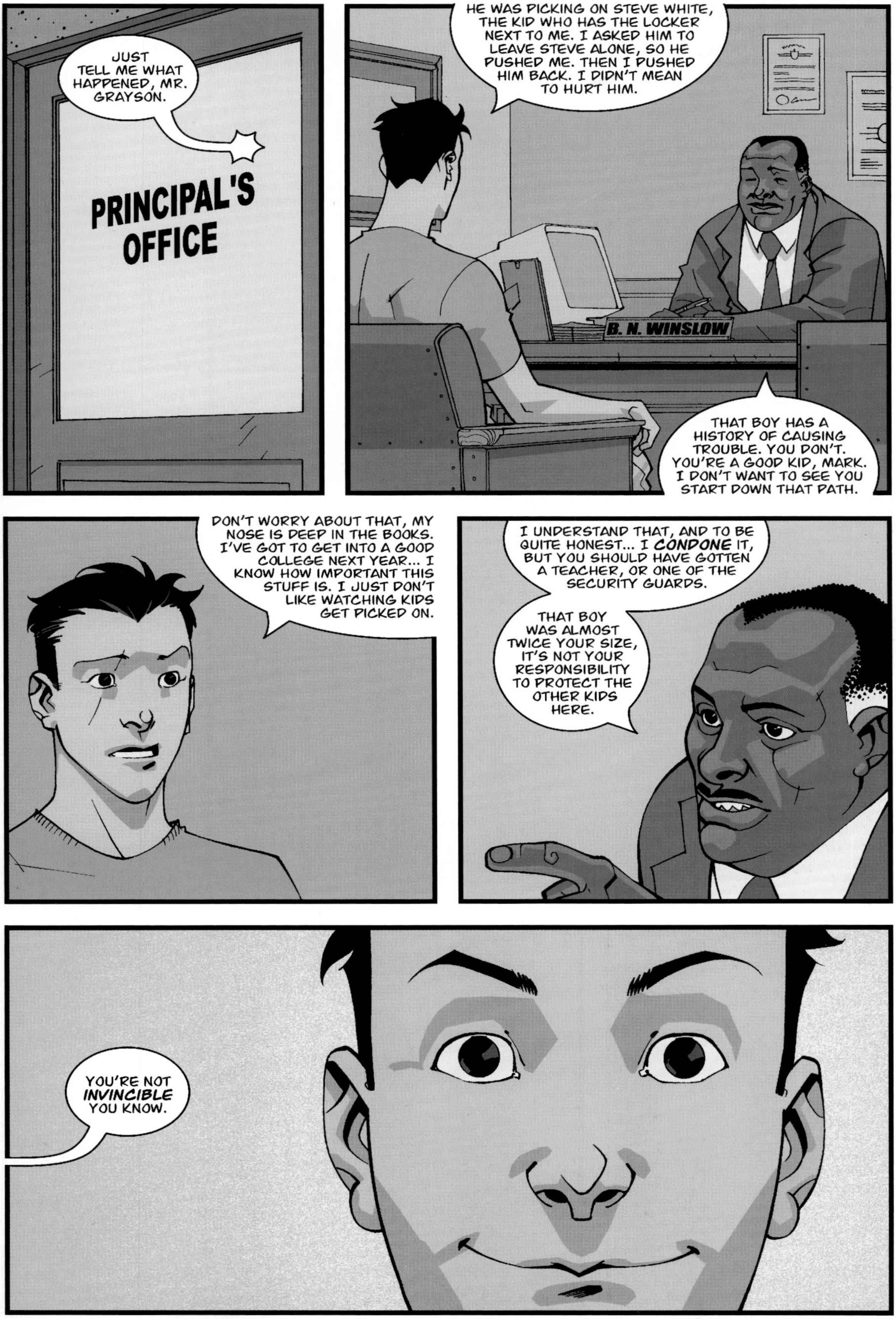
JUST TELL ME WHAT HAPPENED, MR. GRAYSON.
PRINCIPAL'S OFFICE
HE WAS PICKING ON STEVE WHITE, THE KID WHO HAS THE LOCKER NEXT TO ME. I ASKED HIM TO LEAVE STEVE ALONE, SO HE PUSHED ME. THEN I PUSHED HIM BACK. I DIDN'T MEAN TO HURT HIM.
B. N. WINSLOW
THAT BOY HAS A HISTORY OF CAUSING TROUBLE. YOU DON'T. YOU'RE A GOOD KID, MARK. I DON'T WANT TO SEE YOU START DOWN THAT PATH.
DON'T WORRY ABOUT THAT, MY NOSE IS DEEP IN THE BOOKS. I'VE GOT TO GET INTO A GOOD COLLEGE NEXT YEAR... I KNOW HOW IMPORTANT THIS STUFF IS. I JUST DON'T LIKE WATCHING KIDS GET PICKED ON.
I UNDERSTAND THAT, AND TO BE QUITE HONEST... I CONDONE IT, BUT YOU SHOULD HAVE GOTTEN A TEACHER, OR ONE OF THE SECURITY GUARDS.
THAT BOY WAS ALMOST TWICE YOUR SIZE, IT'S NOT YOUR RESPONSIBILITY TO PROTECT THE OTHER KIDS HERE.
YOU'RE NOT INVINCIBLE YOU KNOW.

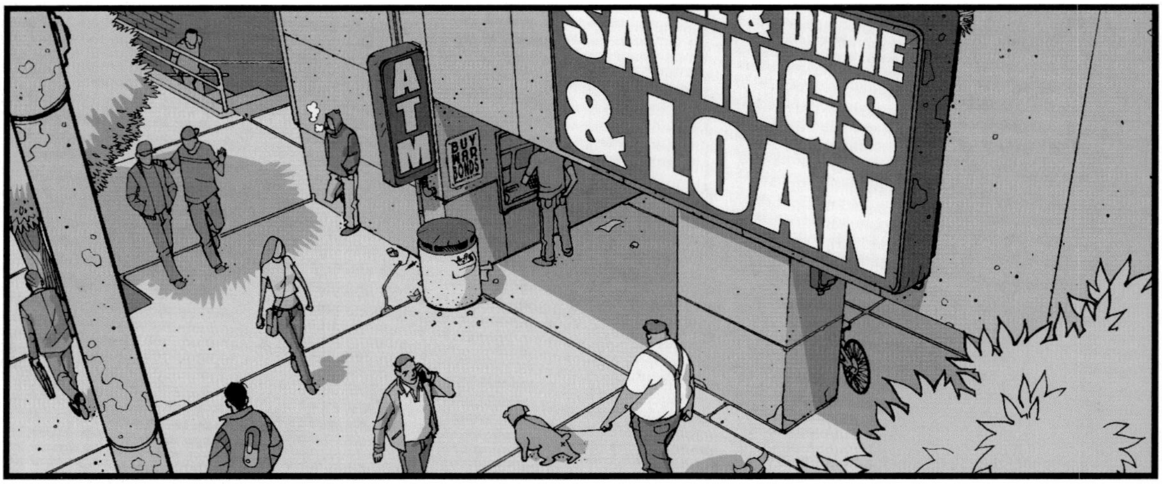
ATM
SAVINGS
& LOAN

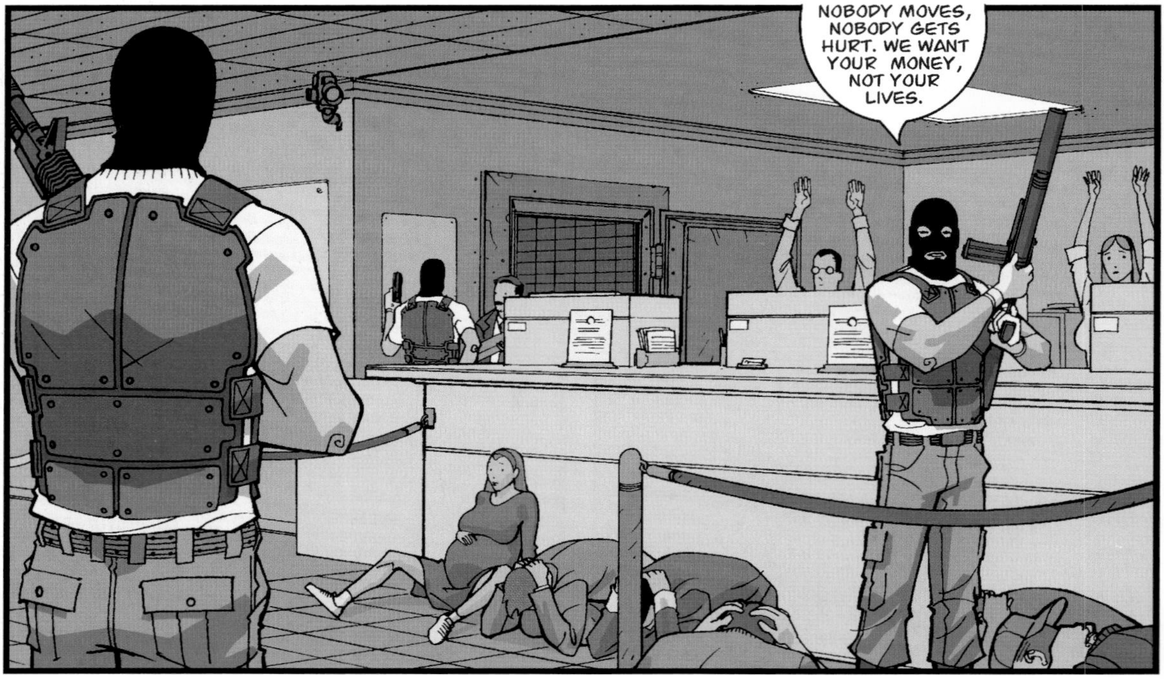
NOBODY MOVES, NOBODY GETS HURT. WE WANT YOUR MONEY, NOT YOUR LIVES.

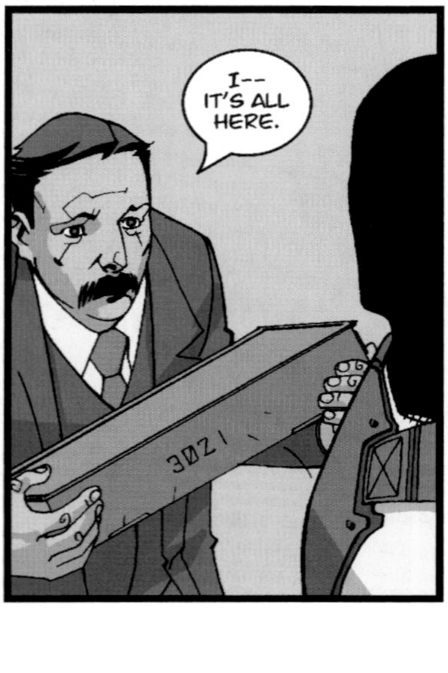
I-- IT'S ALL HERE.

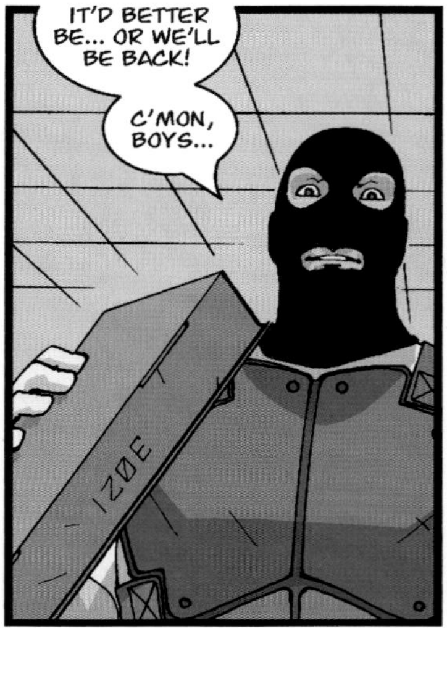
IT'D BETTER BE... OR WE'LL BE BACK!
C'MON, BOYS...

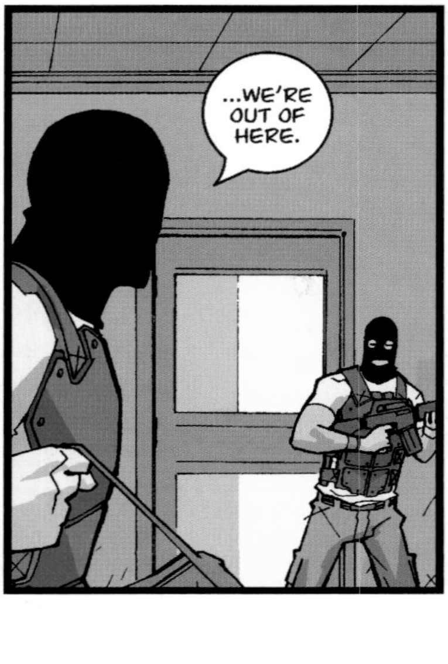
...WE'RE OUT OF HERE.

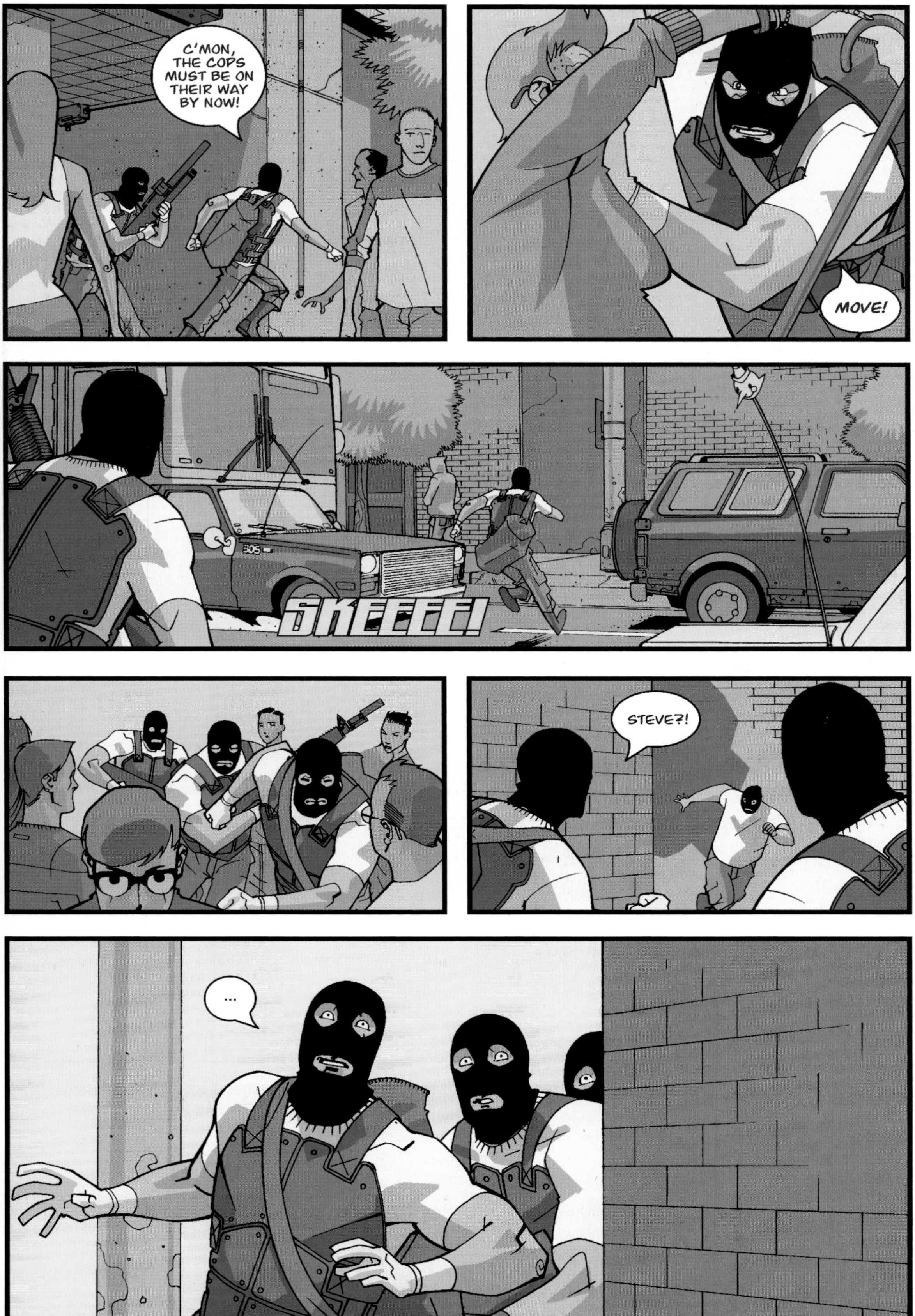
C'MON, THE COPS MUST BE ON THEIR WAY BY NOW!
MOVE!
SKEEEE!
STEVE?!
...

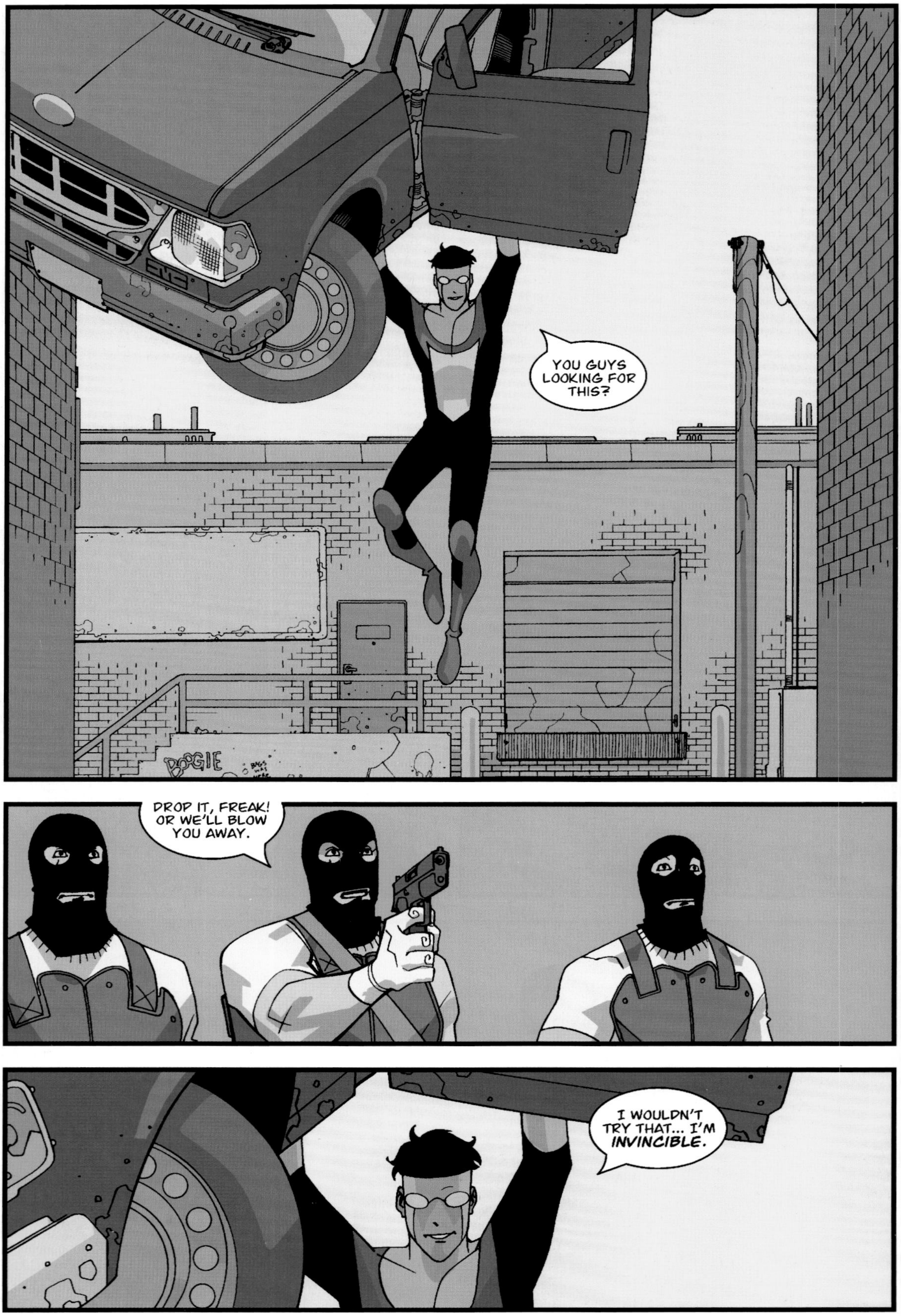
BOOGIE
YOU GUYS LOOKING FOR THIS?
DROP IT, FREAK! OR WE'LL BLOW YOU AWAY.
I WOULDN'T TRY THAT... I'M *INVINCIBLE*.

# CHAPTER TWO

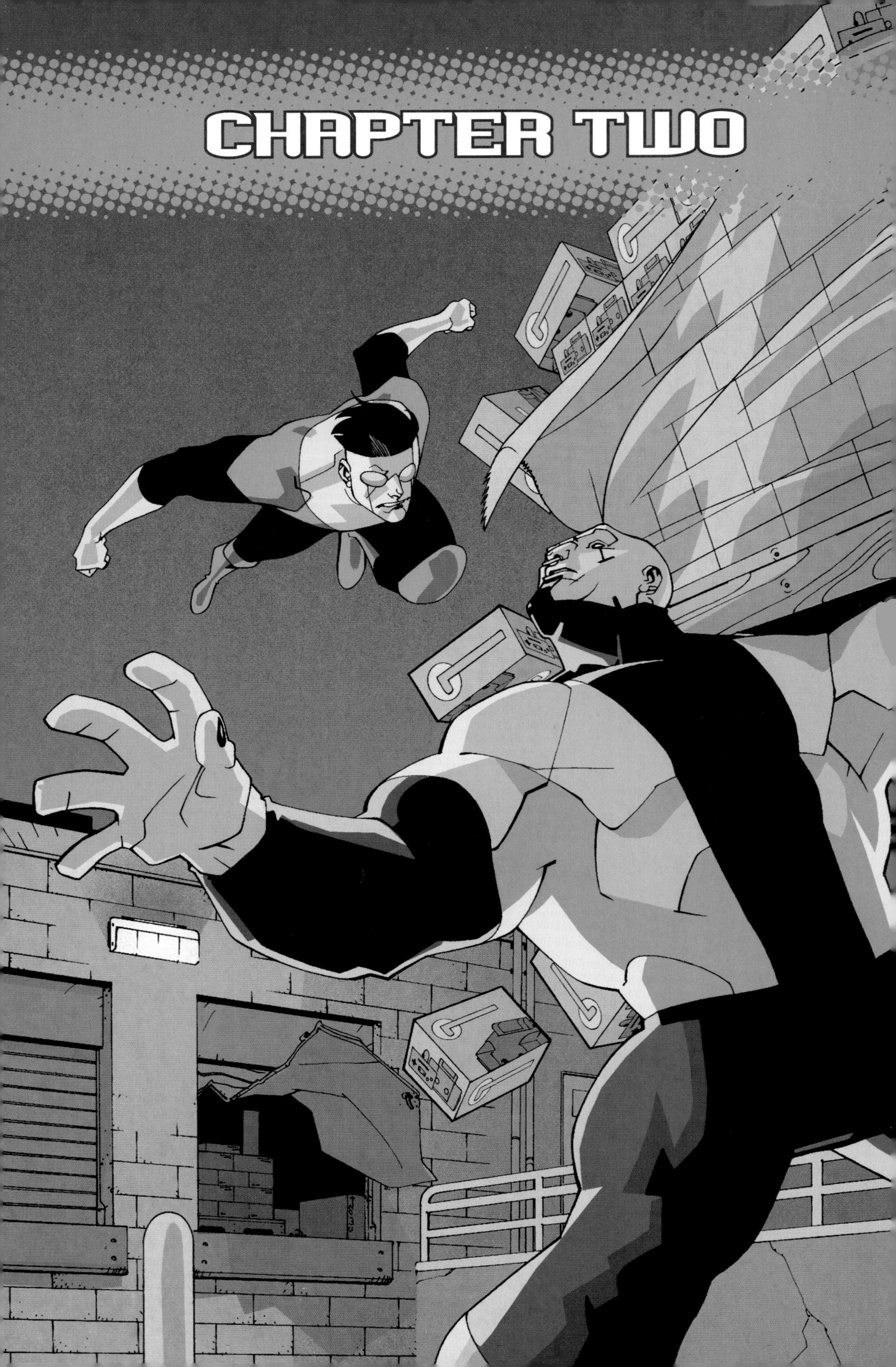

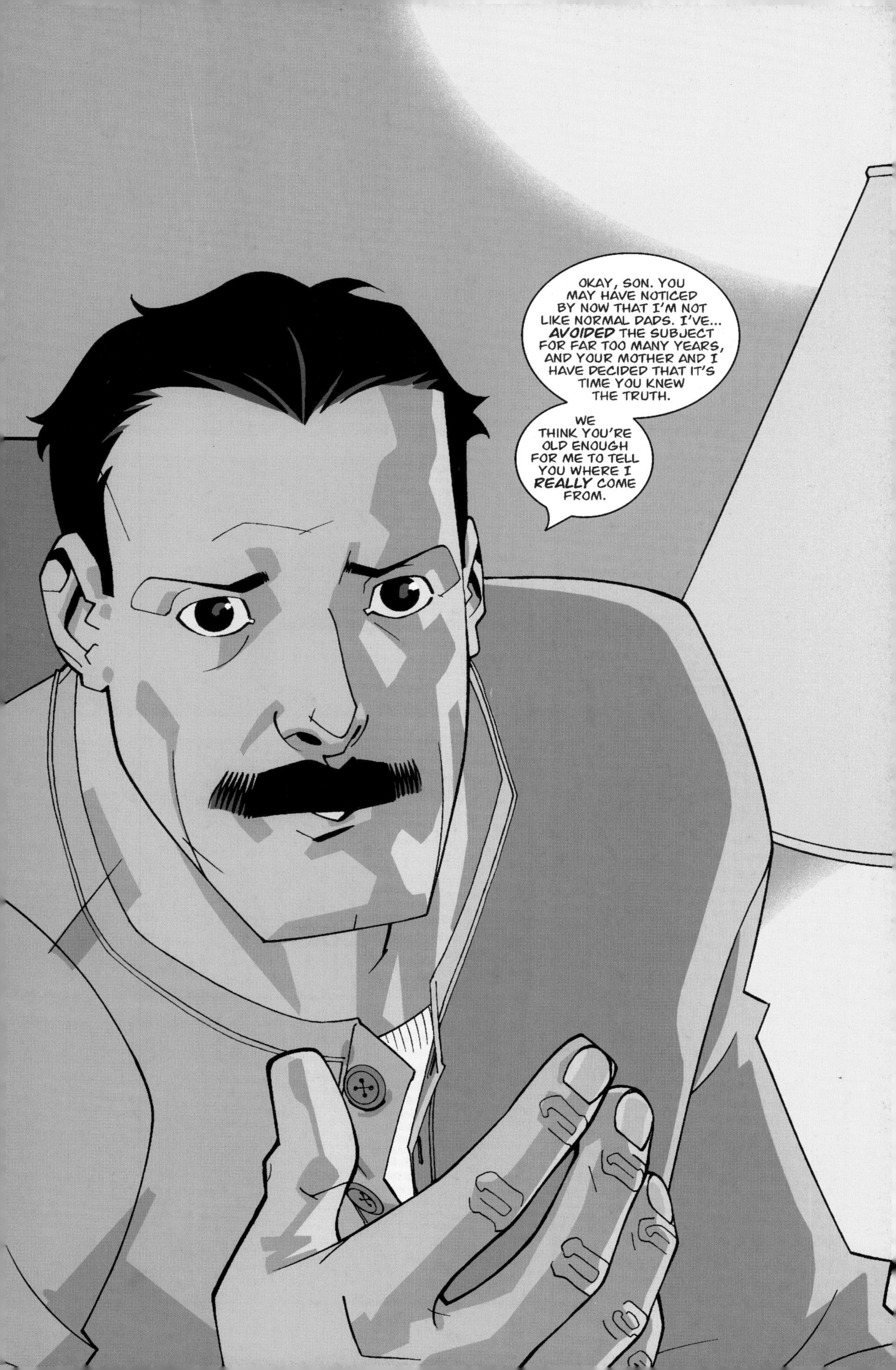
OKAY, SON. YOU MAY HAVE NOTICED BY NOW THAT I'M NOT LIKE NORMAL DADS. I'VE... **AVOIDED** THE SUBJECT FOR FAR TOO MANY YEARS, AND YOUR MOTHER AND I HAVE DECIDED THAT IT'S TIME YOU KNEW THE TRUTH.
WE THINK YOU'RE OLD ENOUGH FOR ME TO TELL YOU WHERE I **REALLY** COME FROM.

BILLIONS OF MILES FROM HERE, OUT IN DEEP SPACE, IS THE PLANET VILTRUM, A COOL BLUE OASIS ALONE IN A SOLAR SYSTEM MUCH LIKE OUR OWN.

I WAS BORN ON THIS PLANET.

ITS PEOPLE ARE NOT COMPLETELY UNLIKE HUMANS, ALTHOUGH, THEY, AND I, HAVE ABILITIES IN ADDITION TO WHAT HUMANS HAVE. WE CAN FLY, MOVE AT SUPER-SPEED, AND POSSESS GREAT STRENGTH... BY HUMAN STANDARDS.

VILTRUM WAS A PLANET THAT HAD ACHIEVED A PERFECT GLOBAL SOCIETY. THERE WAS NO ILLNESS, NO MURDER, NO WAR, IT WAS A RELATIVE UTOPIA.

WITH NO CONFLICT AT HAND, OUR HIGH COUNCIL REFUSED TO LET OUR SOCIETY BECOME COMPLACENT.

COUNCIL MEMBERS ARGUED THAT RATHER THAN REVEL IN OUR NEWFOUND PERFECTION, WE SHOULD TAKE IT UPON OURSELVES TO ENSURE THAT OTHER RACES, LESSER DEVELOPED THAN OUR OWN, SHOULD BE ALLOWED TO DEVELOP TO OUR LEVEL OF ADVANCEMENT.

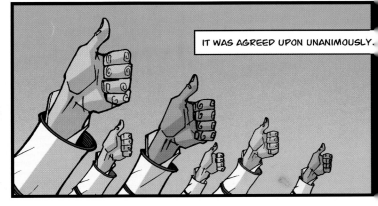

IT WAS AGREED UPON UNANIMOUSLY.

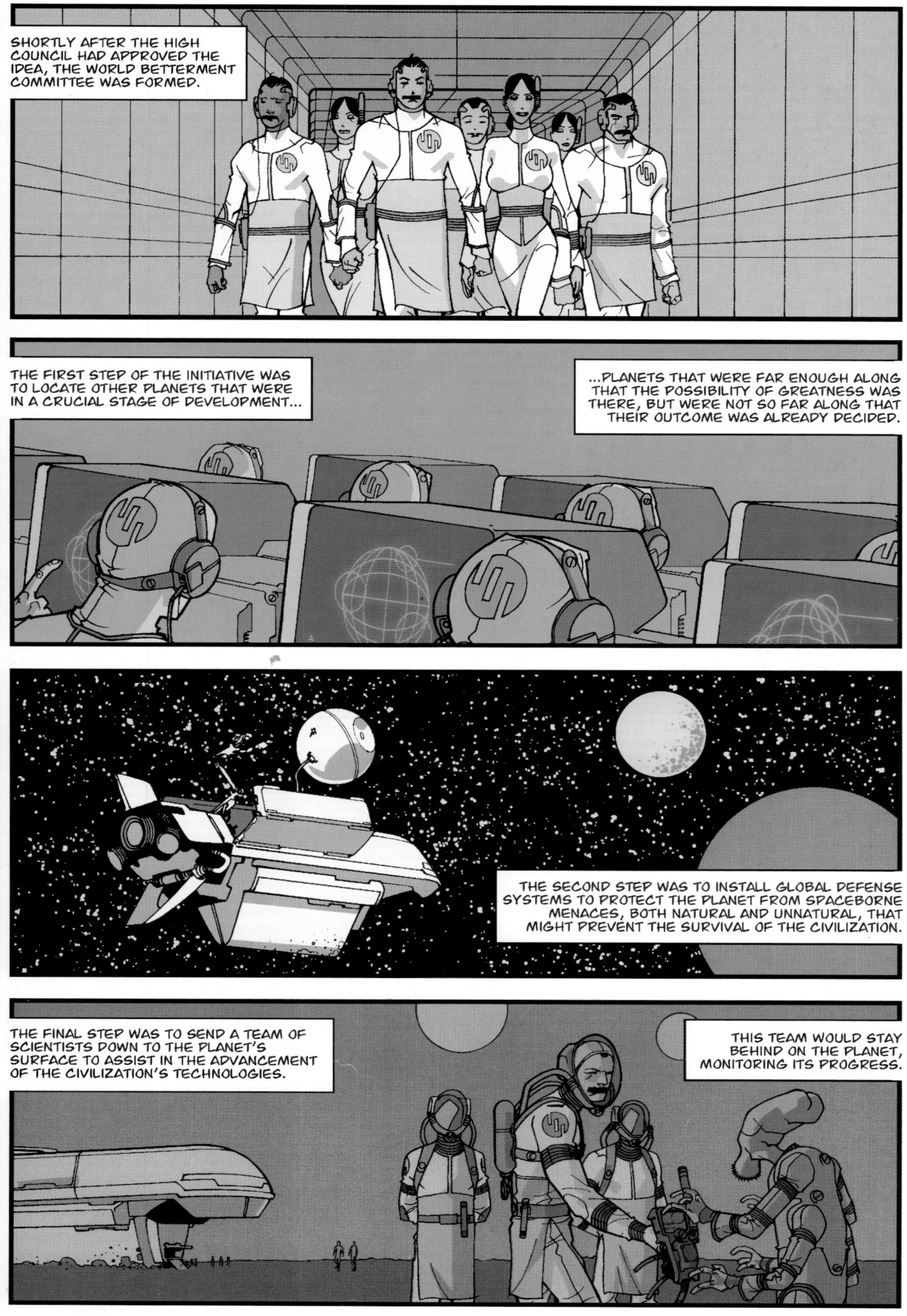
SHORTLY AFTER THE HIGH COUNCIL HAD APPROVED THE IDEA, THE WORLD BETTERMENT COMMITTEE WAS FORMED.
THE FIRST STEP OF THE INITIATIVE WAS TO LOCATE OTHER PLANETS THAT WERE IN A CRUCIAL STAGE OF DEVELOPMENT...
...PLANETS THAT WERE FAR ENOUGH ALONG THAT THE POSSIBILITY OF GREATNESS WAS THERE, BUT WERE NOT SO FAR ALONG THAT THEIR OUTCOME WAS ALREADY DECIDED.
THE SECOND STEP WAS TO INSTALL GLOBAL DEFENSE SYSTEMS TO PROTECT THE PLANET FROM SPACEBORNE MENACES, BOTH NATURAL AND UNNATURAL, THAT MIGHT PREVENT THE SURVIVAL OF THE CIVILIZATION.
THE FINAL STEP WAS TO SEND A TEAM OF SCIENTISTS DOWN TO THE PLANET'S SURFACE TO ASSIST IN THE ADVANCEMENT OF THE CIVILIZATION'S TECHNOLOGIES.
THIS TEAM WOULD STAY BEHIND ON THE PLANET, MONITORING ITS PROGRESS.

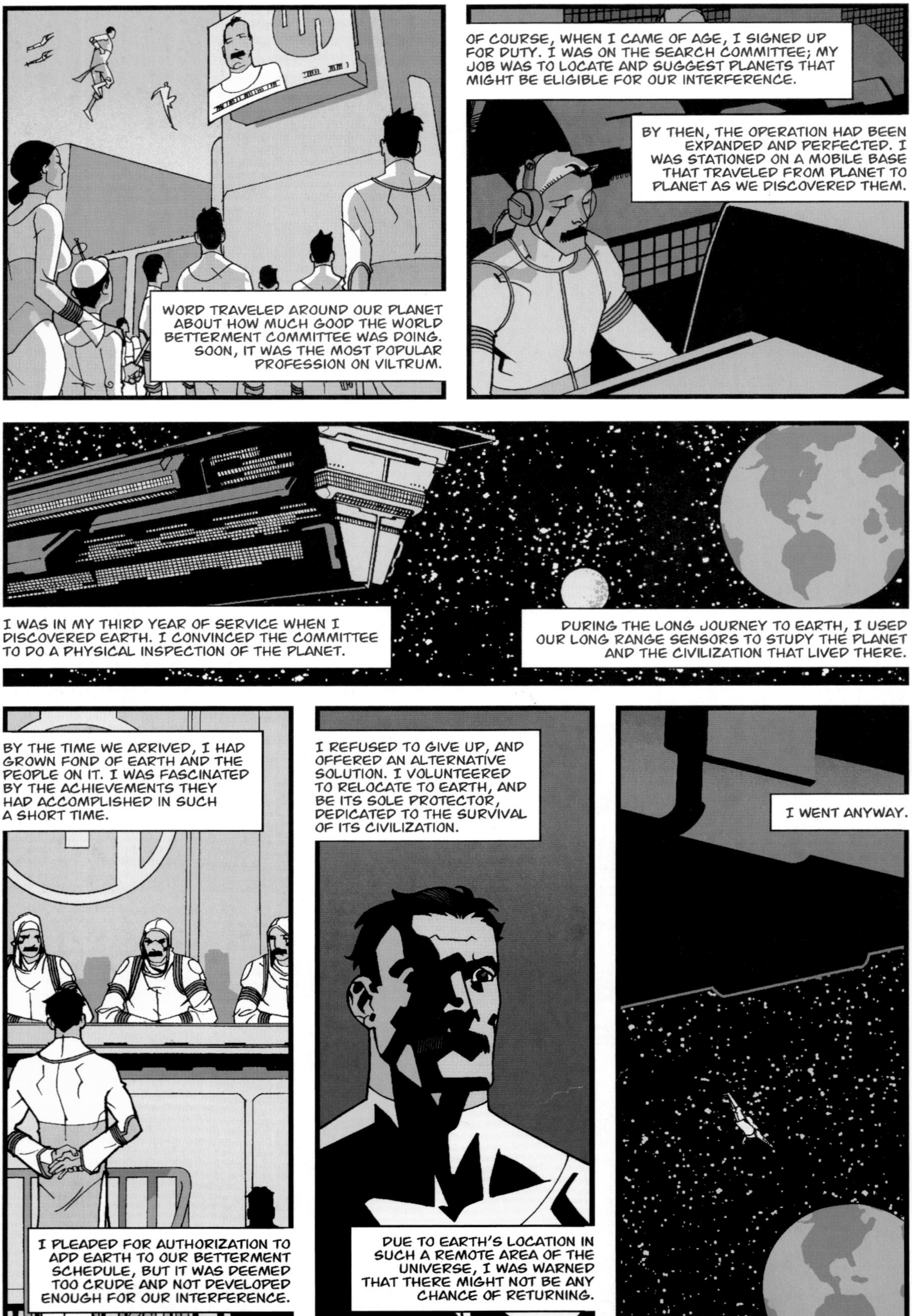
WORD TRAVELED AROUND OUR PLANET ABOUT HOW MUCH GOOD THE WORLD BETTERMENT COMMITTEE WAS DOING. SOON, IT WAS THE MOST POPULAR PROFESSION ON VILTRUM.
OF COURSE, WHEN I CAME OF AGE, I SIGNED UP FOR DUTY. I WAS ON THE SEARCH COMMITTEE; MY JOB WAS TO LOCATE AND SUGGEST PLANETS THAT MIGHT BE ELIGIBLE FOR OUR INTERFERENCE.
BY THEN, THE OPERATION HAD BEEN EXPANDED AND PERFECTED. I WAS STATIONED ON A MOBILE BASE THAT TRAVELED FROM PLANET TO PLANET AS WE DISCOVERED THEM.
I WAS IN MY THIRD YEAR OF SERVICE WHEN I DISCOVERED EARTH. I CONVINCED THE COMMITTEE TO DO A PHYSICAL INSPECTION OF THE PLANET.
DURING THE LONG JOURNEY TO EARTH, I USED OUR LONG RANGE SENSORS TO STUDY THE PLANET AND THE CIVILIZATION THAT LIVED THERE.
BY THE TIME WE ARRIVED, I HAD GROWN FOND OF EARTH AND THE PEOPLE ON IT. I WAS FASCINATED BY THE ACHIEVEMENTS THEY HAD ACCOMPLISHED IN SUCH A SHORT TIME.
I PLEADED FOR AUTHORIZATION TO ADD EARTH TO OUR BETTERMENT SCHEDULE, BUT IT WAS DEEMED TOO CRUDE AND NOT DEVELOPED ENOUGH FOR OUR INTERFERENCE.
I REFUSED TO GIVE UP, AND OFFERED AN ALTERNATIVE SOLUTION. I VOLUNTEERED TO RELOCATE TO EARTH, AND BE ITS SOLE PROTECTOR, DEDICATED TO THE SURVIVAL OF ITS CIVILIZATION.
DUE TO EARTH'S LOCATION IN SUCH A REMOTE AREA OF THE UNIVERSE, I WAS WARNED THAT THERE MIGHT NOT BE ANY CHANCE OF RETURNING.
I WENT ANYWAY.

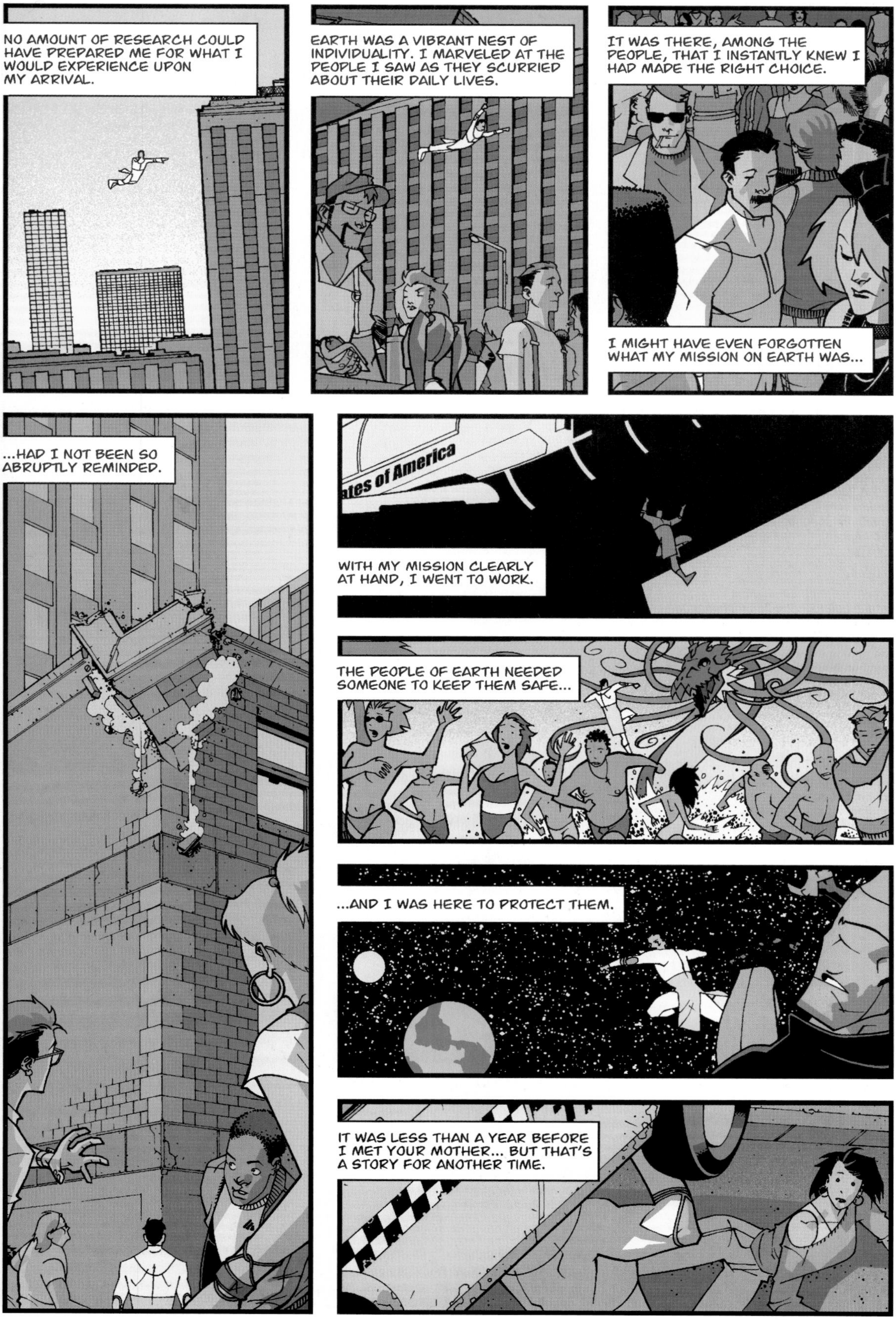
NO AMOUNT OF RESEARCH COULD HAVE PREPARED ME FOR WHAT I WOULD EXPERIENCE UPON MY ARRIVAL.
EARTH WAS A VIBRANT NEST OF INDIVIDUALITY. I MARVELED AT THE PEOPLE I SAW AS THEY SCURRIED ABOUT THEIR DAILY LIVES.
IT WAS THERE, AMONG THE PEOPLE, THAT I INSTANTLY KNEW I HAD MADE THE RIGHT CHOICE.
I MIGHT HAVE EVEN FORGOTTEN WHAT MY MISSION ON EARTH WAS...
...HAD I NOT BEEN SO ABRUPTLY REMINDED.
ates of America
WITH MY MISSION CLEARLY AT HAND, I WENT TO WORK.
THE PEOPLE OF EARTH NEEDED SOMEONE TO KEEP THEM SAFE...
...AND I WAS HERE TO PROTECT THEM.
IT WAS LESS THAN A YEAR BEFORE I MET YOUR MOTHER... BUT THAT'S A STORY FOR ANOTHER TIME.

I KNOW THIS IS A LOT TO TAKE IN AT ONE TIME, BUT YOU'RE OLD ENOUGH TO KNOW THE TRUTH. AND UNFORTUNATELY... I'M NOT DONE YET. ON TOP OF ALL THIS... THERE'S MORE.
YOU SEE, YOU'RE GETTING OLDER, SON...
...THINGS ARE GOING TO START TO CHANGE FOR YOU IN A FEW YEARS AS YOU HIT PUBERTY.
YOU'RE GOING TO START TO GET ACNE.
YOUR VOICE WILL START TO CRACK AND EVENTUALLY CHANGE.
YOU'LL BEGIN TO GROW HAIR IN STRANGE AND NEW PLACES.
YOU'RE GOING TO START LOOKING AT GIRLS IN A WHOLE NEW LIGHT.
THERE'S A GOOD CHANCE THAT YOU'RE GOING TO START TO DEVELOP SUPER POWERS.

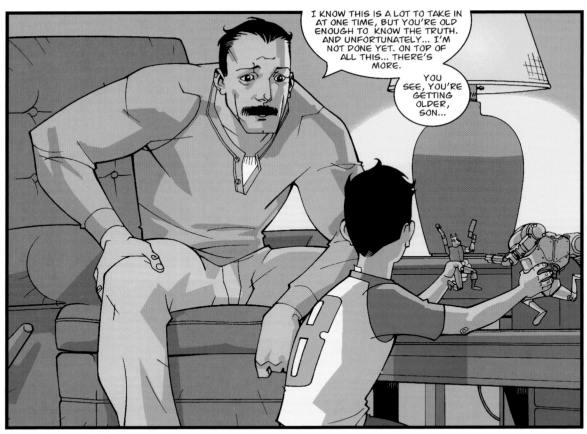

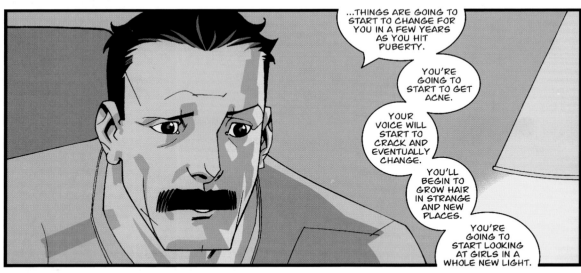

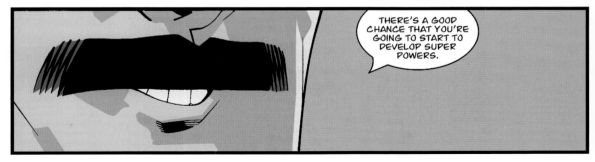

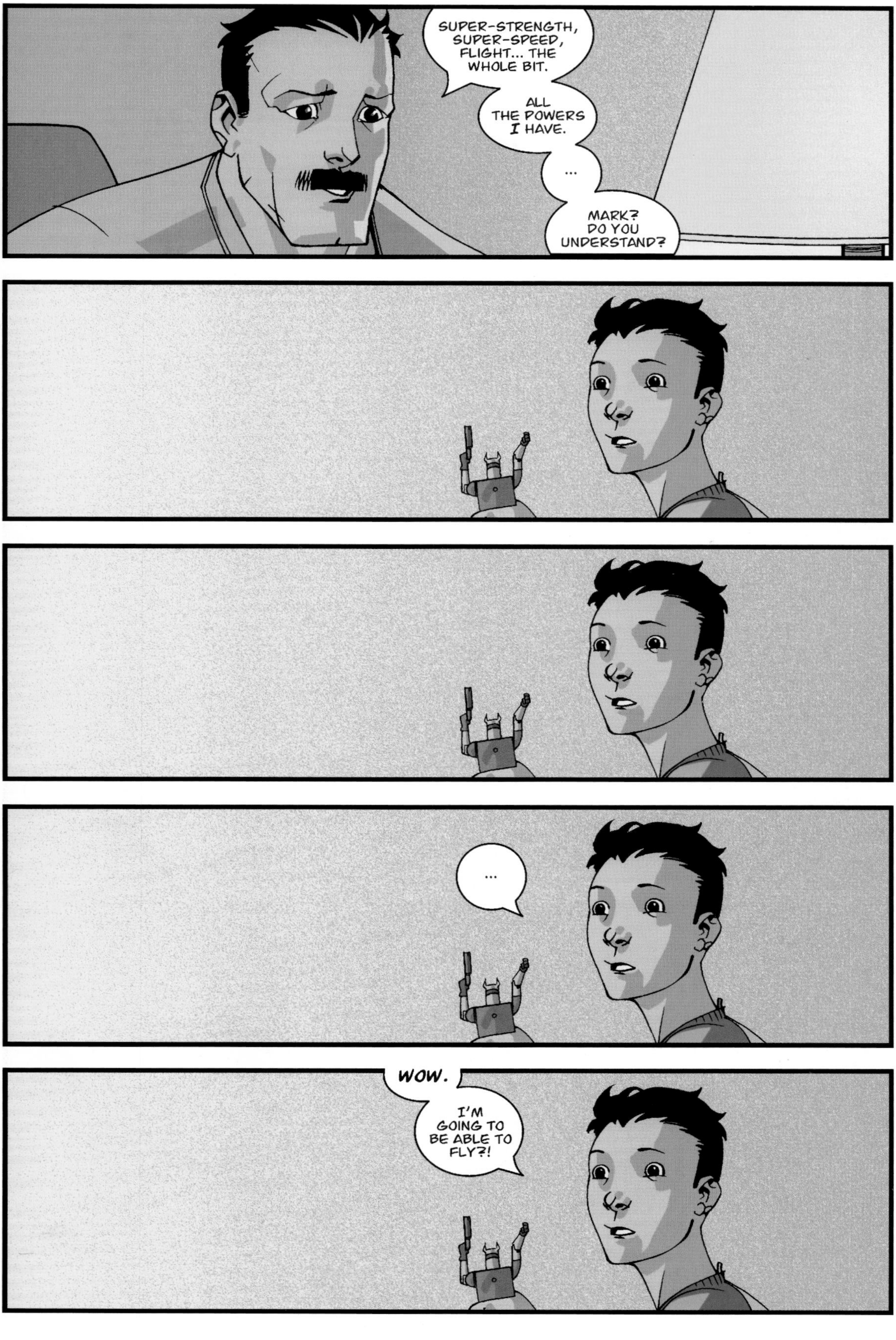
SUPER-STRENGTH, SUPER-SPEED, FLIGHT... THE WHOLE BIT.
ALL THE POWERS I HAVE.
...
MARK? DO YOU UNDERSTAND?
...
WOW.
I'M GOING TO BE ABLE TO FLY?!

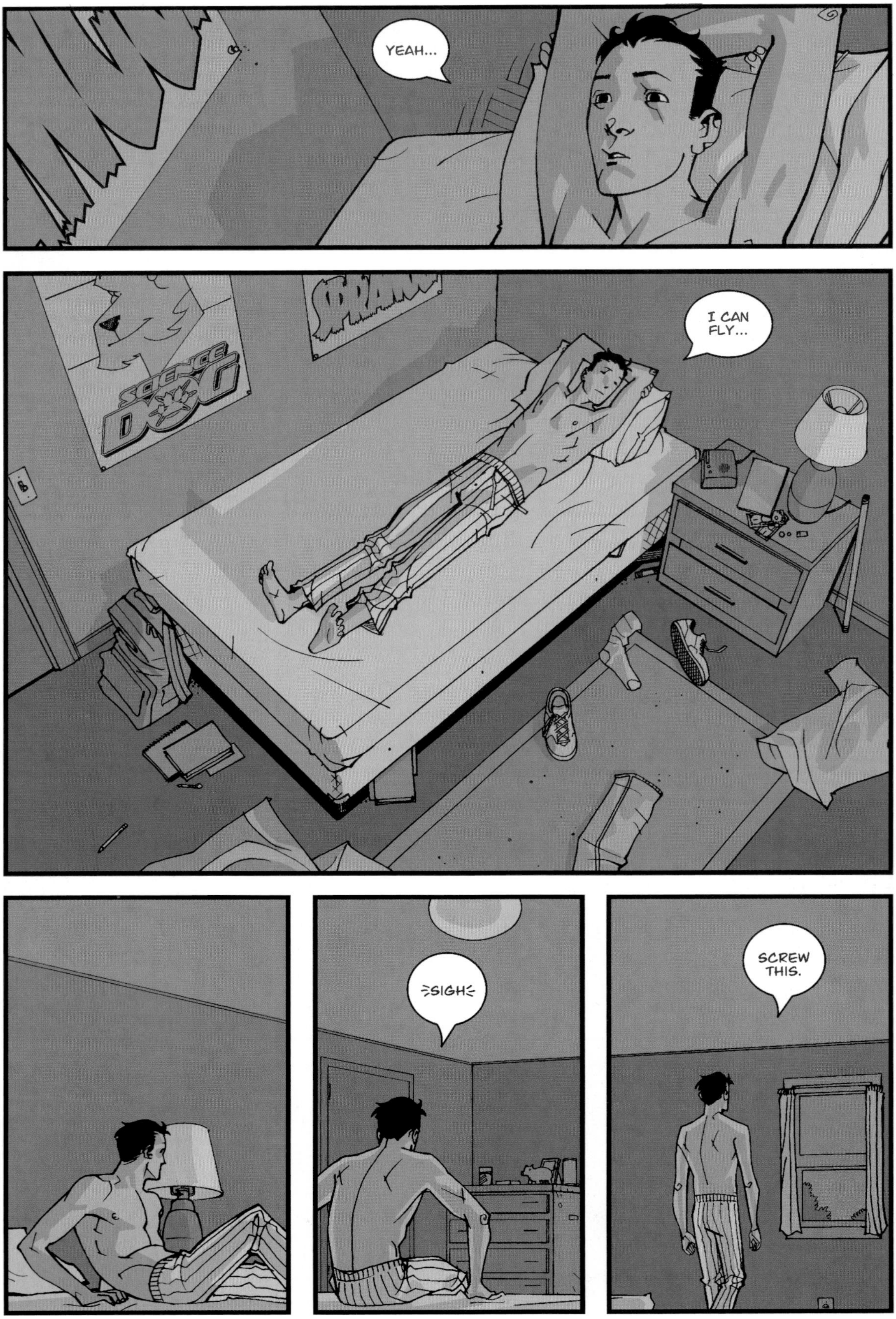
YEAH...
SCIENCE DOG
I CAN FLY...
SIGH
SCREW THIS.

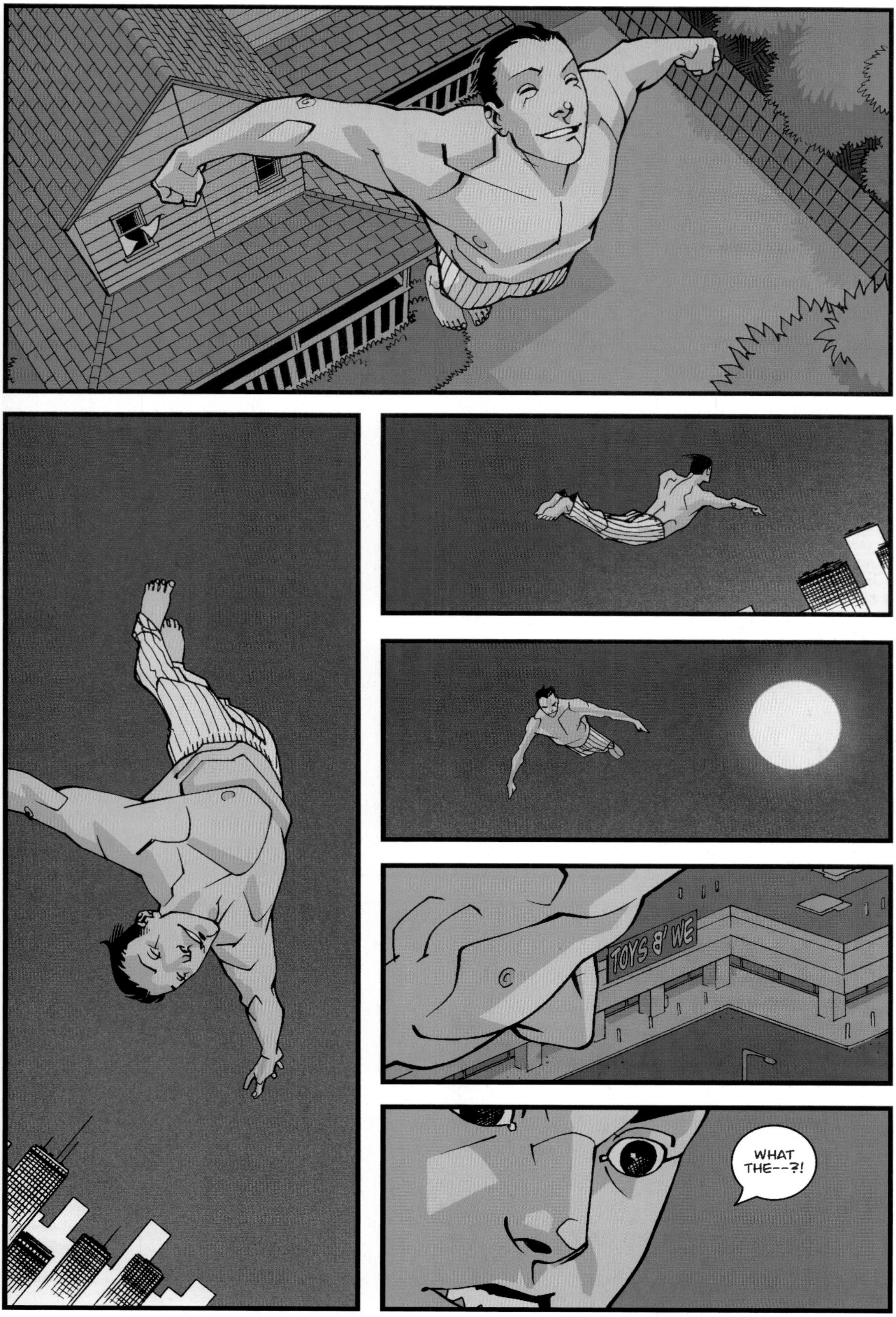
TOYS 'B' WE
WHAT THE--?!

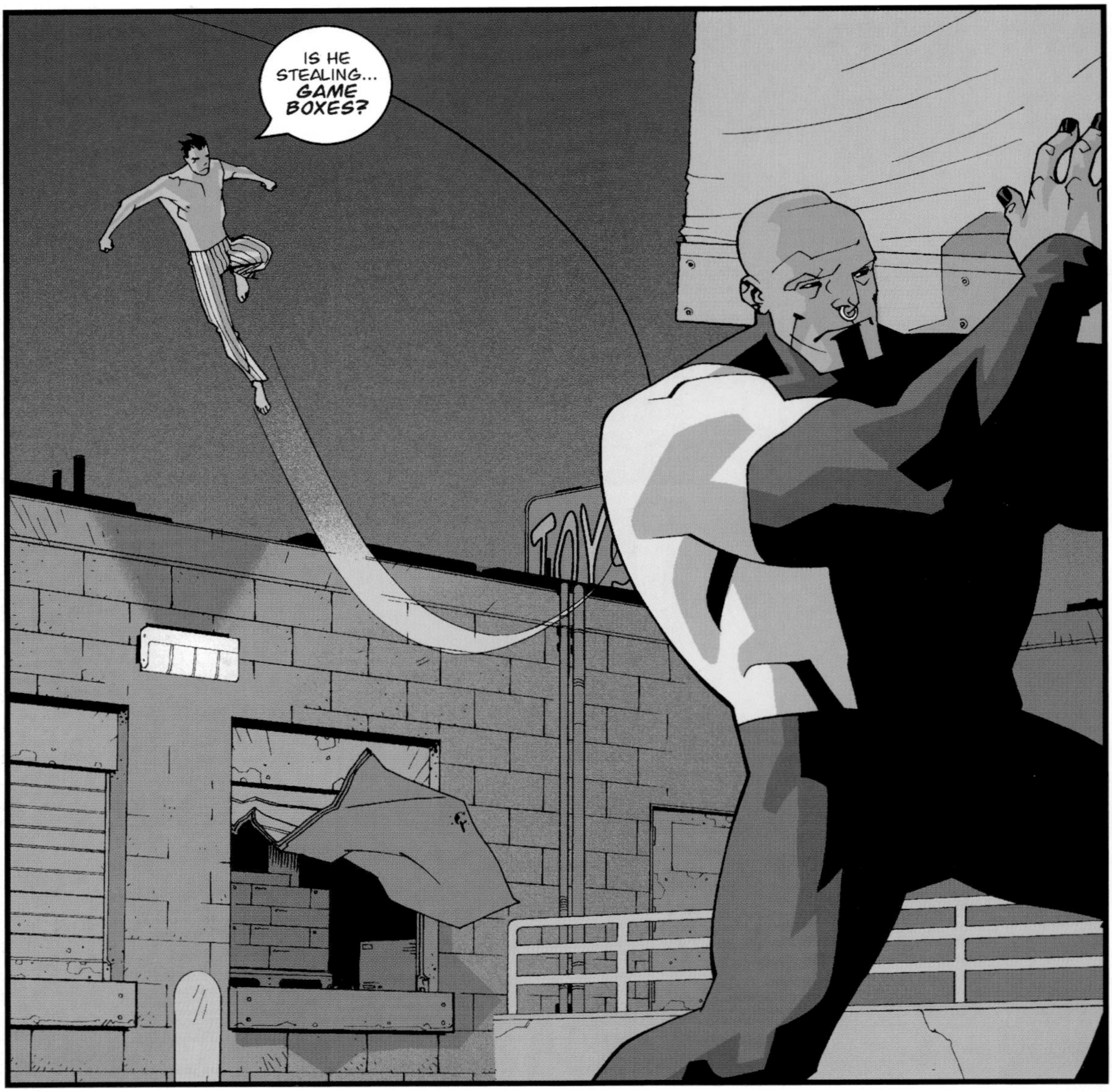
IS HE STEALING... GAME BOXES?
TOYS
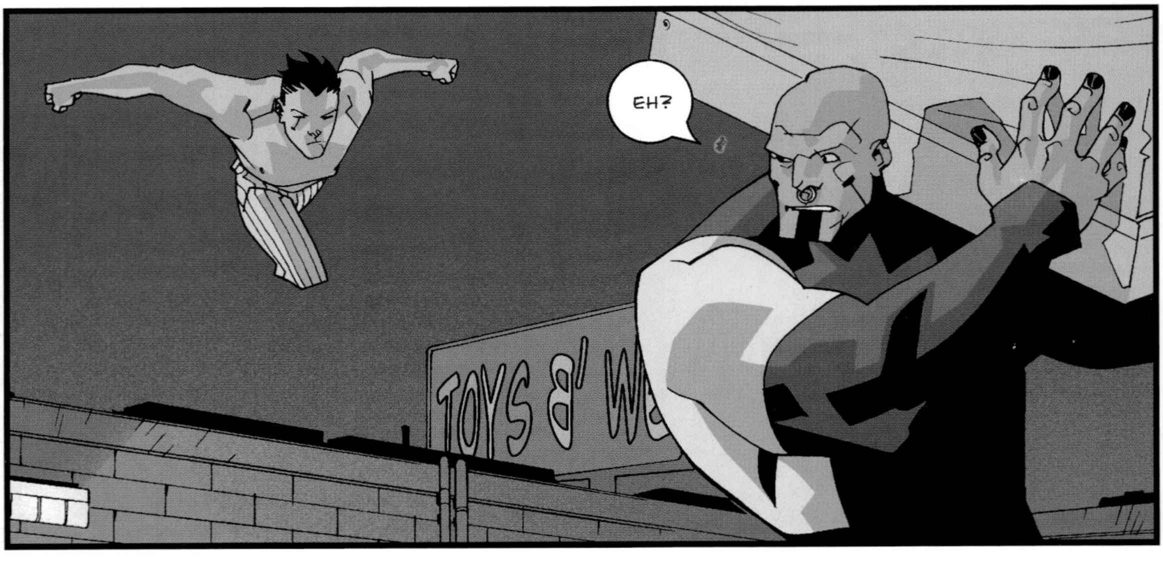
EH?
TOYS B' W

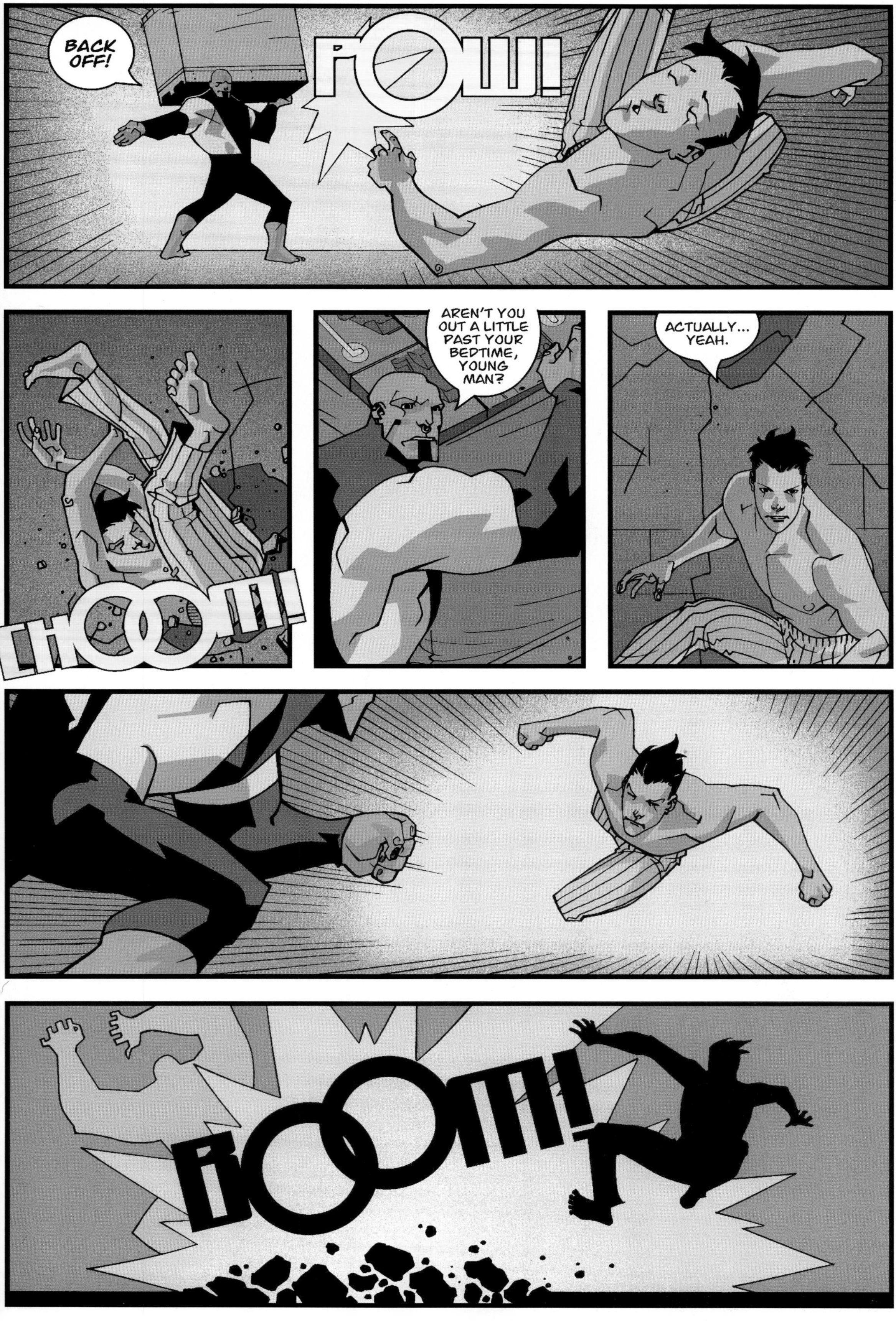
BACK OFF!
POW!
CHOOM!
AREN'T YOU OUT A LITTLE PAST YOUR BEDTIME, YOUNG MAN?
ACTUALLY... YEAH.
BOOM!

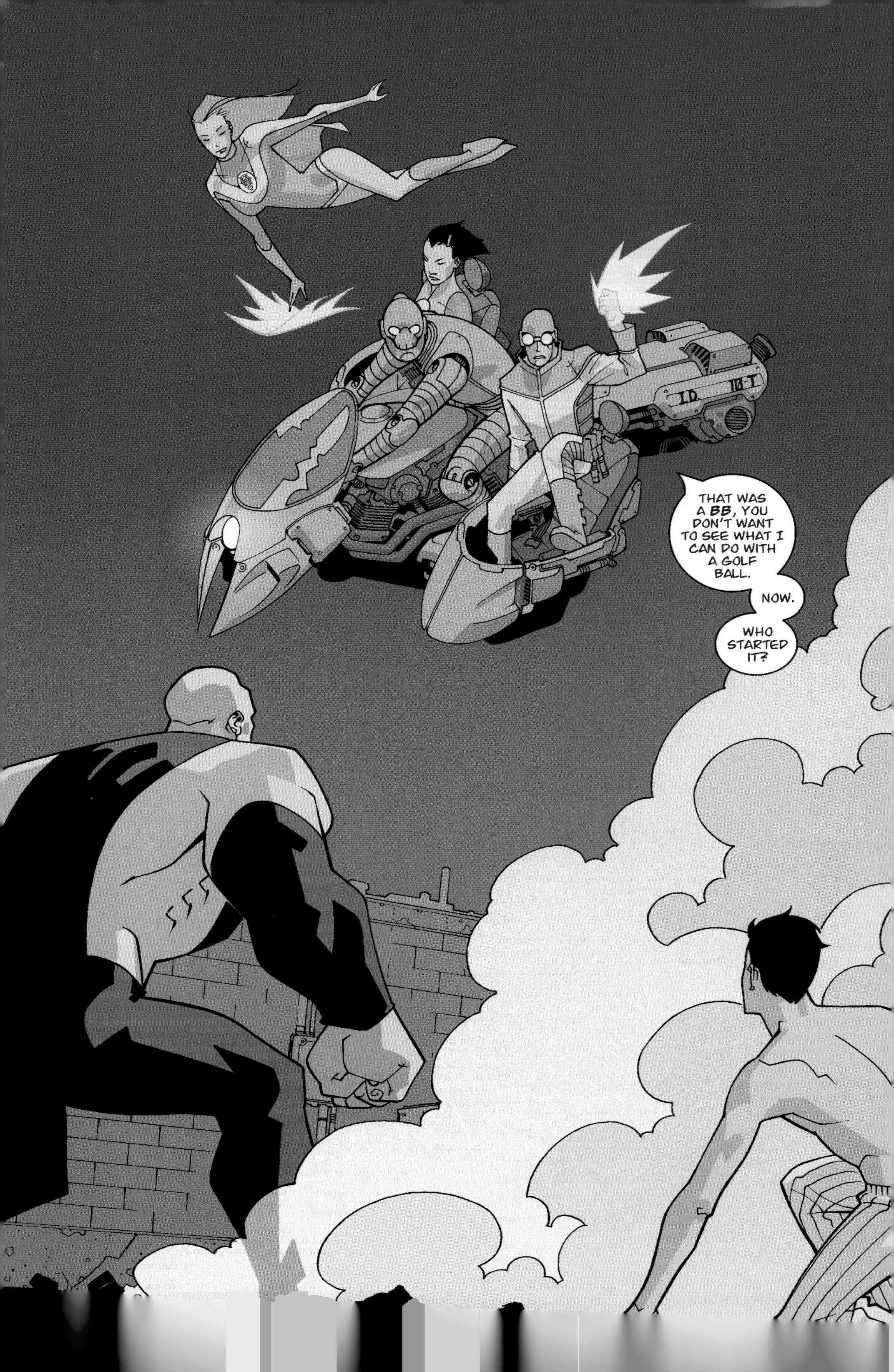
I.D. 10-T
THAT WAS A **BB**, YOU DON'T WANT TO SEE WHAT I CAN DO WITH A GOLF BALL.
NOW.
WHO STARTED IT?

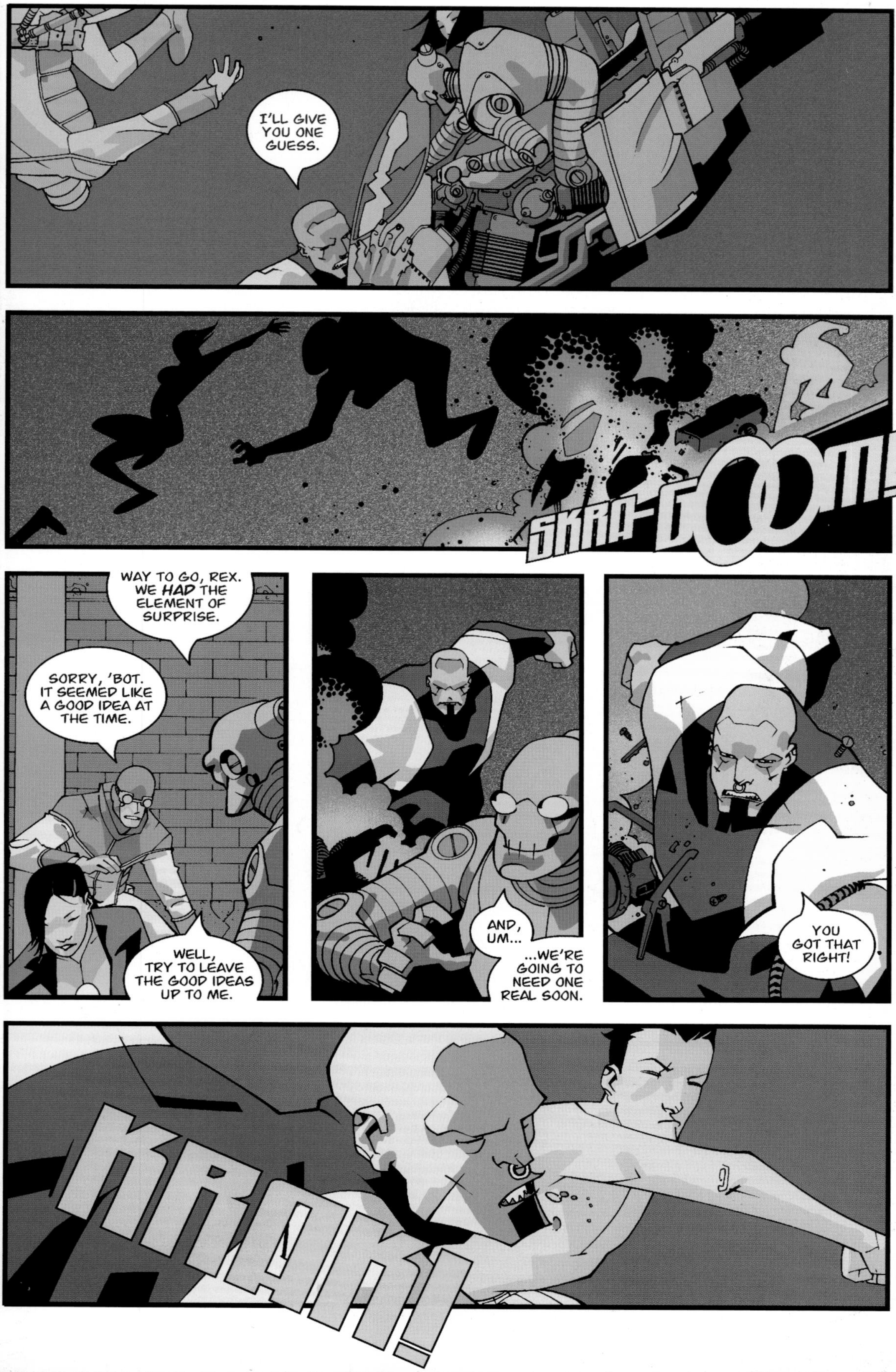

I'LL GIVE YOU ONE GUESS.
SKRA-BOOM!
WAY TO GO, REX. WE HAD THE ELEMENT OF SURPRISE.
SORRY, 'BOT. IT SEEMED LIKE A GOOD IDEA AT THE TIME.
WELL, TRY TO LEAVE THE GOOD IDEAS UP TO ME.
AND, UM...
...WE'RE GOING TO NEED ONE REAL SOON.
YOU GOT THAT RIGHT!
KRAK!

WOW.

NEVER MIND. NICE JOB, KID.

I'LL HAVE ANOTHER VEHICLE SENT TO US BY REMOTE. KATE, PULL OUR FRIEND, MAULER OUT OF THE WAY SO WE WON'T ATTRACT TOO MUCH ATTENTION.

NICE COSTUME, MAN.

SORRY, THERE WASN'T A PHONE BOOTH HANDY.

UM... DO I KNOW YOU?

YOU KNOW... YOU DO LOOK FAMILIAR...

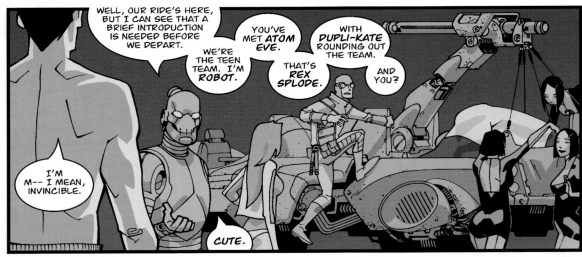

WELL, OUR RIDE'S HERE, BUT I CAN SEE THAT A BRIEF INTRODUCTION IS NEEDED BEFORE WE DEPART.

WE'RE THE TEEN TEAM. I'M ROBOT.

YOU'VE MET ATOM EVE.

THAT'S REX SPLODE.

WITH DUPLI-KATE ROUNDING OUT THE TEAM.

AND YOU?

I'M M-- I MEAN, INVINCIBLE.

CUTE.

NICE TO MEET YOU.

SEE YOU AROUND.

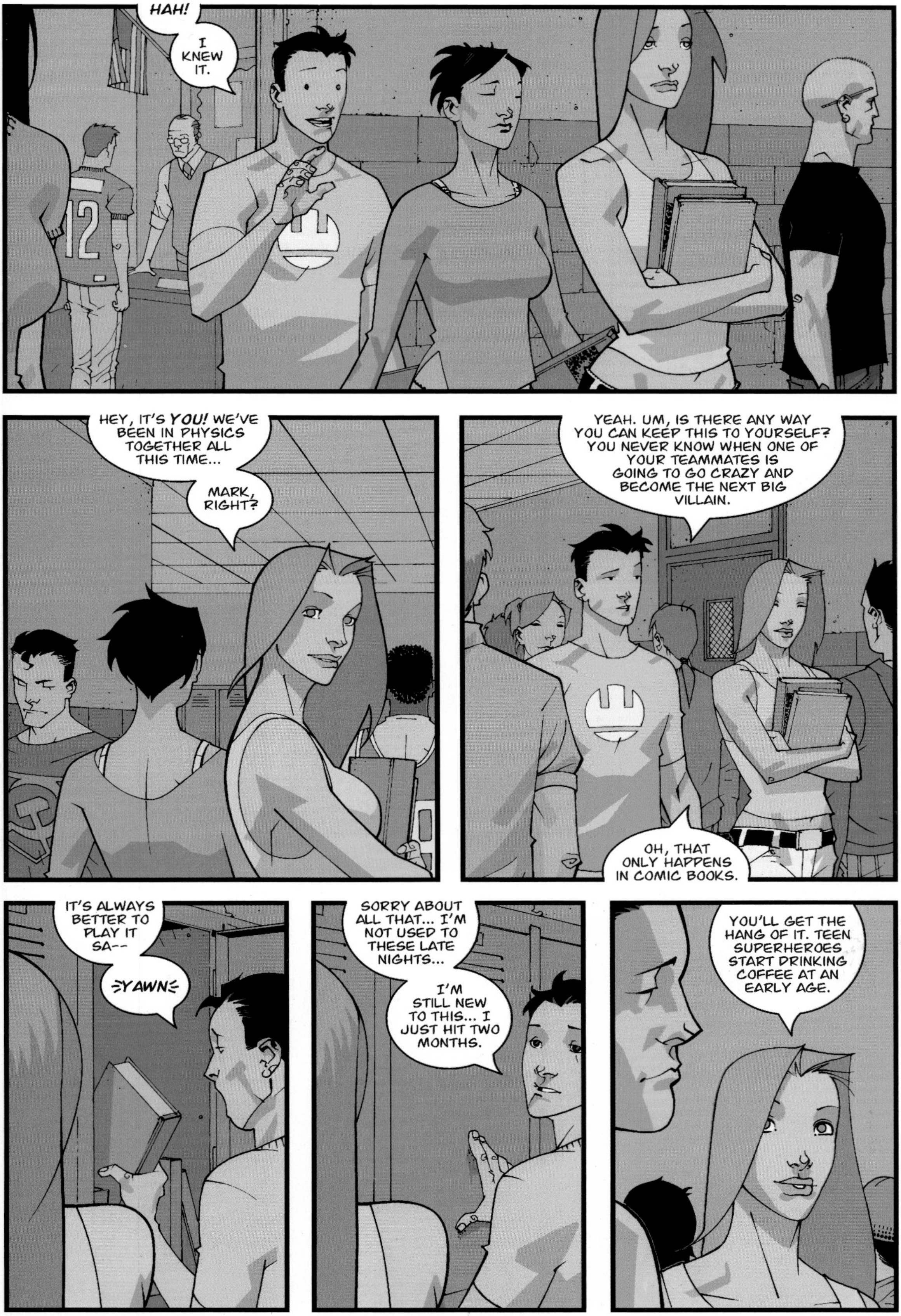
HAH!
I KNEW IT.
HEY, IT'S YOU! WE'VE BEEN IN PHYSICS TOGETHER ALL THIS TIME...
MARK, RIGHT?
YEAH. UM, IS THERE ANY WAY YOU CAN KEEP THIS TO YOURSELF? YOU NEVER KNOW WHEN ONE OF YOUR TEAMMATES IS GOING TO GO CRAZY AND BECOME THE NEXT BIG VILLAIN.
OH, THAT ONLY HAPPENS IN COMIC BOOKS.
IT'S ALWAYS BETTER TO PLAY IT SA--
YAWN
SORRY ABOUT ALL THAT... I'M NOT USED TO THESE LATE NIGHTS...
I'M STILL NEW TO THIS... I JUST HIT TWO MONTHS.
YOU'LL GET THE HANG OF IT. TEEN SUPERHEROES START DRINKING COFFEE AT AN EARLY AGE.

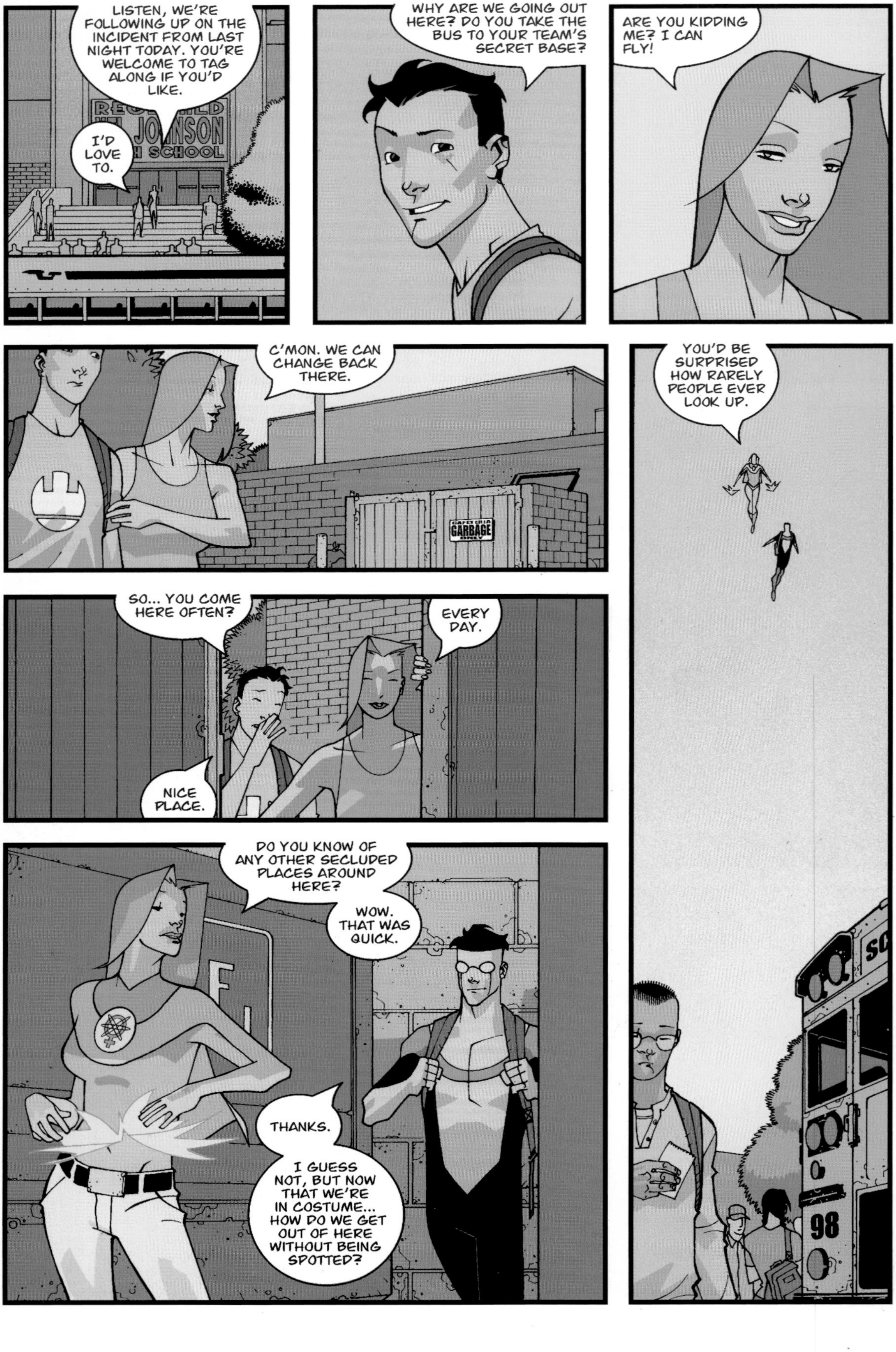
LISTEN, WE'RE FOLLOWING UP ON THE INCIDENT FROM LAST NIGHT TODAY. YOU'RE WELCOME TO TAG ALONG IF YOU'D LIKE.
I'D LOVE TO.
WHY ARE WE GOING OUT HERE? DO YOU TAKE THE BUS TO YOUR TEAM'S SECRET BASE?
ARE YOU KIDDING ME? I CAN FLY!
C'MON. WE CAN CHANGE BACK THERE.
GARBAGE
SO... YOU COME HERE OFTEN?
EVERY DAY.
NICE PLACE.
DO YOU KNOW OF ANY OTHER SECLUDED PLACES AROUND HERE?
WOW. THAT WAS QUICK.
THANKS.
I GUESS NOT, BUT NOW THAT WE'RE IN COSTUME... HOW DO WE GET OUT OF HERE WITHOUT BEING SPOTTED?
YOU'D BE SURPRISED HOW RARELY PEOPLE EVER LOOK UP.
98

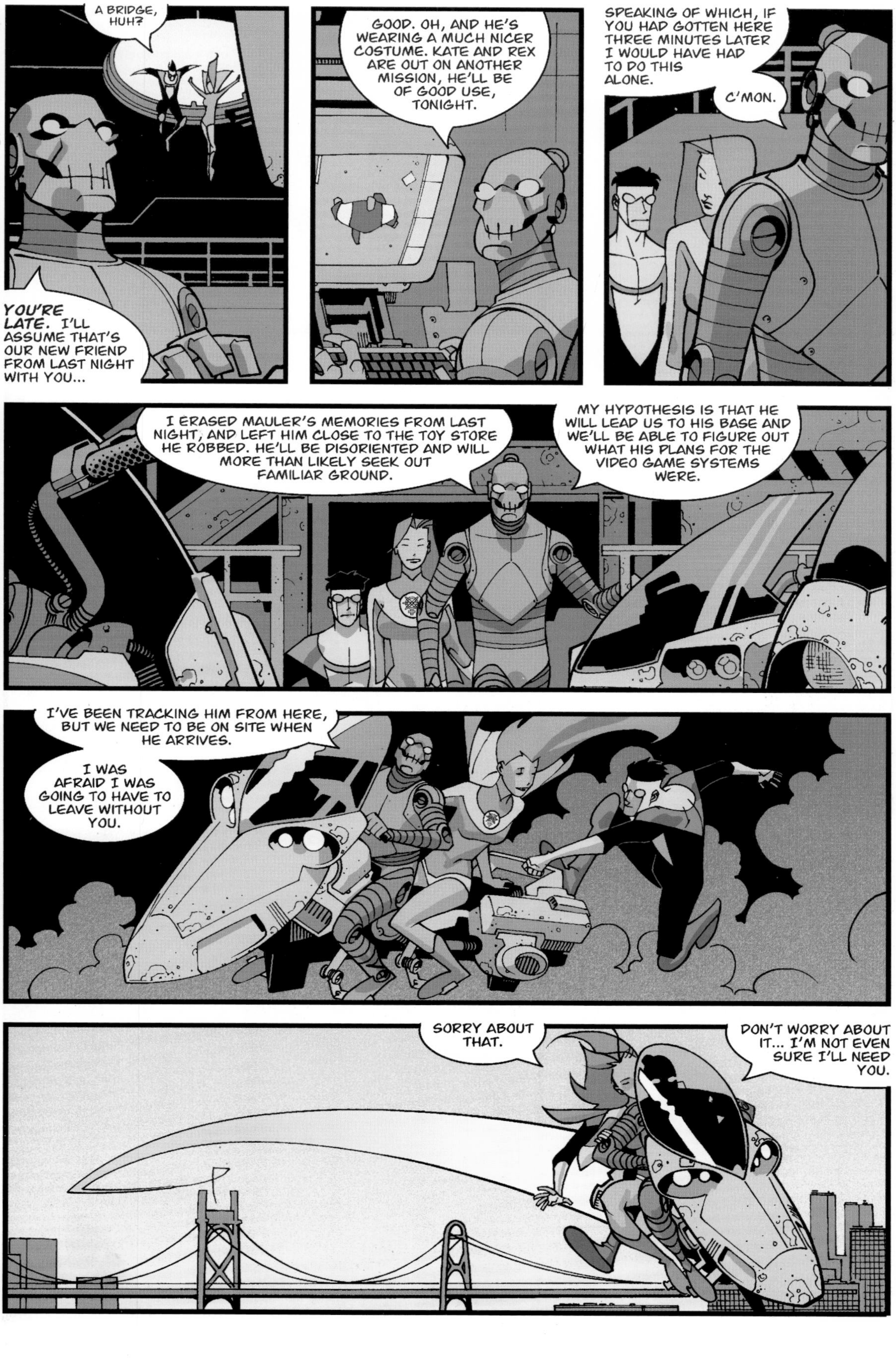
A BRIDGE, HUH?
YOU'RE LATE. I'LL ASSUME THAT'S OUR NEW FRIEND FROM LAST NIGHT WITH YOU...
GOOD. OH, AND HE'S WEARING A MUCH NICER COSTUME. KATE AND REX ARE OUT ON ANOTHER MISSION, HE'LL BE OF GOOD USE, TONIGHT.
SPEAKING OF WHICH, IF YOU HAD GOTTEN HERE THREE MINUTES LATER I WOULD HAVE HAD TO DO THIS ALONE.
C'MON.
I ERASED MAULER'S MEMORIES FROM LAST NIGHT, AND LEFT HIM CLOSE TO THE TOY STORE HE ROBBED. HE'LL BE DISORIENTED AND WILL MORE THAN LIKELY SEEK OUT FAMILIAR GROUND.
MY HYPOTHESIS IS THAT HE WILL LEAD US TO HIS BASE AND WE'LL BE ABLE TO FIGURE OUT WHAT HIS PLANS FOR THE VIDEO GAME SYSTEMS WERE.
I'VE BEEN TRACKING HIM FROM HERE, BUT WE NEED TO BE ON SITE WHEN HE ARRIVES.
I WAS AFRAID I WAS GOING TO HAVE TO LEAVE WITHOUT YOU.
SORRY ABOUT THAT.
DON'T WORRY ABOUT IT... I'M NOT EVEN SURE I'LL NEED YOU.

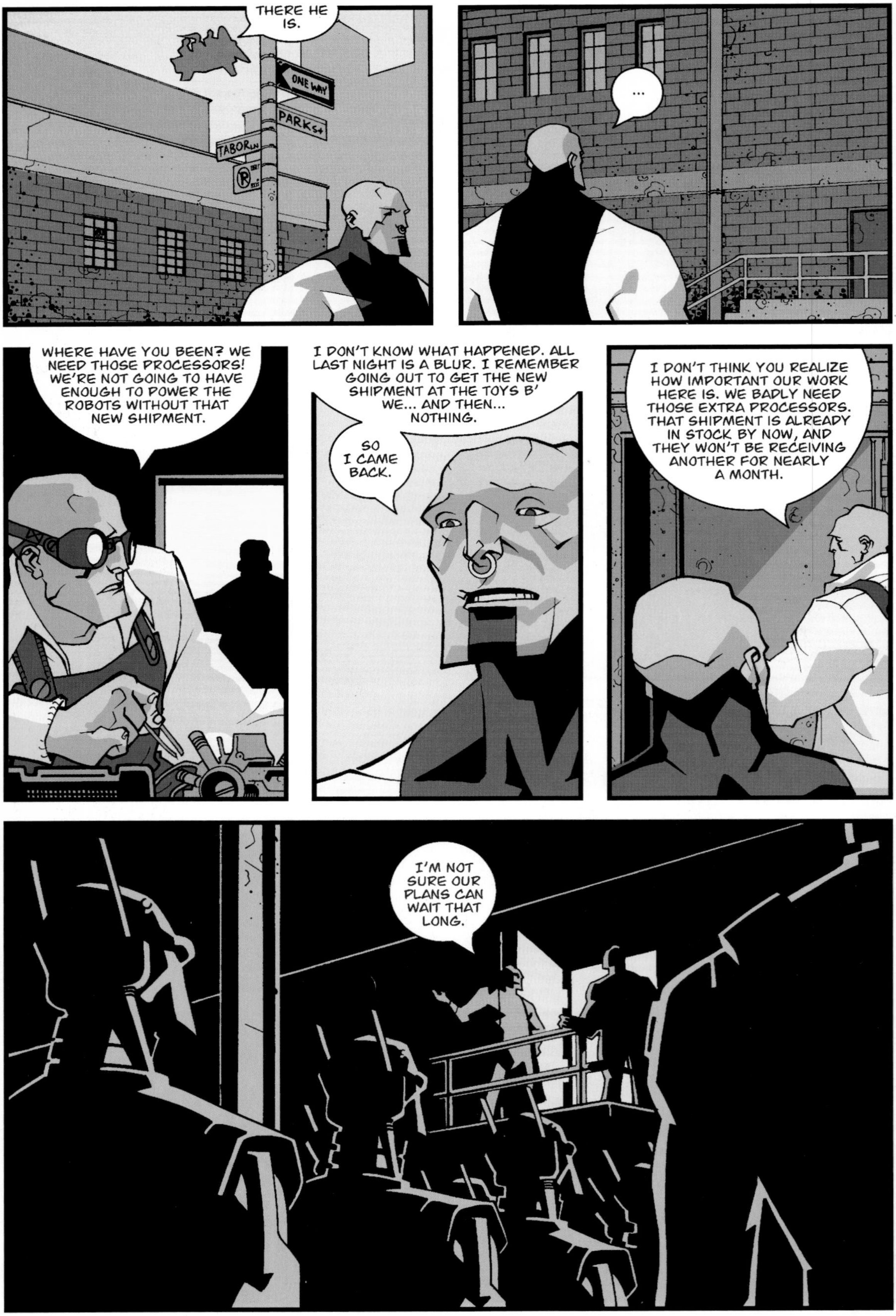
THERE HE IS.
ONE WAY
PARKS St
TABOR LN
...
WHERE HAVE YOU BEEN? WE NEED THOSE PROCESSORS! WE'RE NOT GOING TO HAVE ENOUGH TO POWER THE ROBOTS WITHOUT THAT NEW SHIPMENT.
I DON'T KNOW WHAT HAPPENED. ALL LAST NIGHT IS A BLUR. I REMEMBER GOING OUT TO GET THE NEW SHIPMENT AT THE TOYS B' WE... AND THEN... NOTHING.
SO I CAME BACK.
I DON'T THINK YOU REALIZE HOW IMPORTANT OUR WORK HERE IS. WE BADLY NEED THOSE EXTRA PROCESSORS. THAT SHIPMENT IS ALREADY IN STOCK BY NOW, AND THEY WON'T BE RECEIVING ANOTHER FOR NEARLY A MONTH.
I'M NOT SURE OUR PLANS CAN WAIT THAT LONG.

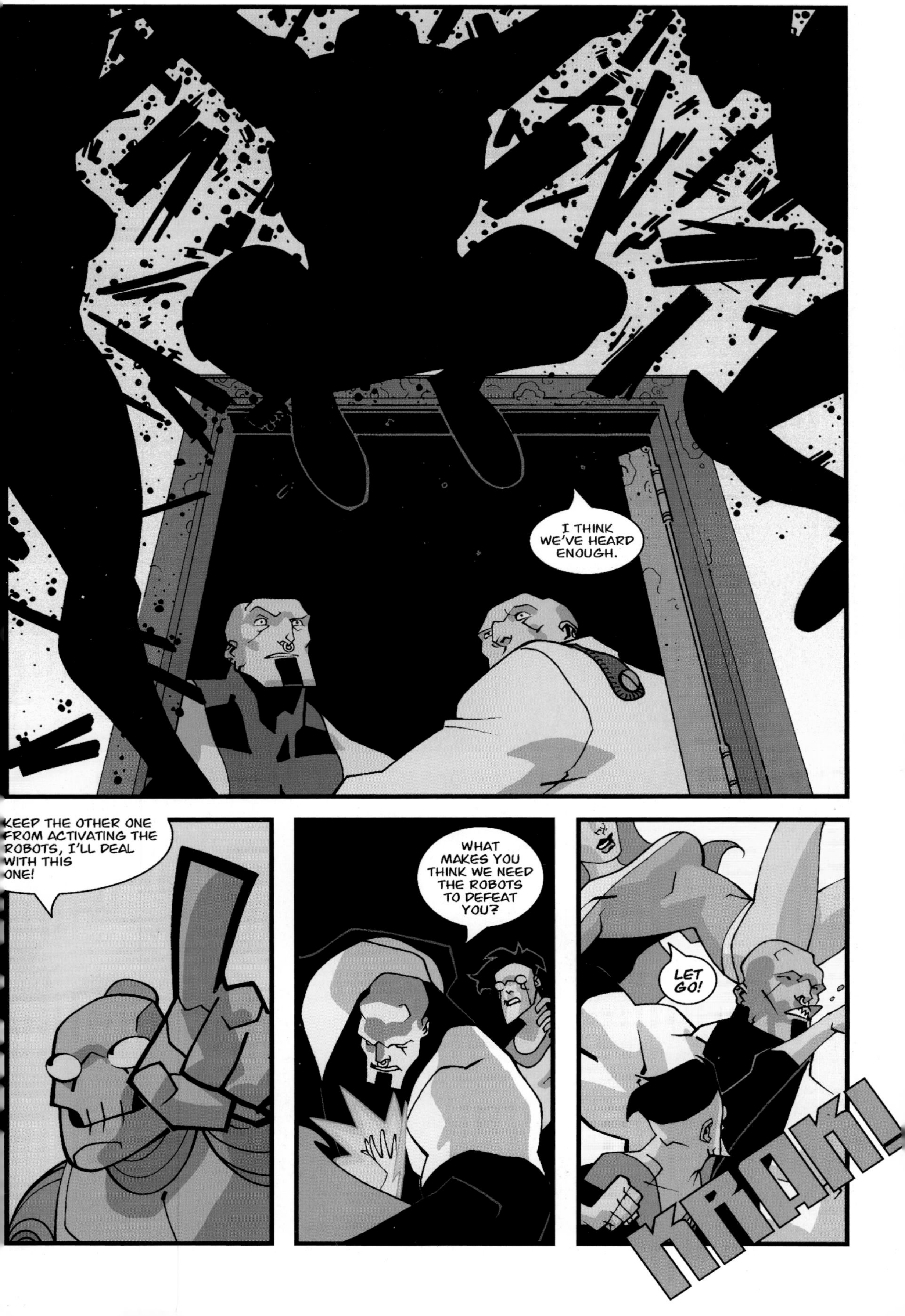
I THINK WE'VE HEARD ENOUGH.
KEEP THE OTHER ONE FROM ACTIVATING THE ROBOTS, I'LL DEAL WITH THIS ONE!
WHAT MAKES YOU THINK WE NEED THE ROBOTS TO DEFEAT YOU?
LET GO!
KRAAK!

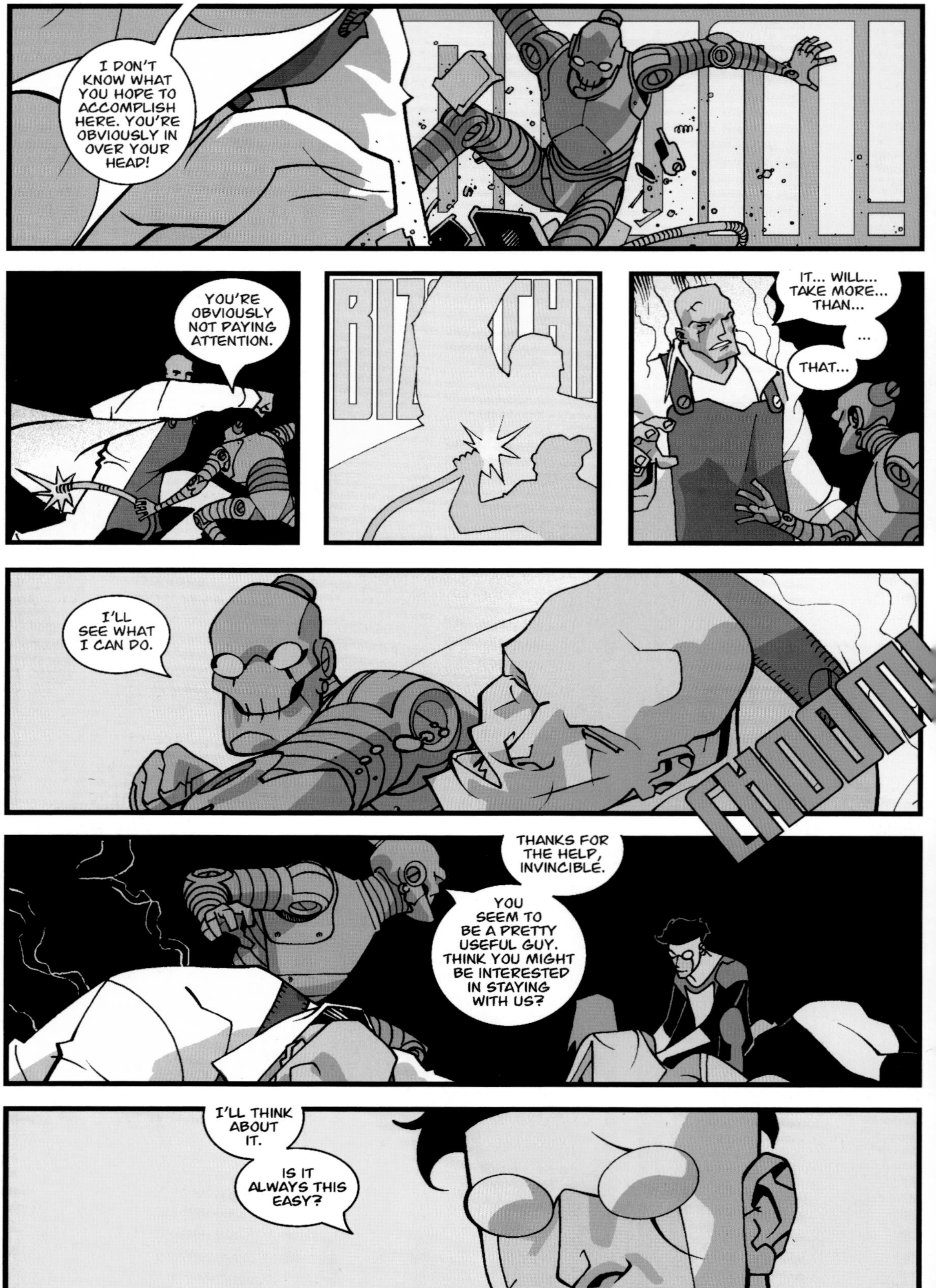
I DON'T KNOW WHAT YOU HOPE TO ACCOMPLISH HERE. YOU'RE OBVIOUSLY IN OVER YOUR HEAD!
YOU'RE OBVIOUSLY NOT PAYING ATTENTION.
IT... WILL... TAKE MORE... THAN...
...
THAT...
I'LL SEE WHAT I CAN DO.
THANKS FOR THE HELP, INVINCIBLE.
YOU SEEM TO BE A PRETTY USEFUL GUY. THINK YOU MIGHT BE INTERESTED IN STAYING WITH US?
I'LL THINK ABOUT IT.
IS IT ALWAYS THIS EASY?

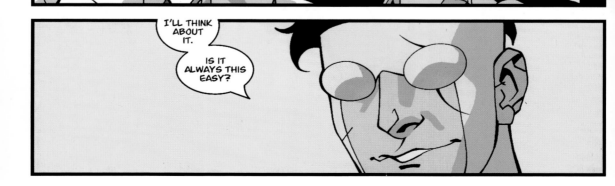

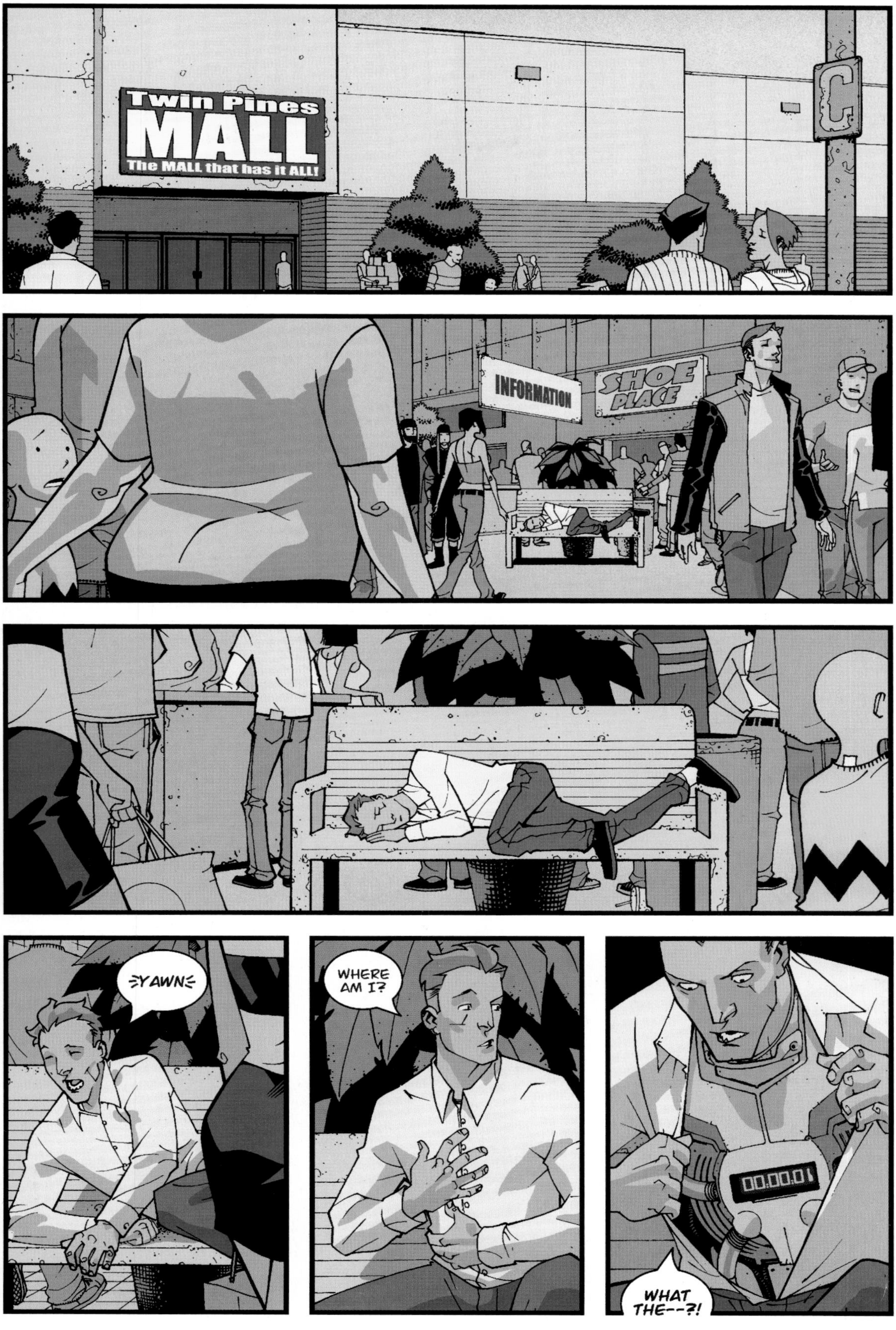
Twin Pines
MALL
The MALL that has it ALL!
C
INFORMATION
SHOE PLACE
YAWN
WHERE AM I?
00.00.01
WHAT THE--?!

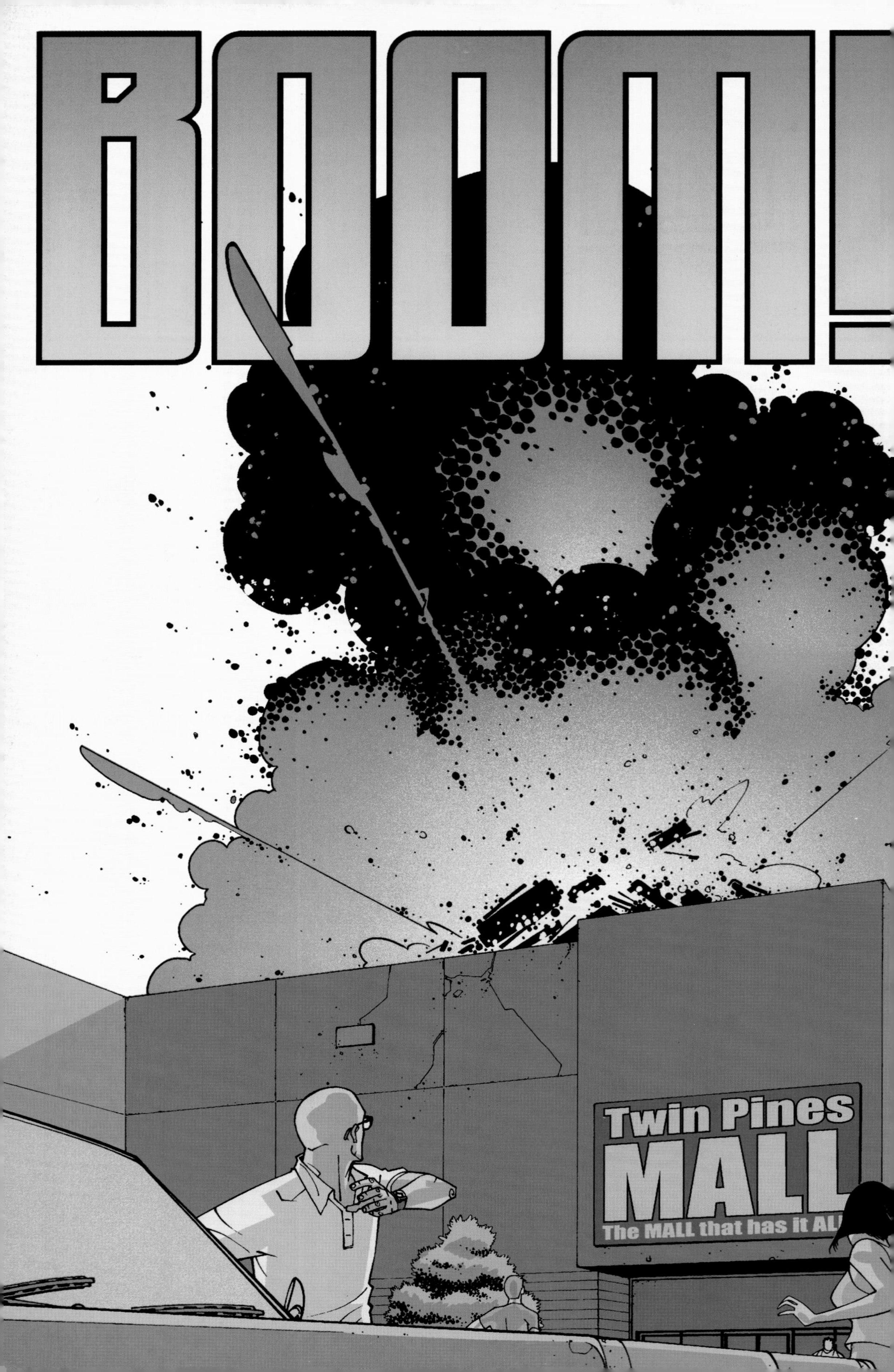
BOOM!
Twin Pines
MALL
The MALL that has it ALL

# CHAPTER THREE

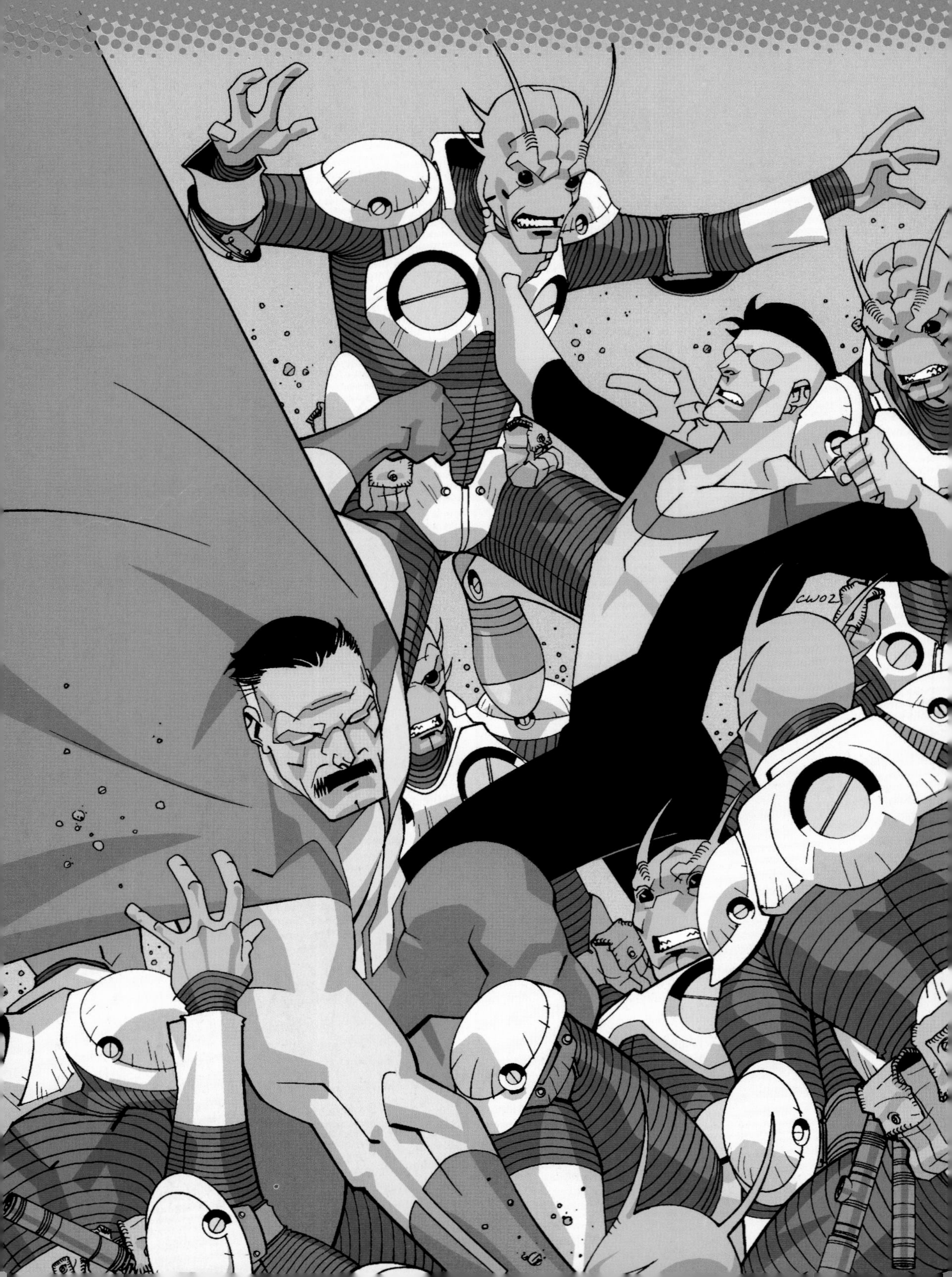

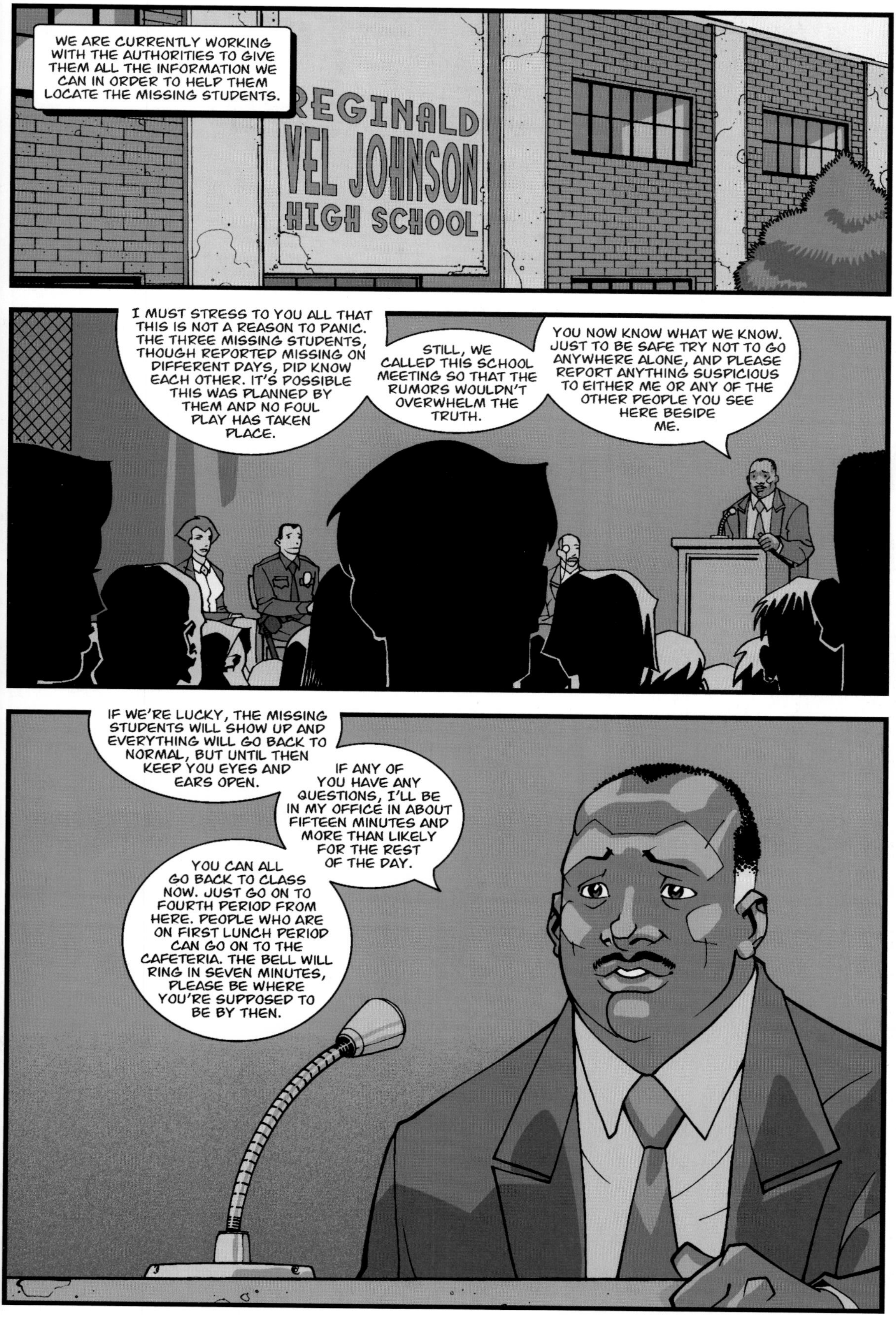
REGINALD VEL JOHNSON HIGH SCHOOL
WE ARE CURRENTLY WORKING WITH THE AUTHORITIES TO GIVE THEM ALL THE INFORMATION WE CAN IN ORDER TO HELP THEM LOCATE THE MISSING STUDENTS.
I MUST STRESS TO YOU ALL THAT THIS IS NOT A REASON TO PANIC. THE THREE MISSING STUDENTS, THOUGH REPORTED MISSING ON DIFFERENT DAYS, DID KNOW EACH OTHER. IT'S POSSIBLE THIS WAS PLANNED BY THEM AND NO FOUL PLAY HAS TAKEN PLACE.
STILL, WE CALLED THIS SCHOOL MEETING SO THAT THE RUMORS WOULDN'T OVERWHELM THE TRUTH.
YOU NOW KNOW WHAT WE KNOW. JUST TO BE SAFE TRY NOT TO GO ANYWHERE ALONE, AND PLEASE REPORT ANYTHING SUSPICIOUS TO EITHER ME OR ANY OF THE OTHER PEOPLE YOU SEE HERE BESIDE ME.
IF WE'RE LUCKY, THE MISSING STUDENTS WILL SHOW UP AND EVERYTHING WILL GO BACK TO NORMAL, BUT UNTIL THEN KEEP YOU EYES AND EARS OPEN.
IF ANY OF YOU HAVE ANY QUESTIONS, I'LL BE IN MY OFFICE IN ABOUT FIFTEEN MINUTES AND MORE THAN LIKELY FOR THE REST OF THE DAY.
YOU CAN ALL GO BACK TO CLASS NOW. JUST GO ON TO FOURTH PERIOD FROM HERE. PEOPLE WHO ARE ON FIRST LUNCH PERIOD CAN GO ON TO THE CAFETERIA. THE BELL WILL RING IN SEVEN MINUTES, PLEASE BE WHERE YOU'RE SUPPOSED TO BE BY THEN.

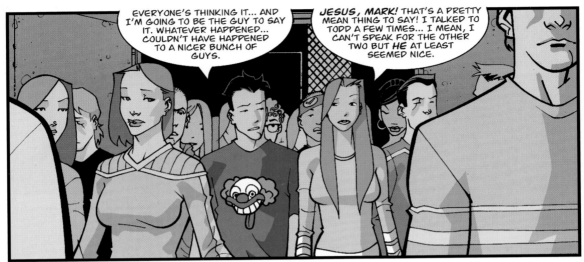

EVERYONE'S THINKING IT... AND I'M GOING TO BE THE GUY TO SAY IT. WHATEVER HAPPENED... COULDN'T HAVE HAPPENED TO A NICER BUNCH OF GUYS.

JESUS, MARK! THAT'S A PRETTY MEAN THING TO SAY! I TALKED TO TODD A FEW TIMES... I MEAN, I CAN'T SPEAK FOR THE OTHER TWO BUT HE AT LEAST SEEMED NICE.

YOU'RE TOTALLY CLUELESS! WHY DO YOU THINK TODD JEFFERSON WOULD BE NICE TO YOU?

OFF THE TOP OF MY HEAD... I THINK IT MAY HAVE SOMETHING TO DO WITH YOU BEING AN EXTREMELY ATTRACTIVE GIRL.

YOU KNOW I'M DATING REX, RIGHT?

WHOA, WHOA! THAT'S NOT WHERE I WAS GOING WITH THAT AT ALL!

...

HEH.

RIIIGHT.

SO, ARE YOU ON YOUR WAY TO THE CAFETERIA, TOO, OR ARE YOU JUST WALKING WITH ME?

WELL, I GUESS WE HAVE THE SAME LUNCH PERIOD, TOO.

I CAN'T BELIEVE WE HADN'T MET BEFORE LAST MONTH.

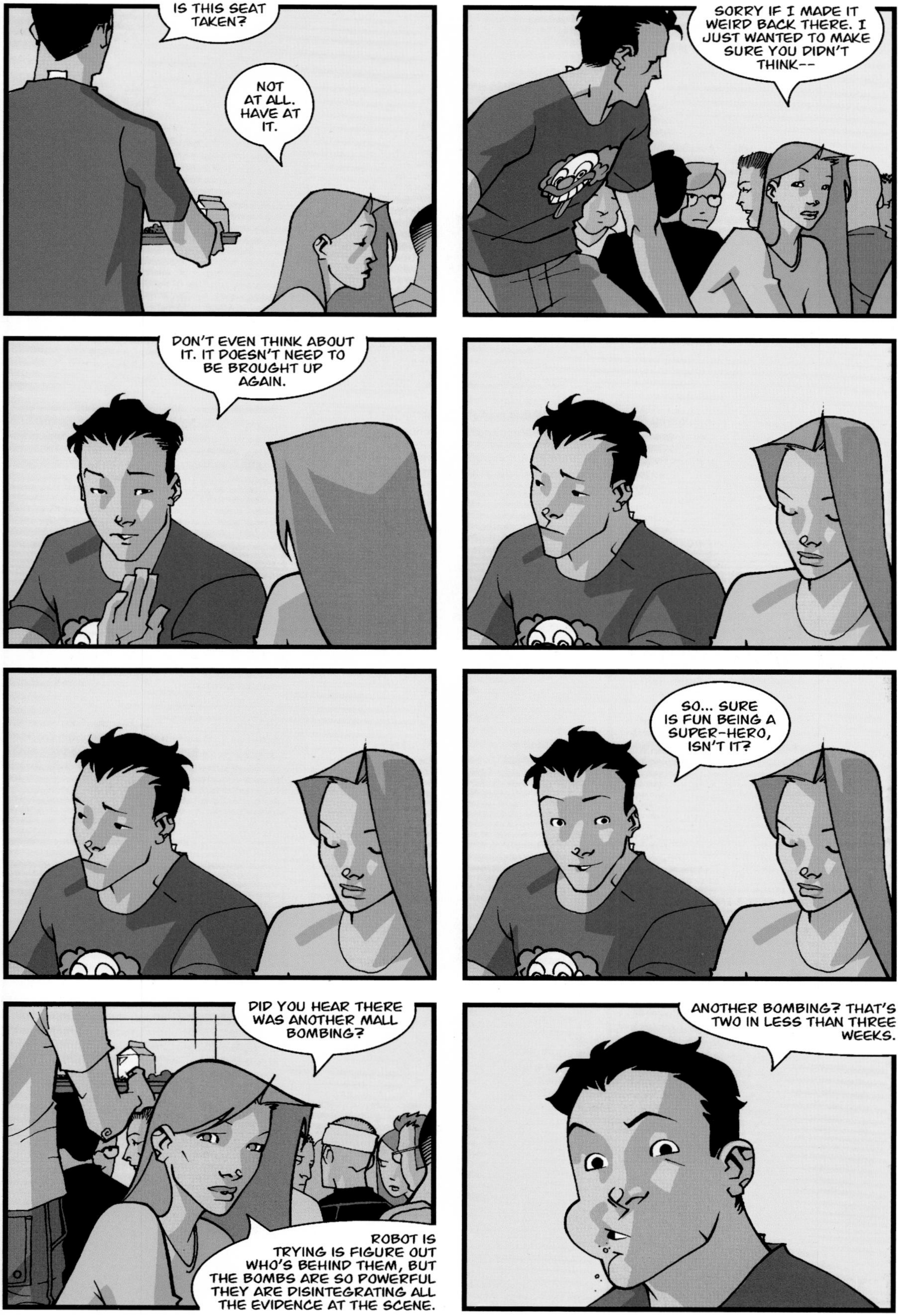
IS THIS SEAT TAKEN?
NOT AT ALL. HAVE AT IT.
SORRY IF I MADE IT WEIRD BACK THERE. I JUST WANTED TO MAKE SURE YOU DIDN'T THINK--
DON'T EVEN THINK ABOUT IT. IT DOESN'T NEED TO BE BROUGHT UP AGAIN.
SO... SURE IS FUN BEING A SUPER-HERO, ISN'T IT?
DID YOU HEAR THERE WAS ANOTHER MALL BOMBING?
ROBOT IS TRYING IS FIGURE OUT WHO'S BEHIND THEM, BUT THE BOMBS ARE SO POWERFUL THEY ARE DISINTEGRATING ALL THE EVIDENCE AT THE SCENE.
ANOTHER BOMBING? THAT'S TWO IN LESS THAN THREE WEEKS.

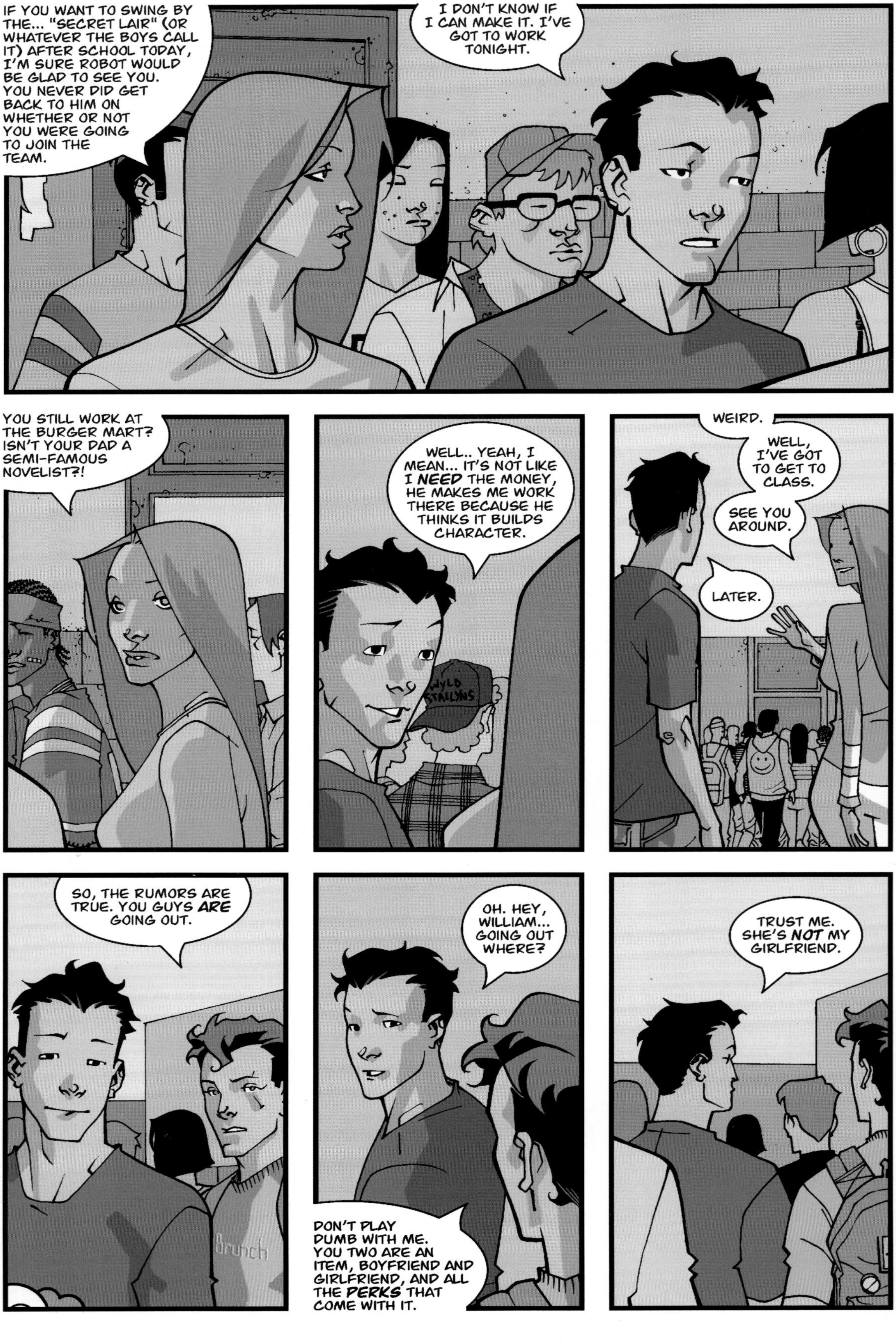

IF YOU WANT TO SWING BY THE... "SECRET LAIR" (OR WHATEVER THE BOYS CALL IT) AFTER SCHOOL TODAY, I'M SURE ROBOT WOULD BE GLAD TO SEE YOU. YOU NEVER DID GET BACK TO HIM ON WHETHER OR NOT YOU WERE GOING TO JOIN THE TEAM.
I DON'T KNOW IF I CAN MAKE IT. I'VE GOT TO WORK TONIGHT.
YOU STILL WORK AT THE BURGER MART? ISN'T YOUR DAD A SEMI-FAMOUS NOVELIST?!
WELL.. YEAH, I MEAN... IT'S NOT LIKE I ***NEED*** THE MONEY, HE MAKES ME WORK THERE BECAUSE HE THINKS IT BUILDS CHARACTER.
WYLD STALLYNS
WEIRD.
WELL, I'VE GOT TO GET TO CLASS.
SEE YOU AROUND.
LATER.
SO, THE RUMORS ARE TRUE. YOU GUYS ***ARE*** GOING OUT.
Brunch
OH. HEY, WILLIAM... GOING OUT WHERE?
DON'T PLAY DUMB WITH ME. YOU TWO ARE AN ITEM, BOYFRIEND AND GIRLFRIEND, AND ALL THE ***PERKS*** THAT COME WITH IT.
TRUST ME. SHE'S ***NOT*** MY GIRLFRIEND.

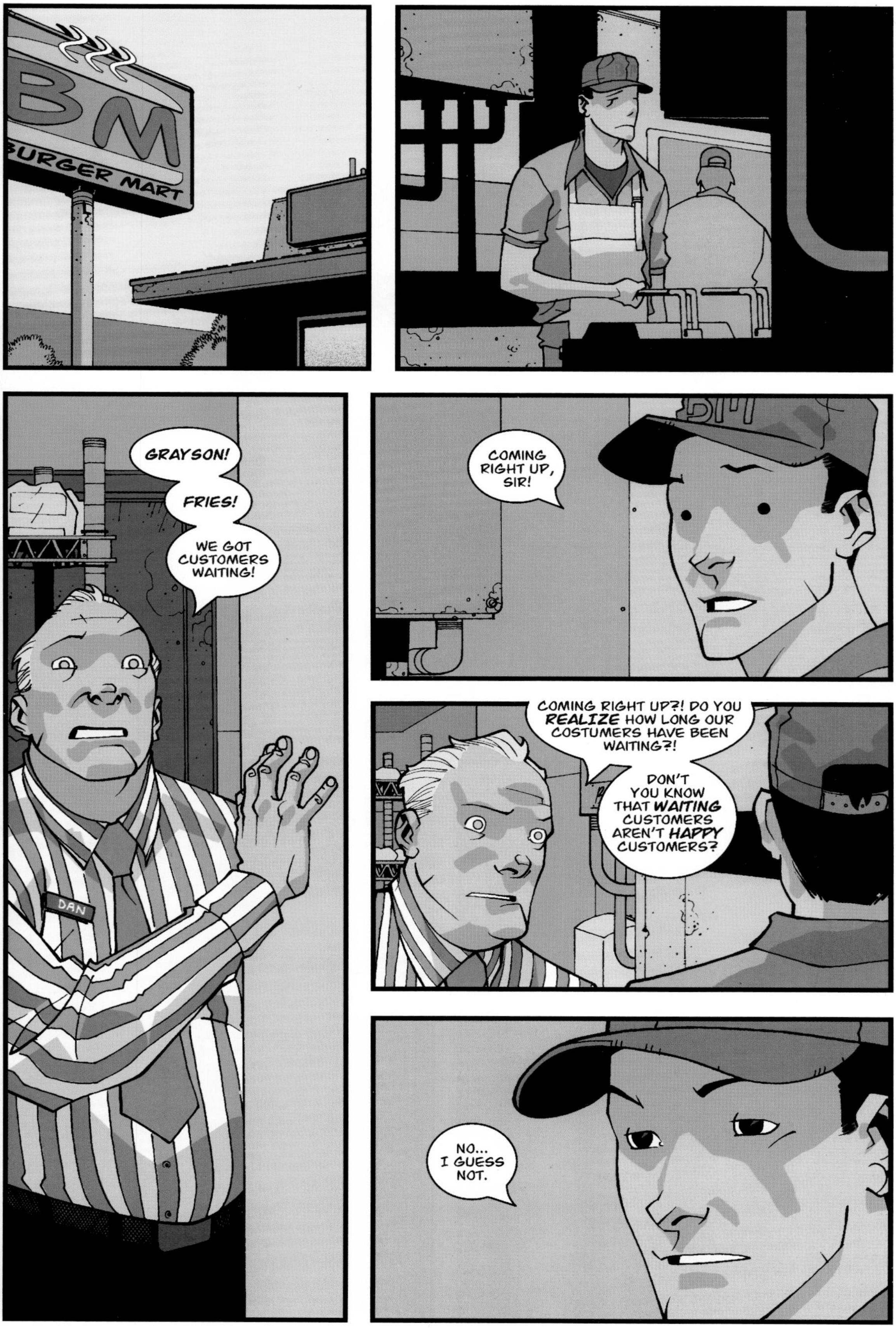
BM
BURGER MART
GRAYSON!
FRIES!
WE GOT CUSTOMERS WAITING!
DAN
BM
COMING RIGHT UP, SIR!
COMING RIGHT UP?! DO YOU **REALIZE** HOW LONG OUR COSTUMERS HAVE BEEN WAITING?!
DON'T YOU KNOW THAT **WAITING** CUSTOMERS AREN'T **HAPPY** CUSTOMERS?
NO... I GUESS NOT.

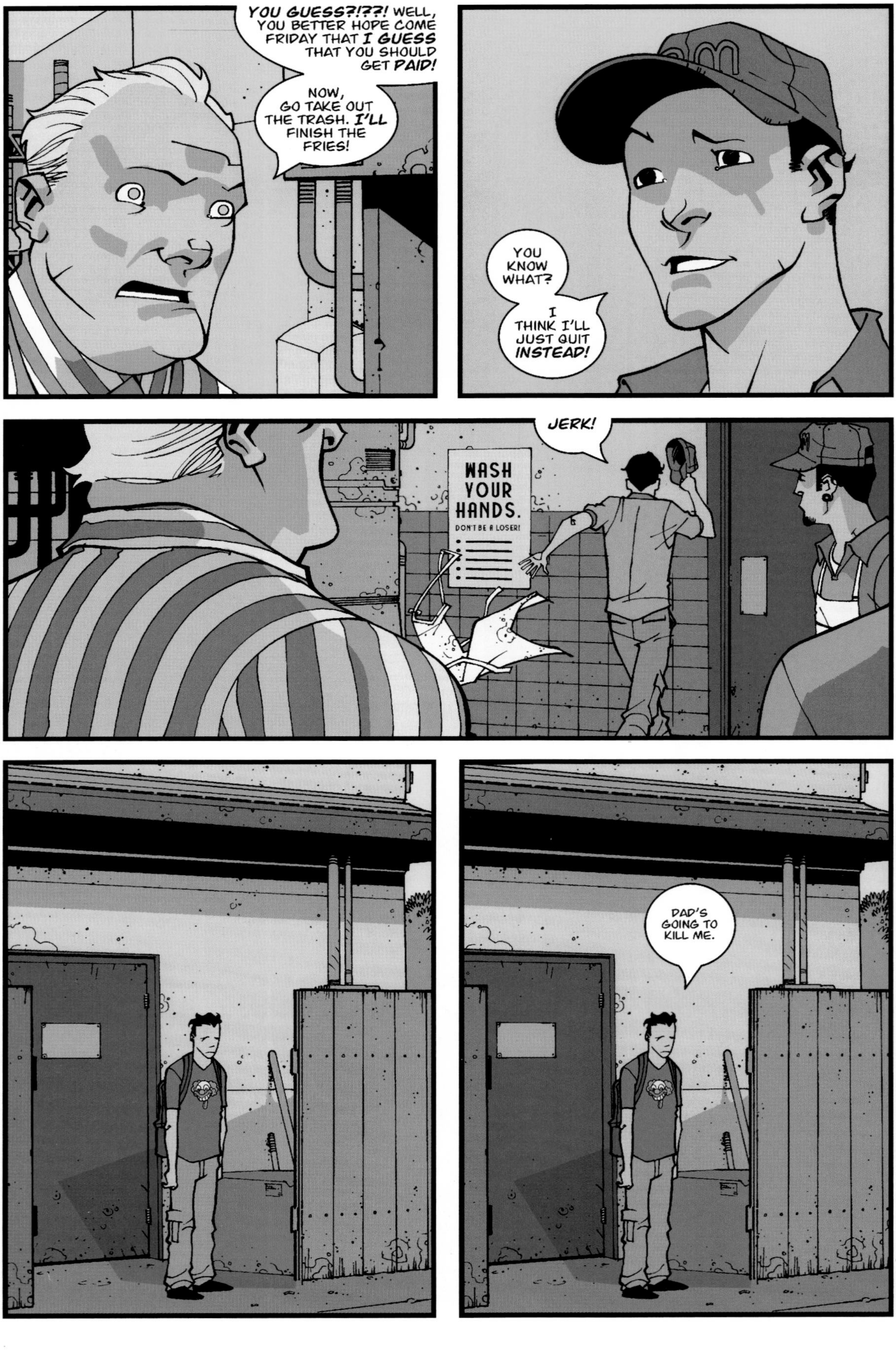
YOU GUESS?!??! WELL, YOU BETTER HOPE COME FRIDAY THAT I GUESS THAT YOU SHOULD GET PAID!
NOW, GO TAKE OUT THE TRASH. I'LL FINISH THE FRIES!
YOU KNOW WHAT?
I THINK I'LL JUST QUIT INSTEAD!
JERK!
WASH YOUR HANDS.
DON'T BE A LOSER!
DAD'S GOING TO KILL ME.

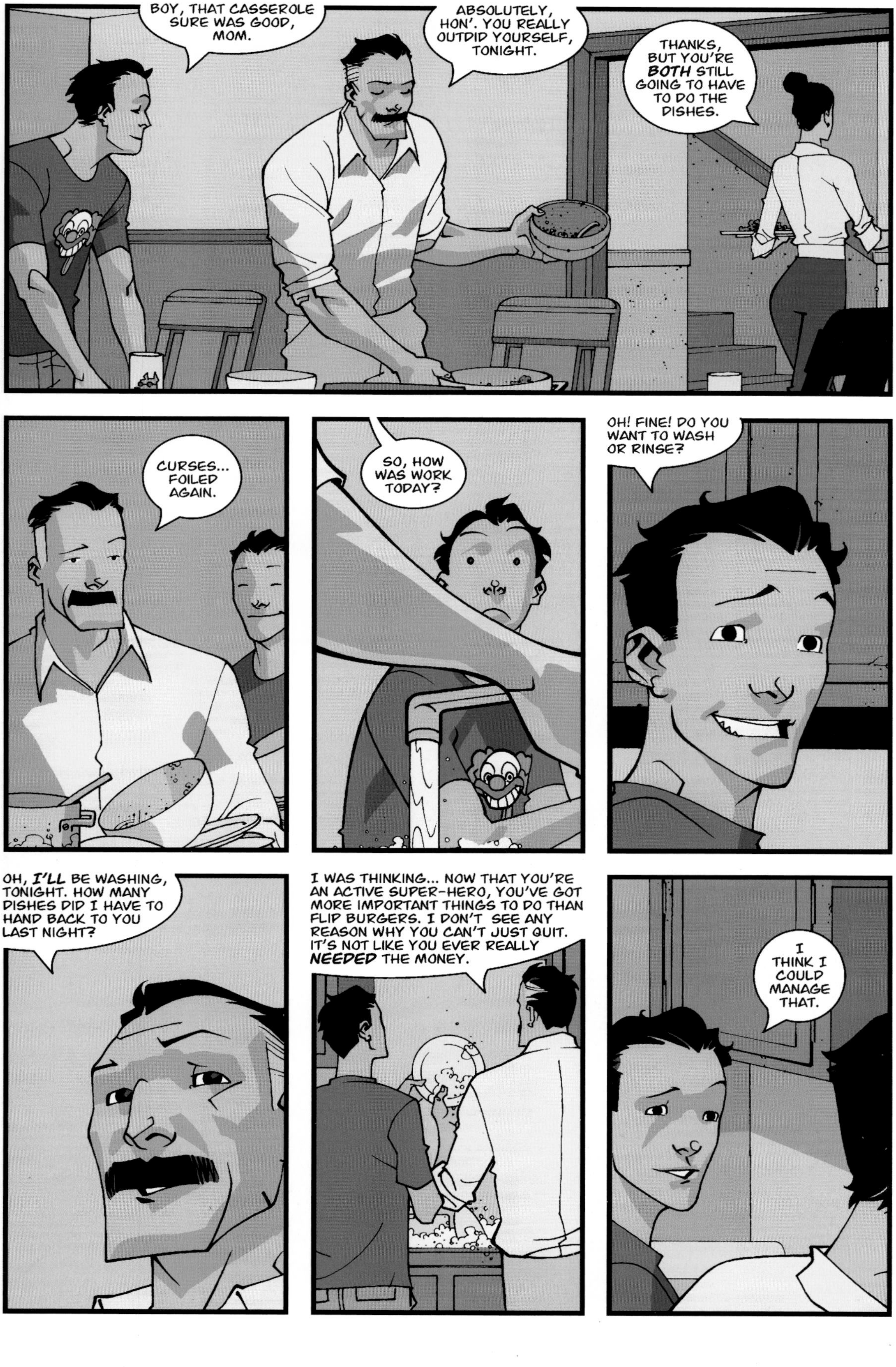
BOY, THAT CASSEROLE SURE WAS GOOD, MOM.
ABSOLUTELY, HON'. YOU REALLY OUTDID YOURSELF, TONIGHT.
THANKS, BUT YOU'RE **BOTH** STILL GOING TO HAVE TO DO THE DISHES.
CURSES... FOILED AGAIN.
SO, HOW WAS WORK TODAY?
OH! FINE! DO YOU WANT TO WASH OR RINSE?
OH, ***I'LL*** BE WASHING, TONIGHT. HOW MANY DISHES DID I HAVE TO HAND BACK TO YOU LAST NIGHT?
I WAS THINKING... NOW THAT YOU'RE AN ACTIVE SUPER-HERO, YOU'VE GOT MORE IMPORTANT THINGS TO DO THAN FLIP BURGERS. I DON'T SEE ANY REASON WHY YOU CAN'T JUST QUIT. IT'S NOT LIKE YOU EVER REALLY ***NEEDED*** THE MONEY.
I THINK I COULD MANAGE THAT.

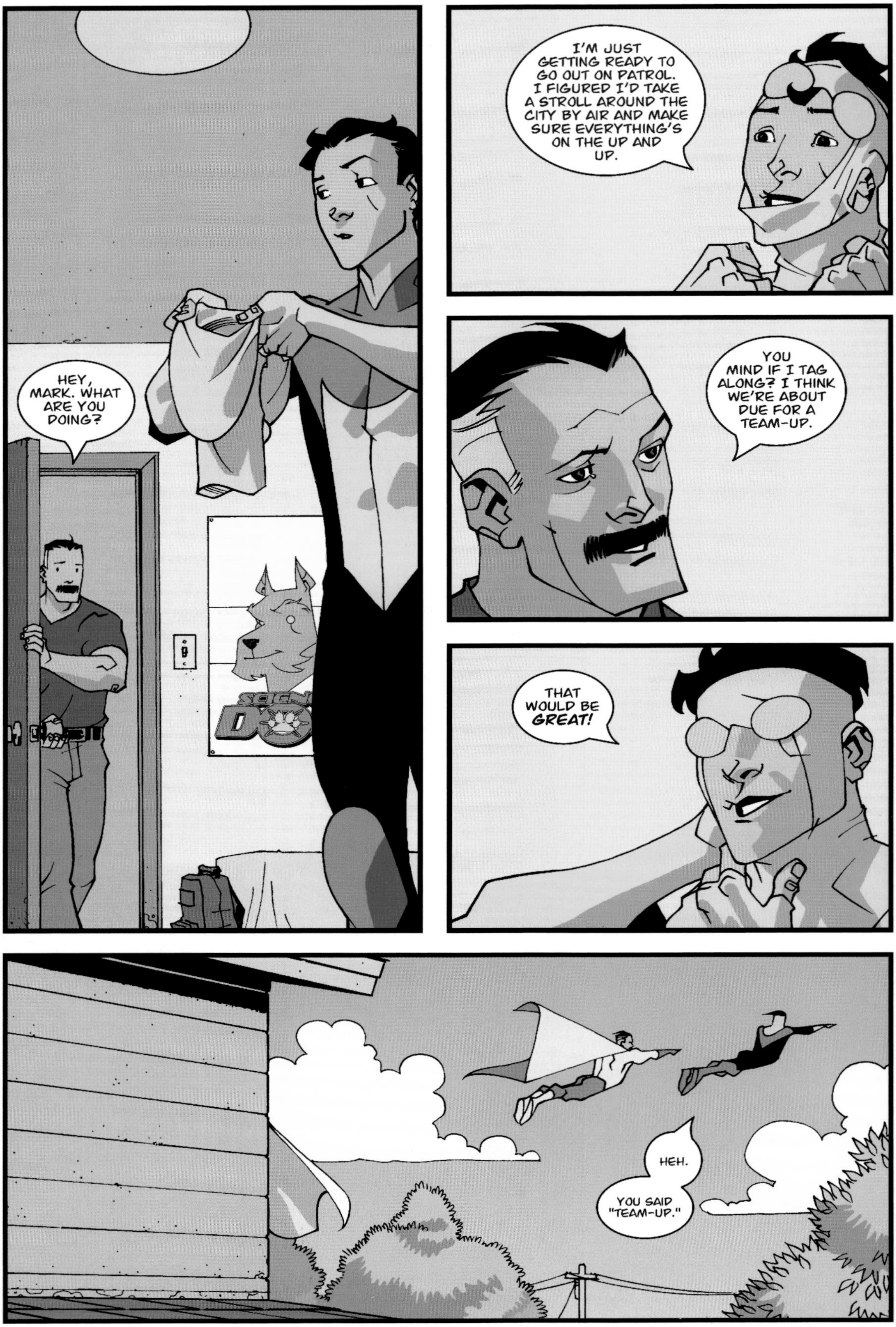
HEY, MARK. WHAT ARE YOU DOING?
I'M JUST GETTING READY TO GO OUT ON PATROL. I FIGURED I'D TAKE A STROLL AROUND THE CITY BY AIR AND MAKE SURE EVERYTHING'S ON THE UP AND UP.
YOU MIND IF I TAG ALONG? I THINK WE'RE ABOUT DUE FOR A TEAM-UP.
THAT WOULD BE **GREAT!**
HEH.
YOU SAID "TEAM-UP."

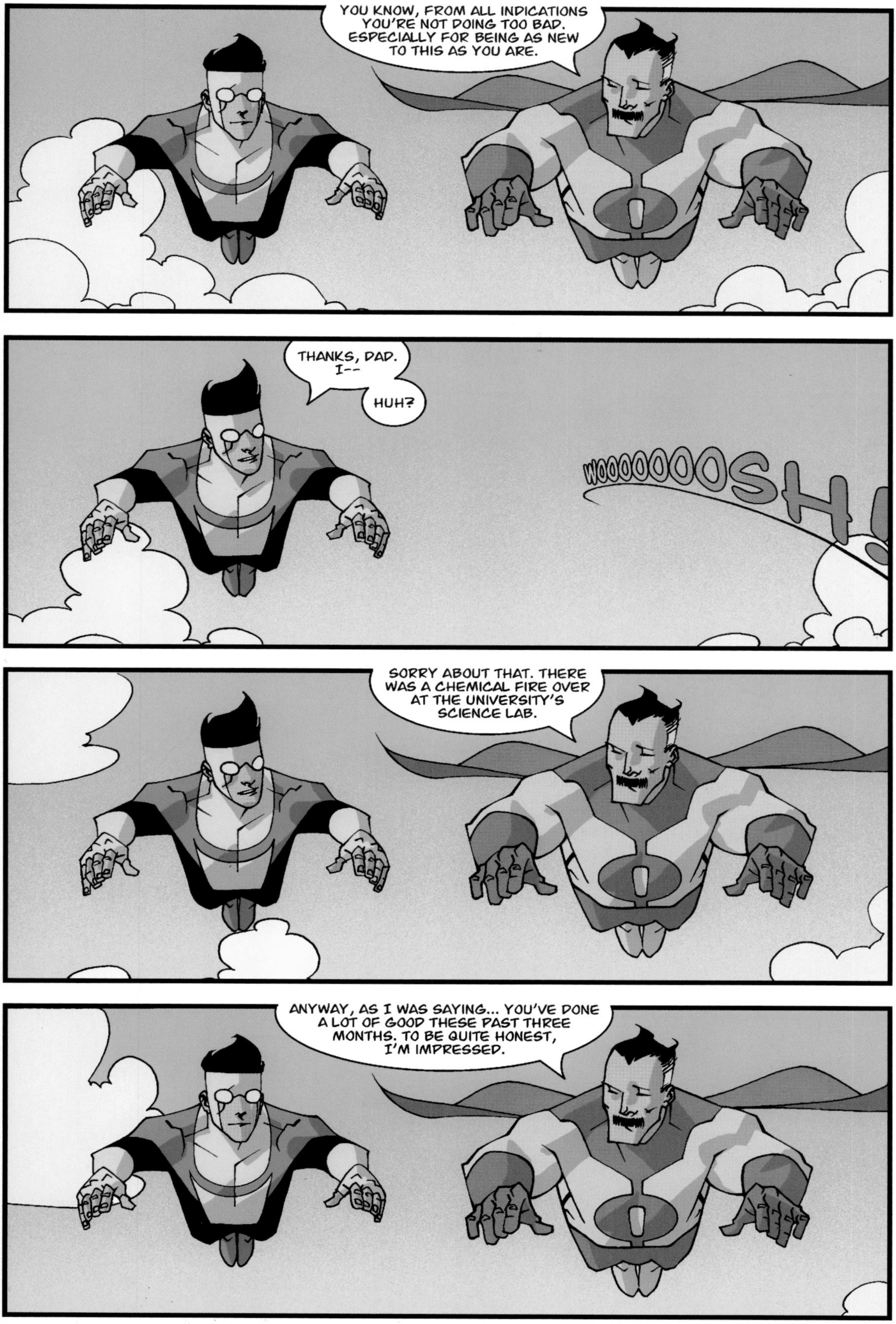
YOU KNOW, FROM ALL INDICATIONS YOU'RE NOT DOING TOO BAD. ESPECIALLY FOR BEING AS NEW TO THIS AS YOU ARE.
THANKS, DAD. I--
HUH?
WOOOOOOOSH
SORRY ABOUT THAT. THERE WAS A CHEMICAL FIRE OVER AT THE UNIVERSITY'S SCIENCE LAB.
ANYWAY, AS I WAS SAYING... YOU'VE DONE A LOT OF GOOD THESE PAST THREE MONTHS. TO BE QUITE HONEST, I'M IMPRESSED.

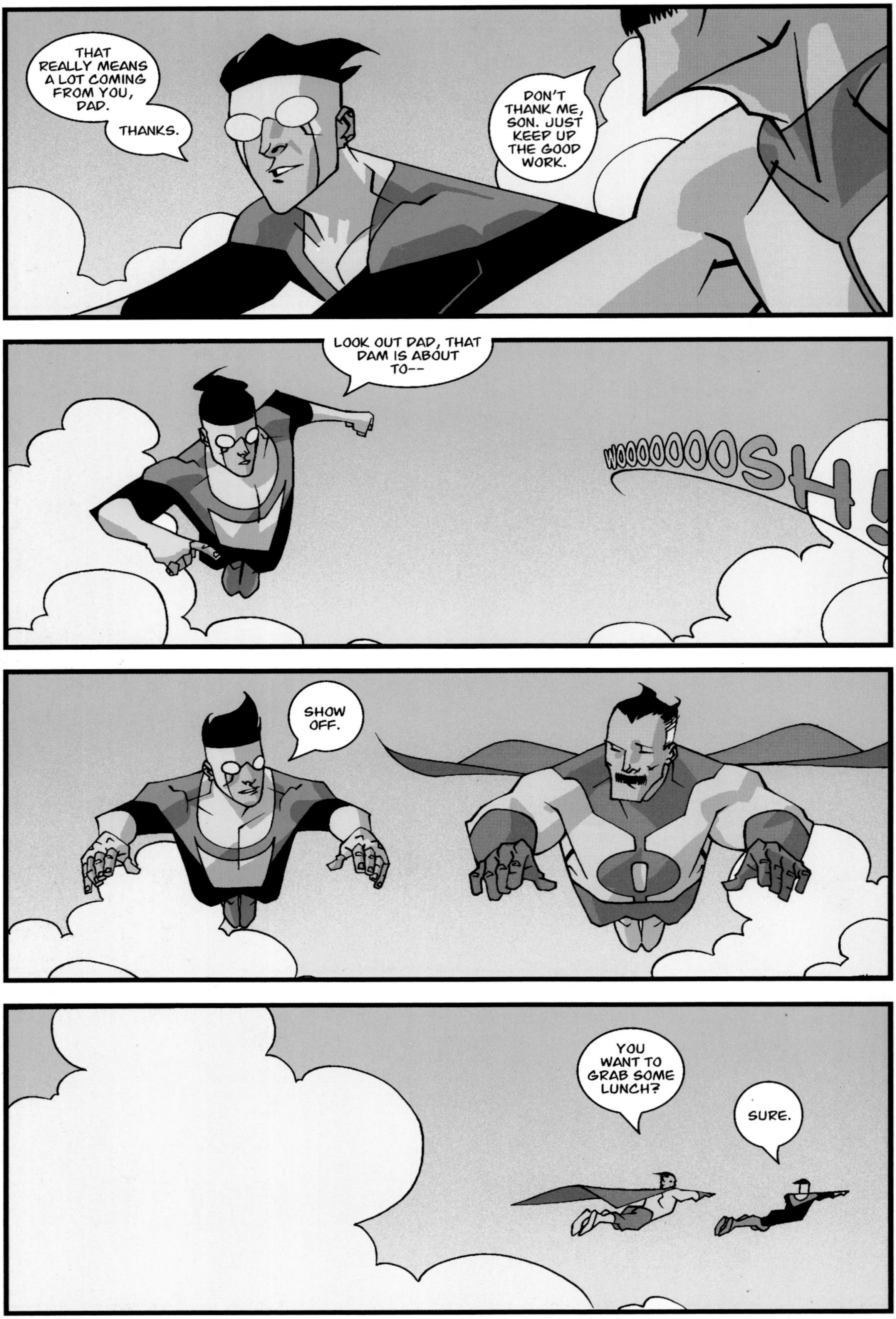
THAT REALLY MEANS A LOT COMING FROM YOU, DAD.
THANKS.
DON'T THANK ME, SON. JUST KEEP UP THE GOOD WORK.
LOOK OUT DAD, THAT DAM IS ABOUT TO--
WOOOOOOOOSH!
SHOW OFF.
YOU WANT TO GRAB SOME LUNCH?
SURE.

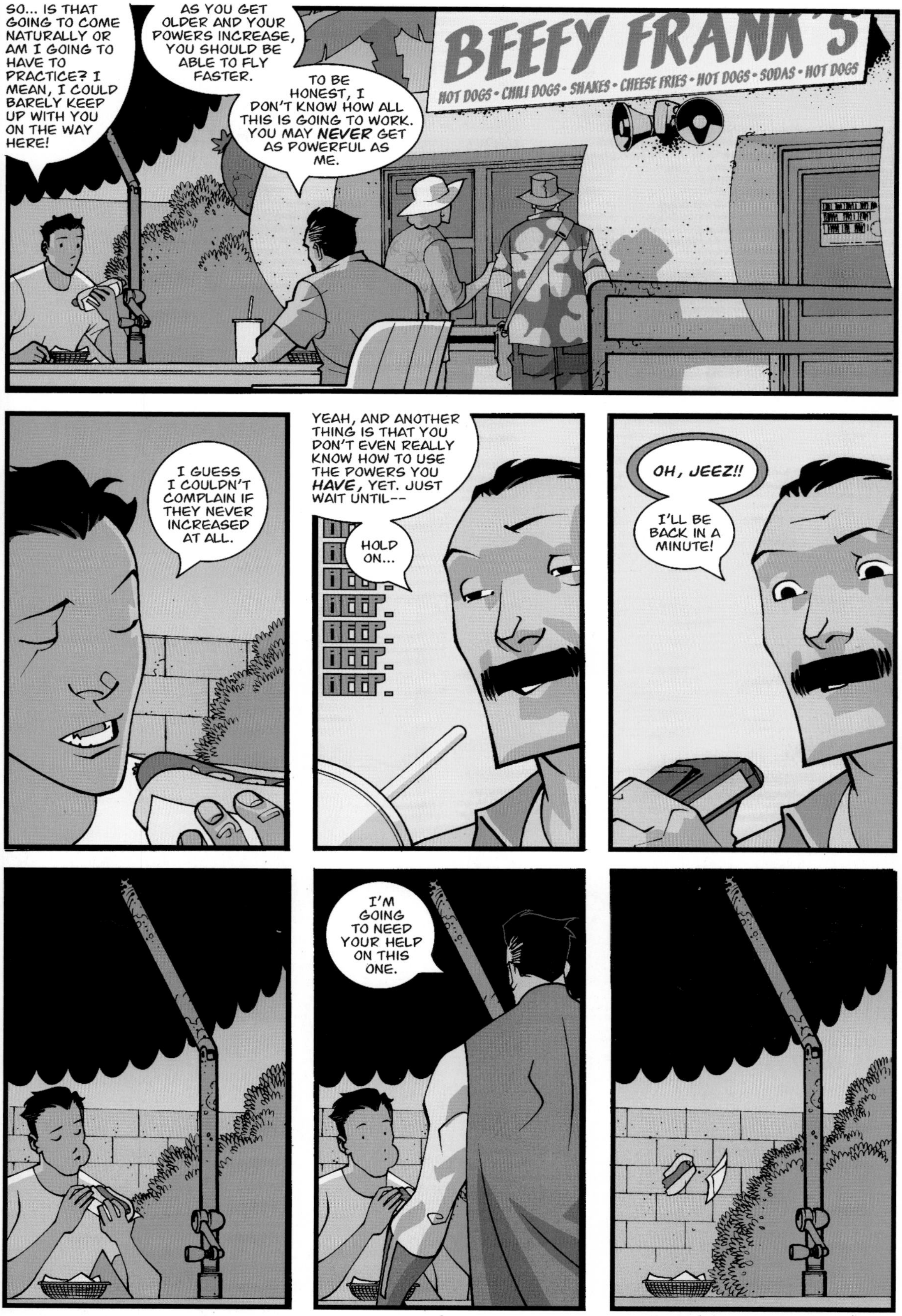
SO... IS THAT GOING TO COME NATURALLY OR AM I GOING TO HAVE TO PRACTICE? I MEAN, I COULD BARELY KEEP UP WITH YOU ON THE WAY HERE!
AS YOU GET OLDER AND YOUR POWERS INCREASE, YOU SHOULD BE ABLE TO FLY FASTER.
BEEFY FRANK'S
HOT DOGS • CHILI DOGS • SHAKES • CHEESE FRIES • HOT DOGS • SODAS • HOT DOGS
TO BE HONEST, I DON'T KNOW HOW ALL THIS IS GOING TO WORK. YOU MAY **NEVER** GET AS POWERFUL AS ME.
I GUESS I COULDN'T COMPLAIN IF THEY NEVER INCREASED AT ALL.
YEAH, AND ANOTHER THING IS THAT YOU DON'T EVEN REALLY KNOW HOW TO USE THE POWERS YOU ***HAVE***, YET. JUST WAIT UNTIL--
BEEP BEEP BEEP BEEP BEEP BEEP BEEP
HOLD ON...
*OH, JEEZ!!*
I'LL BE BACK IN A MINUTE!
I'M GOING TO NEED YOUR HELP ON THIS ONE.

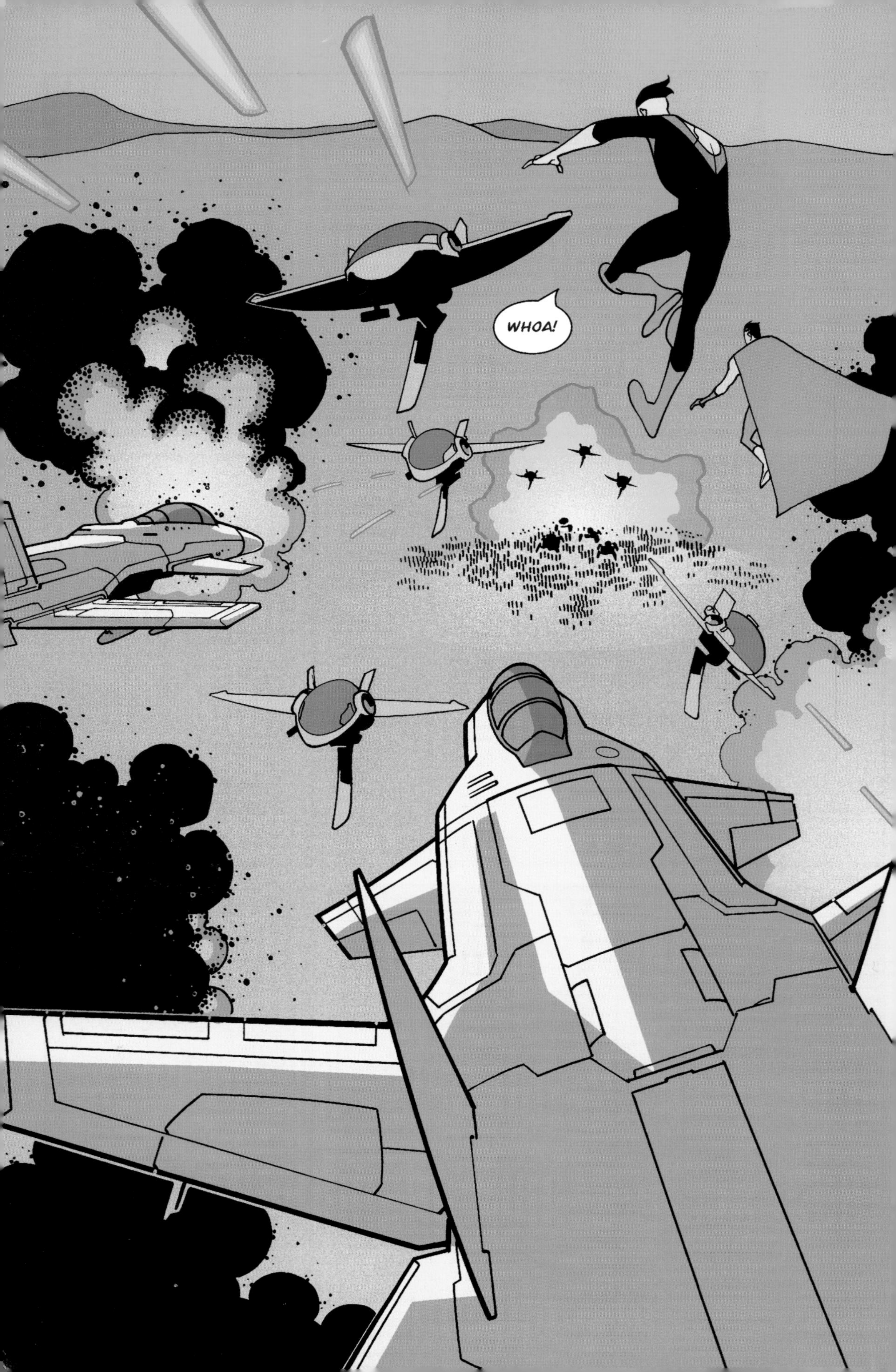
WHOA!

NO TIME FOR THAT, SON! LET'S HELP THESE BOYS OUT!

GOOM!

I'LL DO WHAT I CAN!

THAT'S THE SPIRIT!

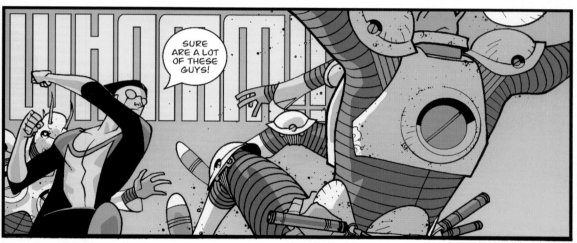

WHOMP!

SURE ARE A LOT OF THESE GUYS!

NO KIDDING!

THERE SEEMS TO BE AN ENDLESS STREAM OF THEM COMING OUT OF THAT PORTAL.

BOOM!

BOOM!

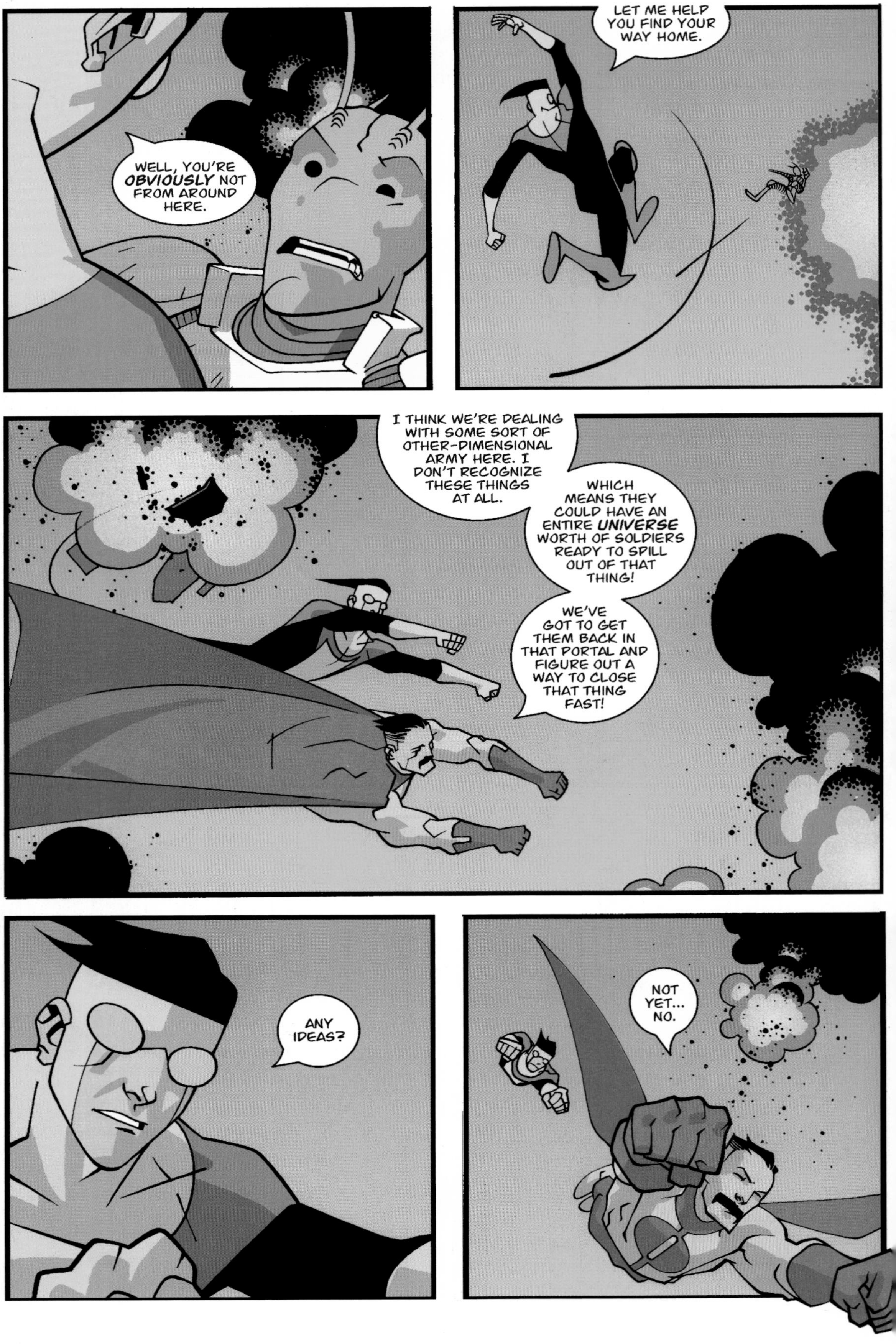
WELL, YOU'RE OBVIOUSLY NOT FROM AROUND HERE.
LET ME HELP YOU FIND YOUR WAY HOME.
I THINK WE'RE DEALING WITH SOME SORT OF OTHER-DIMENSIONAL ARMY HERE. I DON'T RECOGNIZE THESE THINGS AT ALL.
WHICH MEANS THEY COULD HAVE AN ENTIRE UNIVERSE WORTH OF SOLDIERS READY TO SPILL OUT OF THAT THING!
WE'VE GOT TO GET THEM BACK IN THAT PORTAL AND FIGURE OUT A WAY TO CLOSE THAT THING FAST!
ANY IDEAS?
NOT YET... NO.

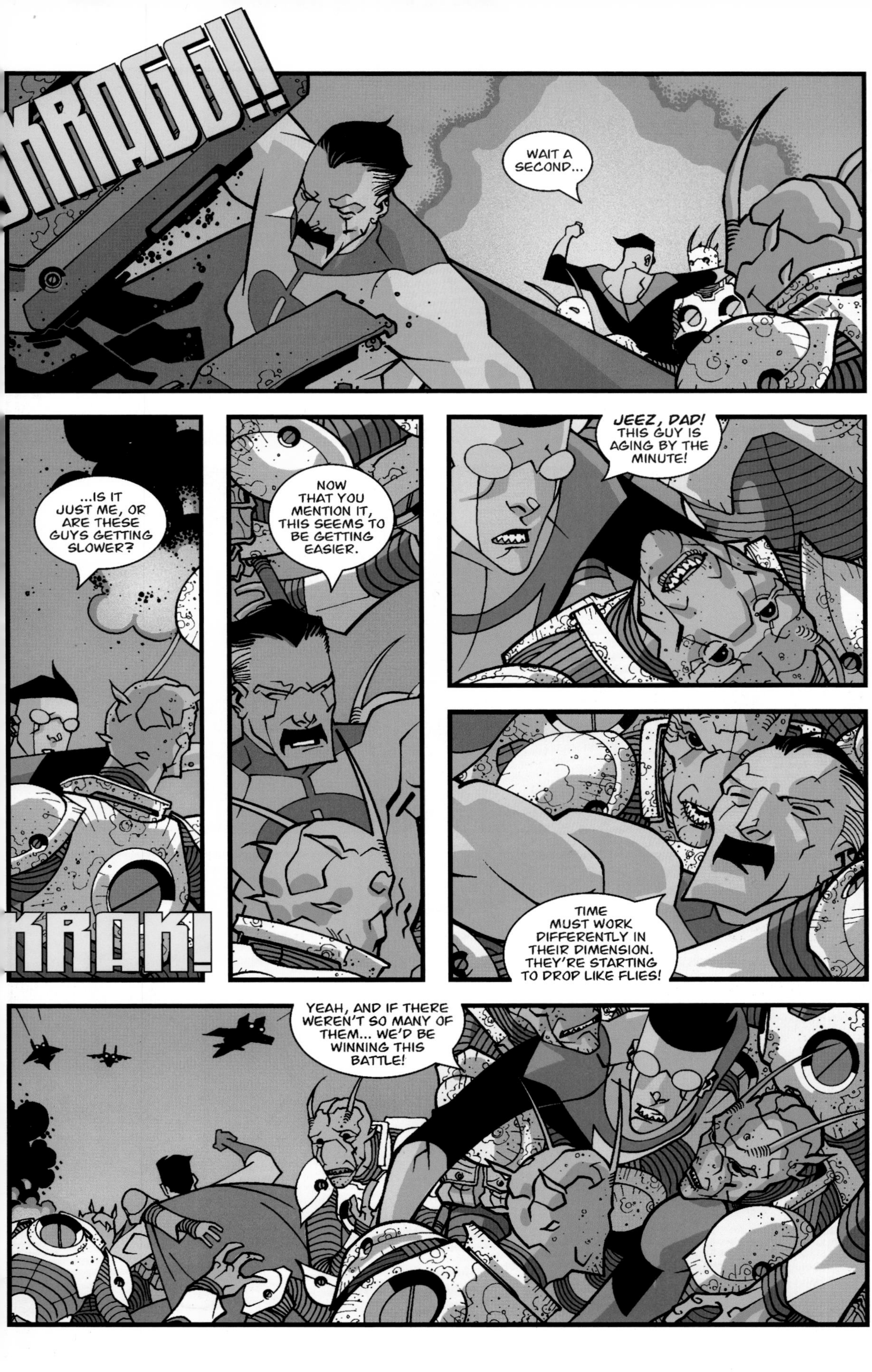
KRAGG!!
WAIT A SECOND...
...IS IT JUST ME, OR ARE THESE GUYS GETTING SLOWER?
KRAK!
NOW THAT YOU MENTION IT, THIS SEEMS TO BE GETTING EASIER.
JEEZ, DAD! THIS GUY IS AGING BY THE MINUTE!
TIME MUST WORK DIFFERENTLY IN THEIR DIMENSION. THEY'RE STARTING TO DROP LIKE FLIES!
YEAH, AND IF THERE WEREN'T SO MANY OF THEM... WE'D BE WINNING THIS BATTLE!

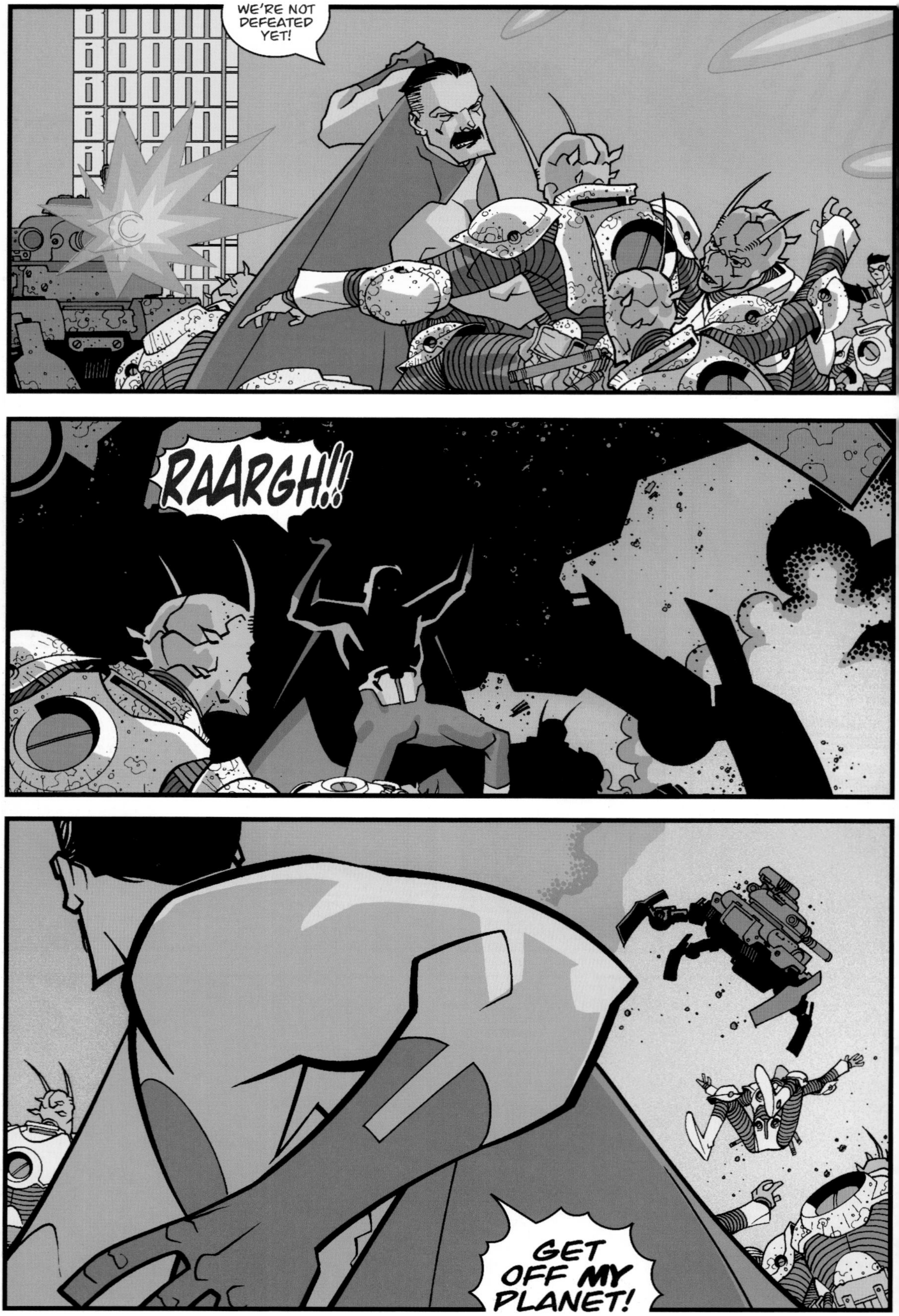
BOOM!
BOOM!
BOOM!
WE'RE NOT DEFEATED YET!
RAARGH!!
GET OFF MY PLANET!

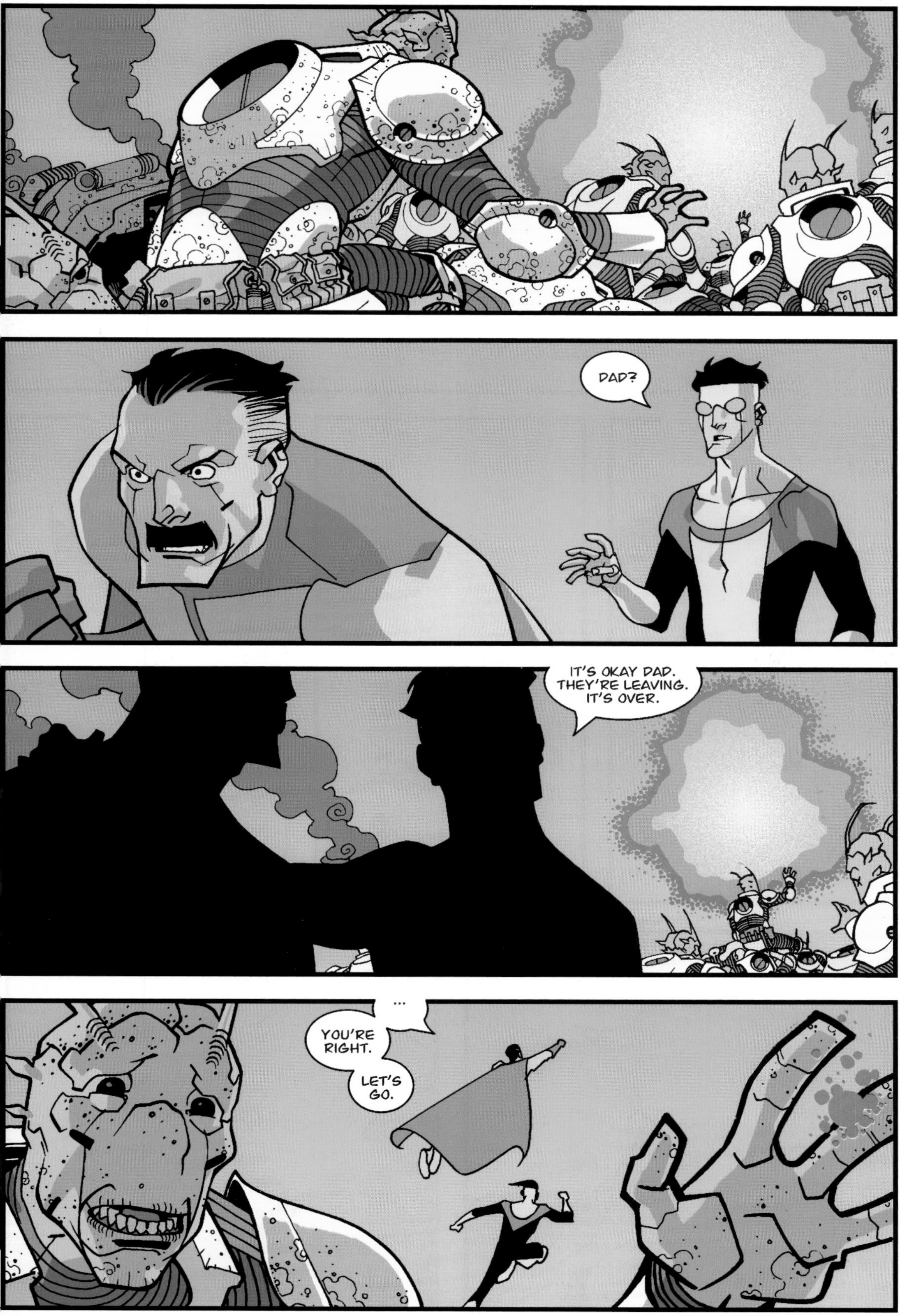
DAD?
IT'S OKAY DAD. THEY'RE LEAVING. IT'S OVER.
...
YOU'RE RIGHT.
LET'S GO.

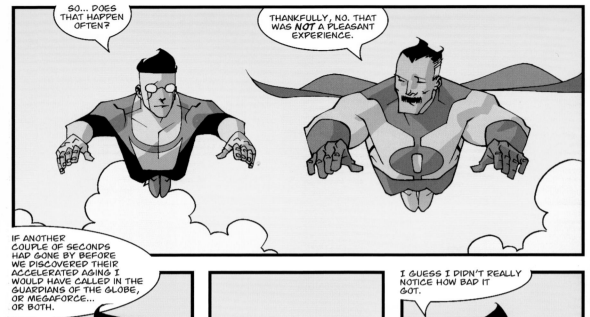

SO... DOES THAT HAPPEN OFTEN?

THANKFULLY, NO. THAT WAS *NOT* A PLEASANT EXPERIENCE.

IF ANOTHER COUPLE OF SECONDS HAD GONE BY BEFORE WE DISCOVERED THEIR ACCELERATED AGING I WOULD HAVE CALLED IN THE GUARDIANS OF THE GLOBE, OR MEGAFORCE... OR BOTH.

WOW.

I GUESS I DIDN'T REALLY NOTICE HOW BAD IT GOT.

WELL... WE MADE IT THROUGH. DON'T DWELL ON IT.

LET'S JUST WORRY ABOUT GETTING HOME WITHOUT RUNNING INTO ANY MORE TROUBLE. WE'RE ALMOST THERE, AND I'LL BET YOUR MOM'S ALMOST DONE WITH--

LAKESIDE MALL.

TRY TO KEEP UP.

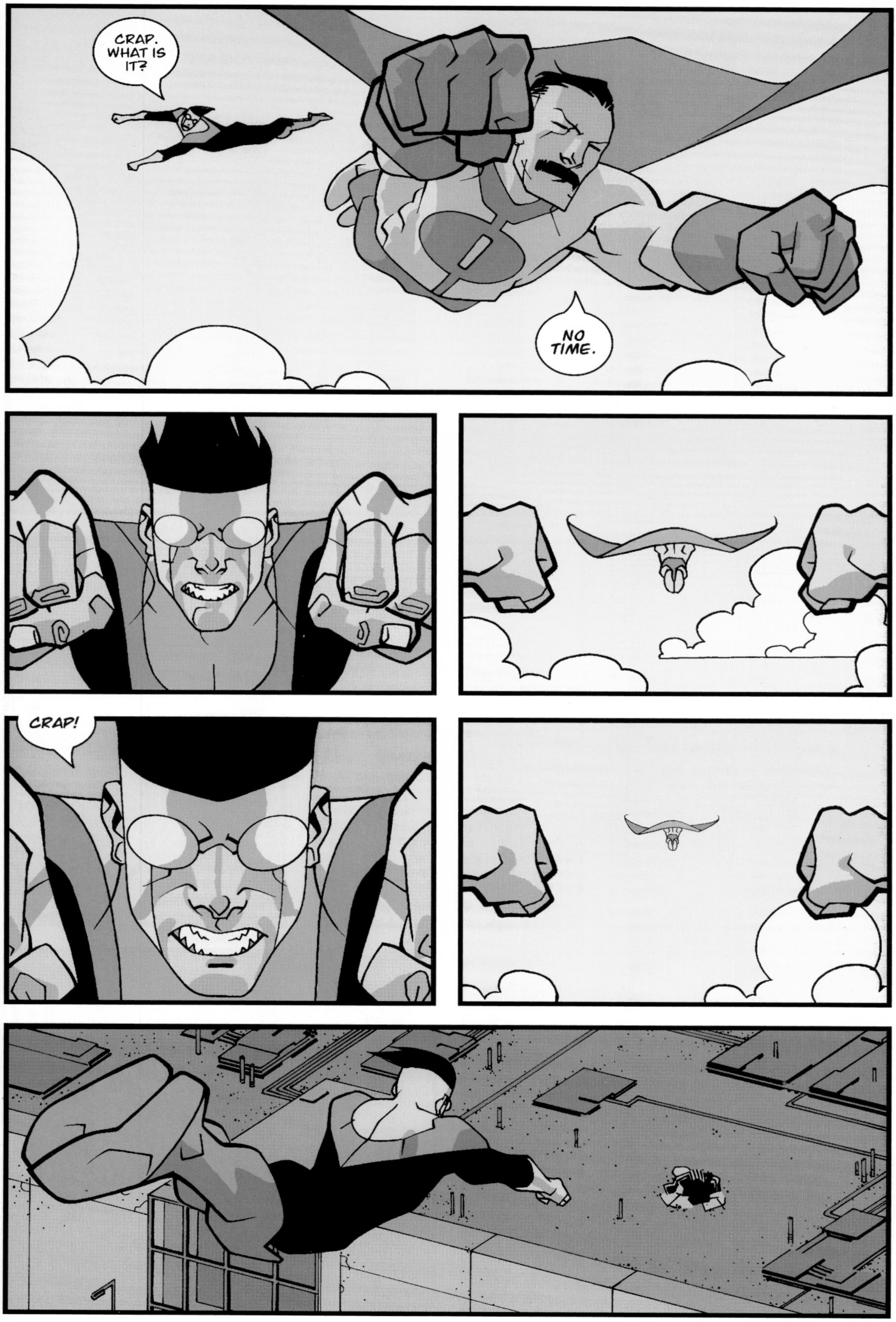
CRAP. WHAT IS IT?
NO TIME.
CRAP!

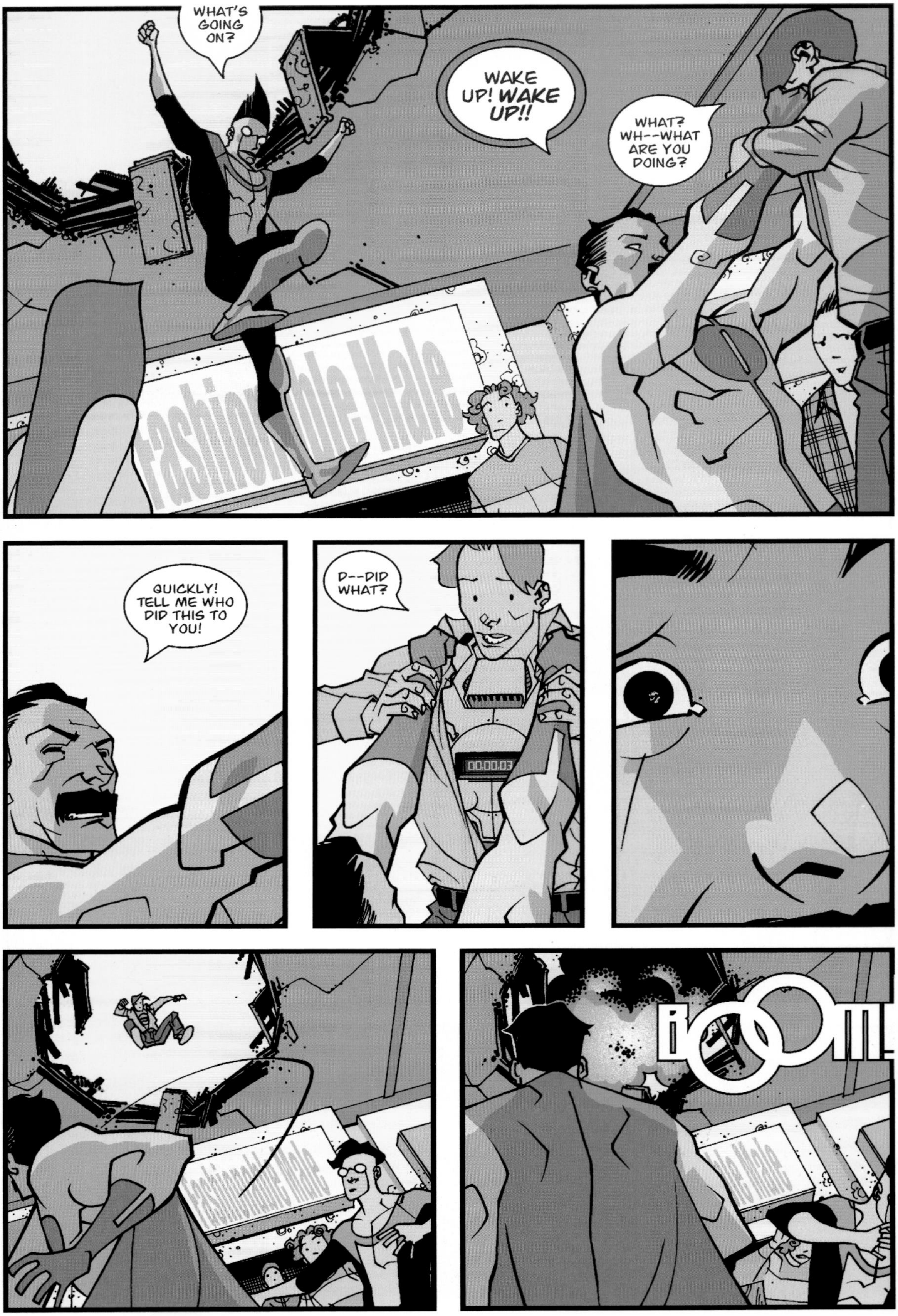
WHAT'S GOING ON?
WAKE UP! WAKE UP!!
WHAT? WH--WHAT ARE YOU DOING?
Fashionable Male
QUICKLY! TELL ME WHO DID THIS TO YOU!
D--DID WHAT?
00.00.03
Fashionable Male
BOOM!

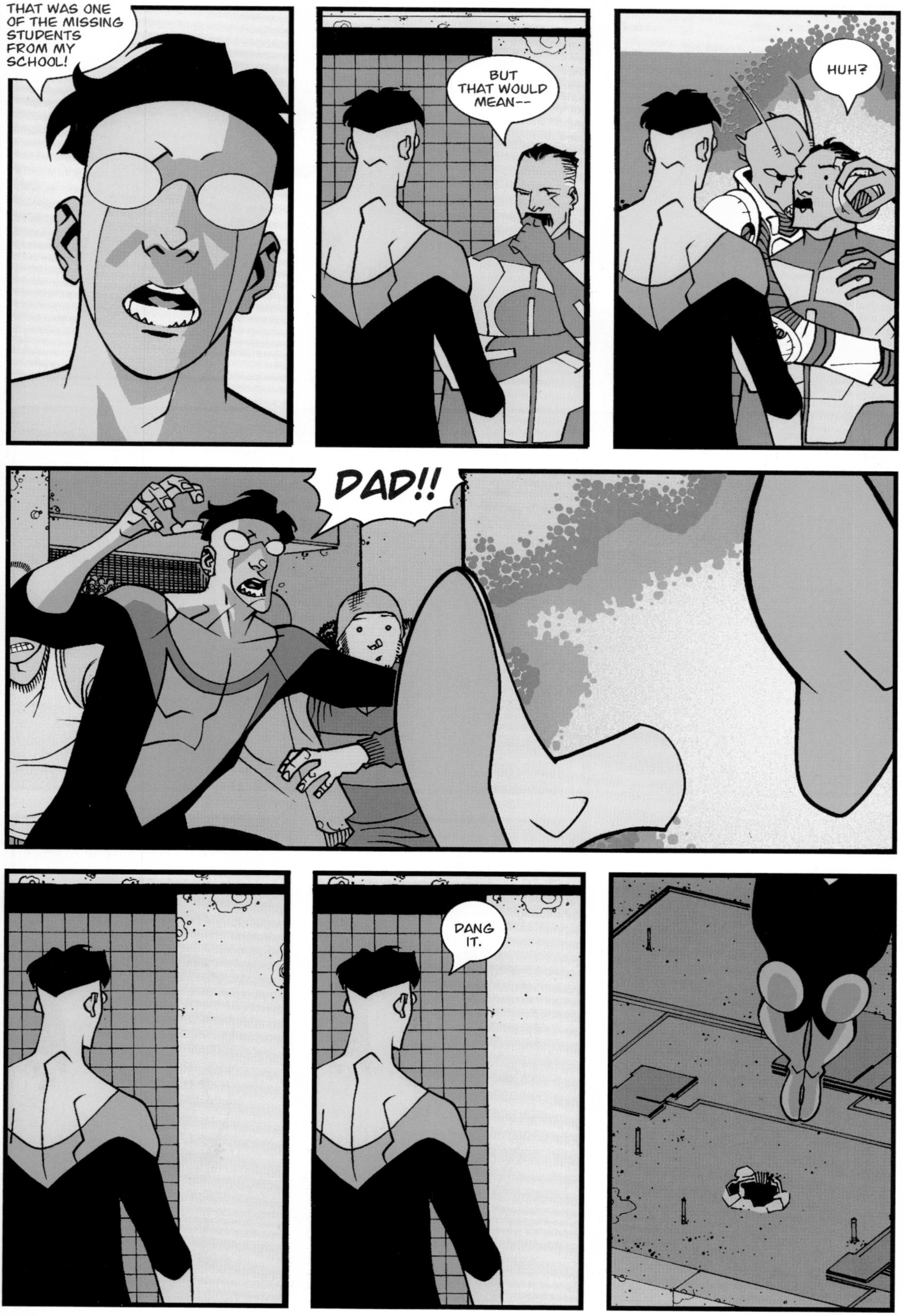
THAT WAS ONE OF THE MISSING STUDENTS FROM MY SCHOOL!
BUT THAT WOULD MEAN--
HUH?
DAD!!
DANG IT.

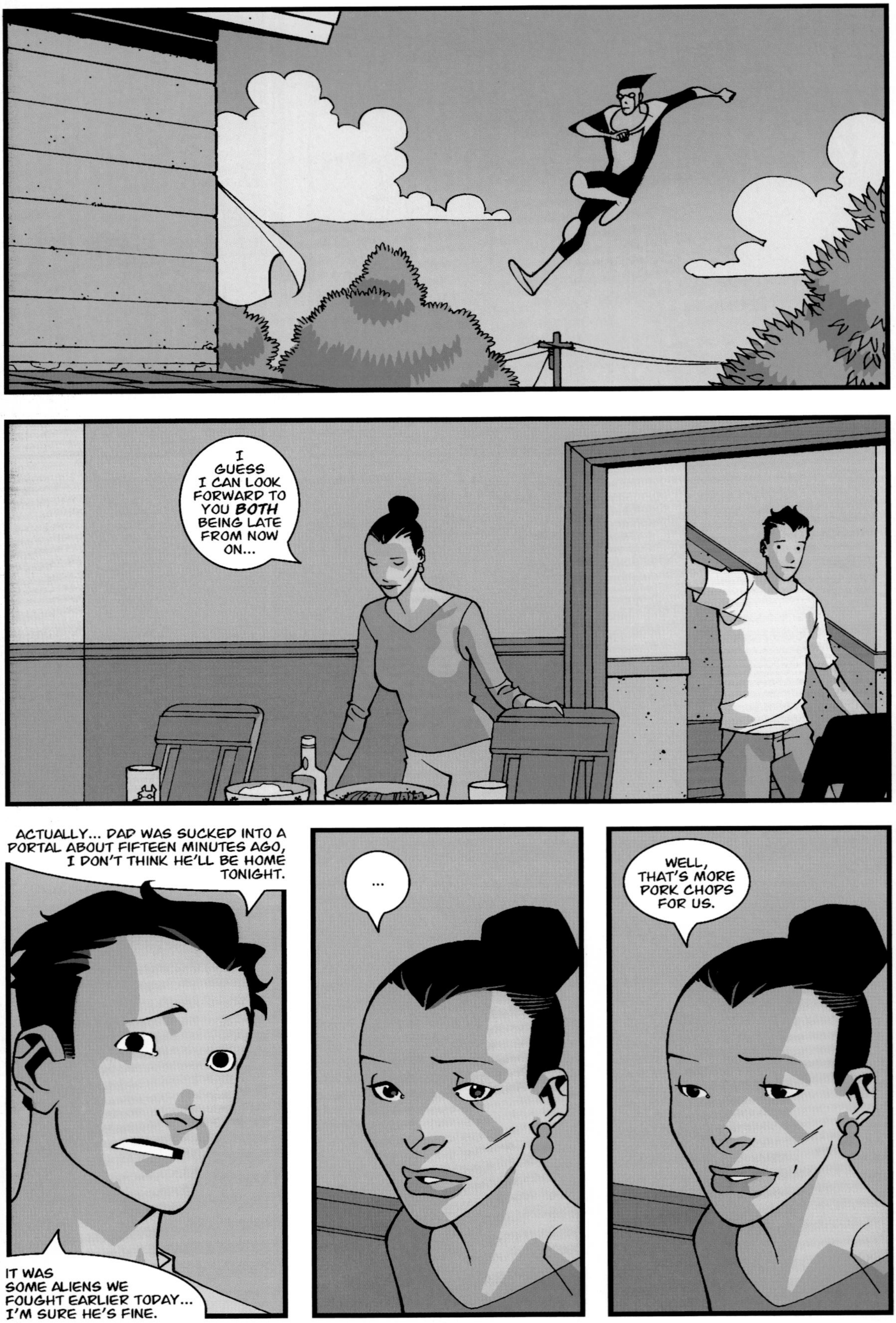
I GUESS I CAN LOOK FORWARD TO YOU BOTH BEING LATE FROM NOW ON...
ACTUALLY... DAD WAS SUCKED INTO A PORTAL ABOUT FIFTEEN MINUTES AGO, I DON'T THINK HE'LL BE HOME TONIGHT.
IT WAS SOME ALIENS WE FOUGHT EARLIER TODAY... I'M SURE HE'S FINE.
...
WELL, THAT'S MORE PORK CHOPS FOR US.

# CHAPTER FOUR

00:00:01

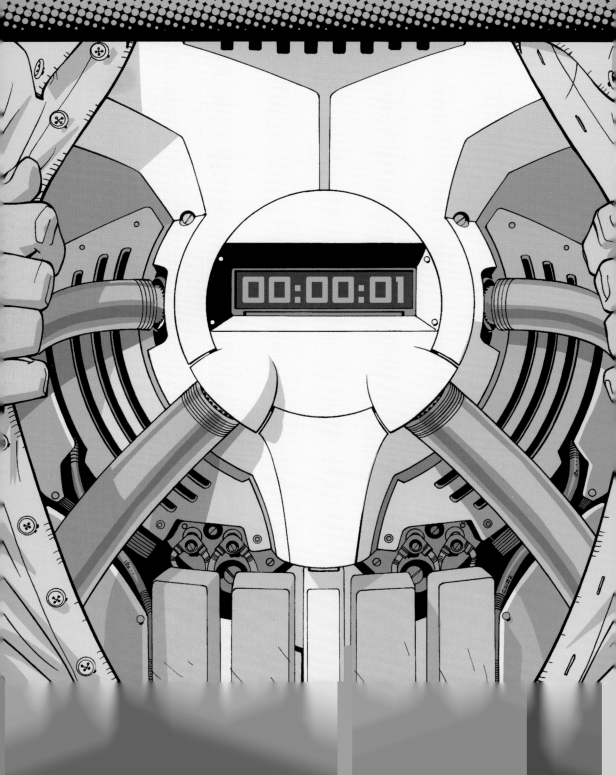

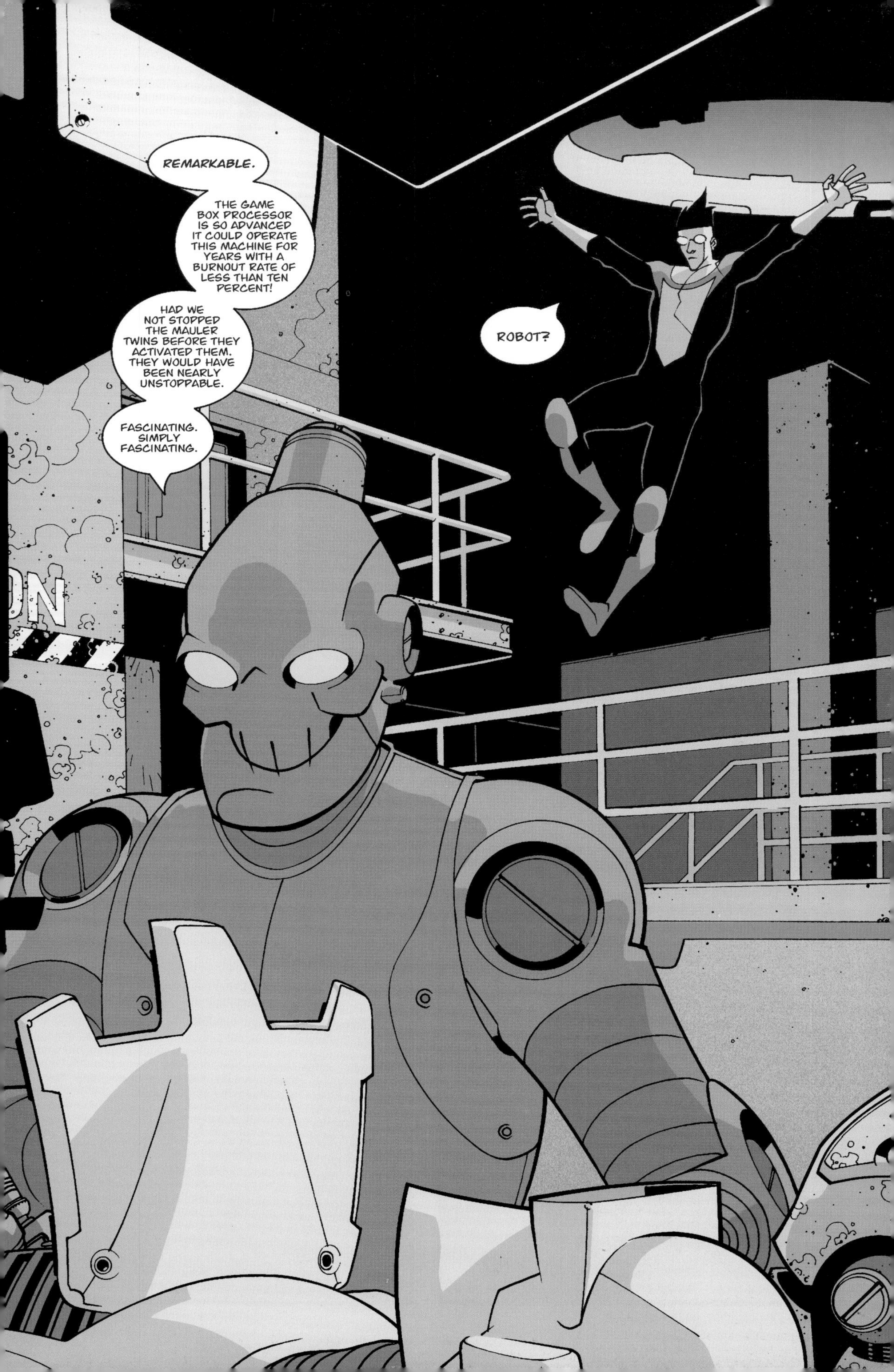
REMARKABLE.
THE GAME BOX PROCESSOR IS SO ADVANCED IT COULD OPERATE THIS MACHINE FOR YEARS WITH A BURNOUT RATE OF LESS THAN TEN PERCENT!
HAD WE NOT STOPPED THE MAULER TWINS BEFORE THEY ACTIVATED THEM. THEY WOULD HAVE BEEN NEARLY UNSTOPPABLE.
FASCINATING. SIMPLY FASCINATING.
ROBOT?

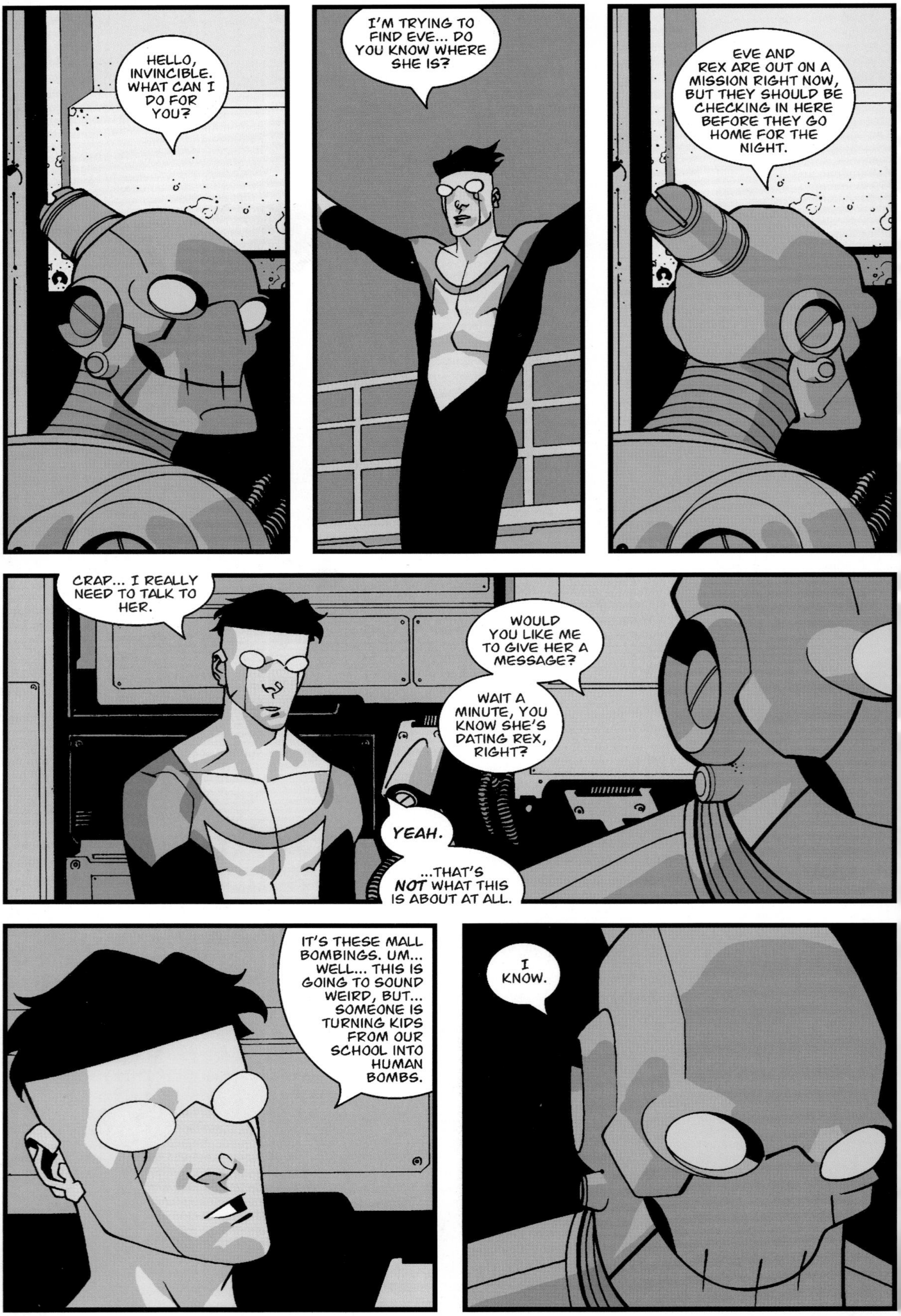

HELLO, INVINCIBLE. WHAT CAN I DO FOR YOU?
I'M TRYING TO FIND EVE... DO YOU KNOW WHERE SHE IS?
EVE AND REX ARE OUT ON A MISSION RIGHT NOW, BUT THEY SHOULD BE CHECKING IN HERE BEFORE THEY GO HOME FOR THE NIGHT.
CRAP... I REALLY NEED TO TALK TO HER.
WOULD YOU LIKE ME TO GIVE HER A MESSAGE?
WAIT A MINUTE, YOU KNOW SHE'S DATING REX, RIGHT?
YEAH.
...THAT'S NOT WHAT THIS IS ABOUT AT ALL.
IT'S THESE MALL BOMBINGS. UM... WELL... THIS IS GOING TO SOUND WEIRD, BUT... SOMEONE IS TURNING KIDS FROM OUR SCHOOL INTO HUMAN BOMBS.
I KNOW.

I MEAN, IT'S LATE AND ALL BUT I JUST WANTED TO LET HER KNOW SO THAT--

WAIT... WHAT?

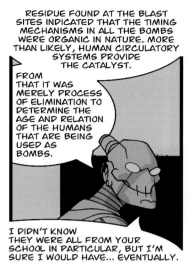

RESIDUE FOUND AT THE BLAST SITES INDICATED THAT THE TIMING MECHANISMS IN ALL THE BOMBS WERE ORGANIC IN NATURE. MORE THAN LIKELY, HUMAN CIRCULATORY SYSTEMS PROVIDE THE CATALYST.

FROM THAT IT WAS MERELY PROCESS OF ELIMINATION TO DETERMINE THE AGE AND RELATION OF THE HUMANS THAT ARE BEING USED AS BOMBS.

I DIDN'T KNOW THEY WERE ALL FROM YOUR SCHOOL IN PARTICULAR, BUT I'M SURE I WOULD HAVE... EVENTUALLY.

WELL... I'M ONLY SURE THAT THE MOST RECENT ONE WENT TO MY SCHOOL, BUT HE'S ONE OF THE THREE KIDS THAT ARE MISSING.

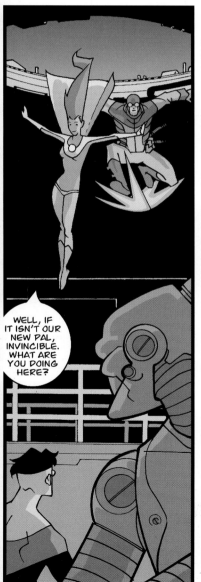

WELL, IF IT ISN'T OUR NEW PAL, INVINCIBLE. WHAT ARE YOU DOING HERE?

I THINK THE MALL BOMBINGS ARE CONNECTED TO MISSING KIDS AT OUR SCHOOL.

OH, GOD. THAT'S AWFUL.

BYE, BABE.

≥SMECK≤

ANY IDEA WHO'S BEHIND IT?

NO, AND THERE'S NOTHING WE CAN DO ABOUT THAT TONIGHT.

I SUGGEST YOU TWO GO HOME AND GET SOME SLEEP. THEN KEEP YOUR EYES OPEN AT SCHOOL TOMORROW. I'LL LET YOU KNOW IF I FIGURE OUT ANYTHING ON MY OWN.

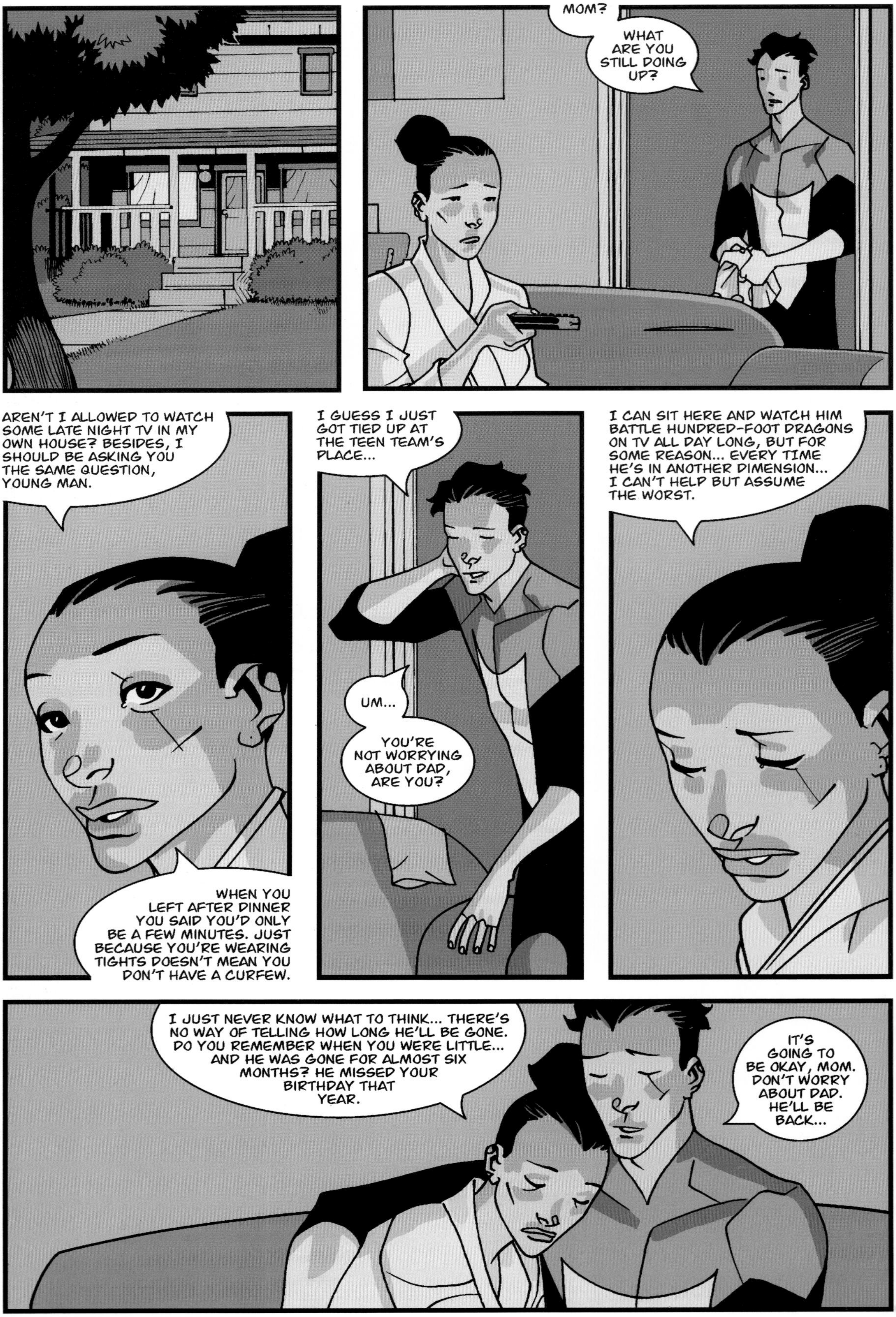
MOM?
WHAT ARE YOU STILL DOING UP?
AREN'T I ALLOWED TO WATCH SOME LATE NIGHT TV IN MY OWN HOUSE? BESIDES, I SHOULD BE ASKING YOU THE SAME QUESTION, YOUNG MAN.
WHEN YOU LEFT AFTER DINNER YOU SAID YOU'D ONLY BE A FEW MINUTES. JUST BECAUSE YOU'RE WEARING TIGHTS DOESN'T MEAN YOU DON'T HAVE A CURFEW.
I GUESS I JUST GOT TIED UP AT THE TEEN TEAM'S PLACE...
UM...
YOU'RE NOT WORRYING ABOUT DAD, ARE YOU?
I CAN SIT HERE AND WATCH HIM BATTLE HUNDRED-FOOT DRAGONS ON TV ALL DAY LONG, BUT FOR SOME REASON... EVERY TIME HE'S IN ANOTHER DIMENSION... I CAN'T HELP BUT ASSUME THE WORST.
I JUST NEVER KNOW WHAT TO THINK... THERE'S NO WAY OF TELLING HOW LONG HE'LL BE GONE. DO YOU REMEMBER WHEN YOU WERE LITTLE... AND HE WAS GONE FOR ALMOST SIX MONTHS? HE MISSED YOUR BIRTHDAY THAT YEAR.
IT'S GOING TO BE OKAY, MOM. DON'T WORRY ABOUT DAD. HE'LL BE BACK...

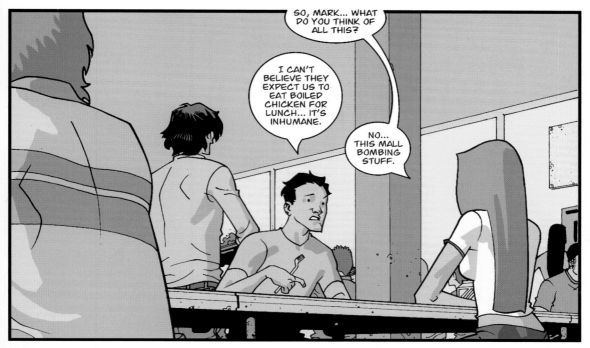

SO, MARK... WHAT DO YOU THINK OF ALL THIS?

I CAN'T BELIEVE THEY EXPECT US TO EAT BOILED CHICKEN FOR LUNCH... IT'S INHUMANE.

NO... THIS MALL BOMBING STUFF.

I DON'T KNOW... IT'S UNSETTLING. I MEAN, I KNOW THIS IS GOING TO SOUND BAD, BUT I'M TRYING NOT TO THINK ABOUT IT.

WELL, THAT'S A **GREAT** WAY TO FIGURE THIS THING OUT!

SORRY, BUT LET'S BE REALISTIC. SHOULD WE BE SEARCHING FOR CLUES RIGHT NOW? I FOR ONE AM NOT DRESSED FOR THAT SORT OF THING, AND WE DON'T EVEN HAVE A DOG.

DON'T THINK FOR A SECOND THAT I DON'T WANT TO CATCH THIS GUY. I JUST THINK THAT WE DON'T REALLY HAVE ANYTHING TO GO ON RIGHT NOW...

...RIGHT?

I GUESS.

I MEAN, THERE ARE PLENTY OF POSSIBILITIES BUT REALLY NOTHING TO POINT US IN ANY DIRECTION.

≷SIGH≷

NO KIDDING. I WISH IT WERE JUST A BIG MONSTER WE COULD PUNCH.

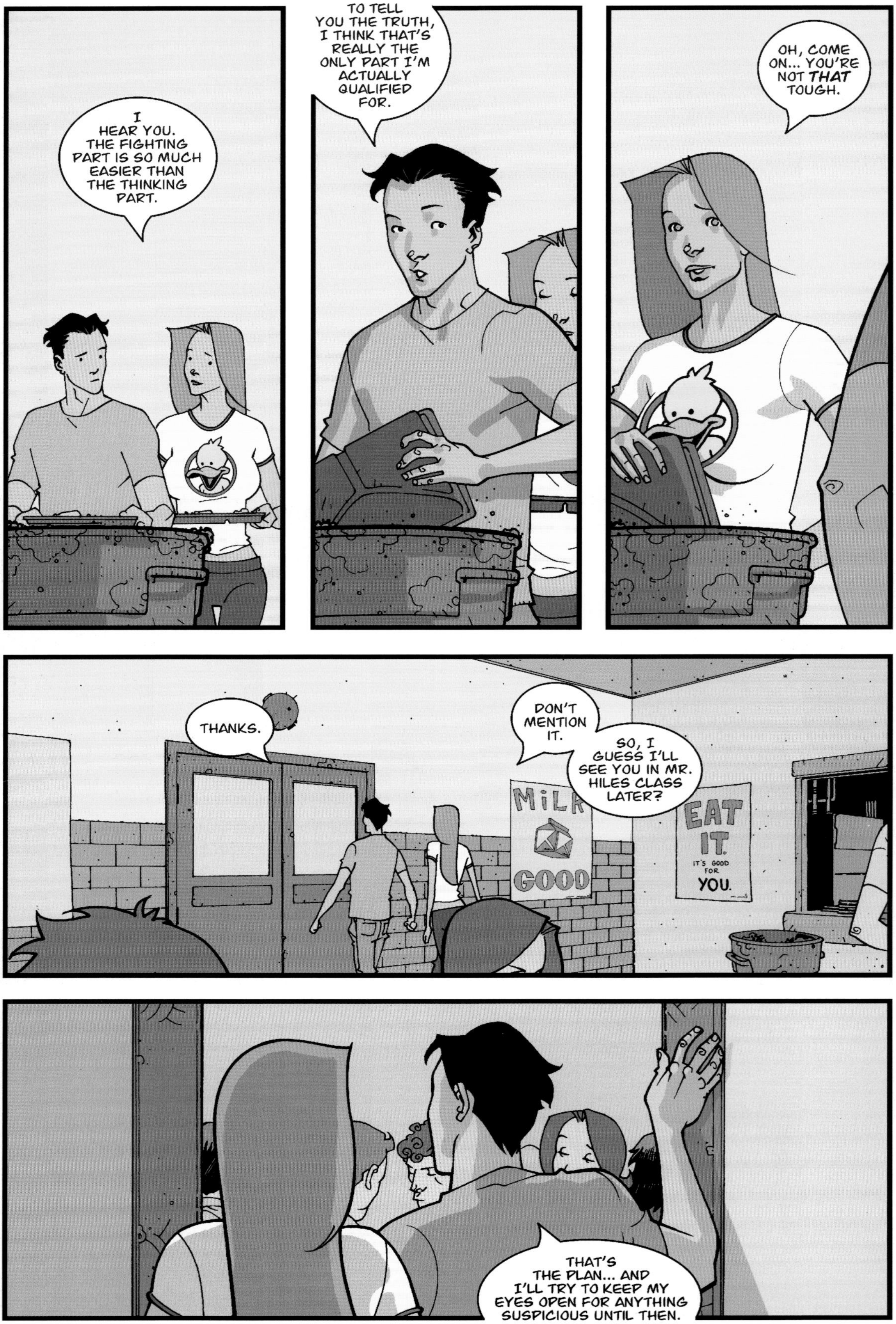
I HEAR YOU. THE FIGHTING PART IS SO MUCH EASIER THAN THE THINKING PART.
TO TELL YOU THE TRUTH, I THINK THAT'S REALLY THE ONLY PART I'M ACTUALLY QUALIFIED FOR.
OH, COME ON... YOU'RE NOT THAT TOUGH.
THANKS.
MILK GOOD
DON'T MENTION IT.
SO, I GUESS I'LL SEE YOU IN MR. HILES CLASS LATER?
EAT IT. IT'S GOOD FOR YOU.
THAT'S THE PLAN... AND I'LL TRY TO KEEP MY EYES OPEN FOR ANYTHING SUSPICIOUS UNTIL THEN.

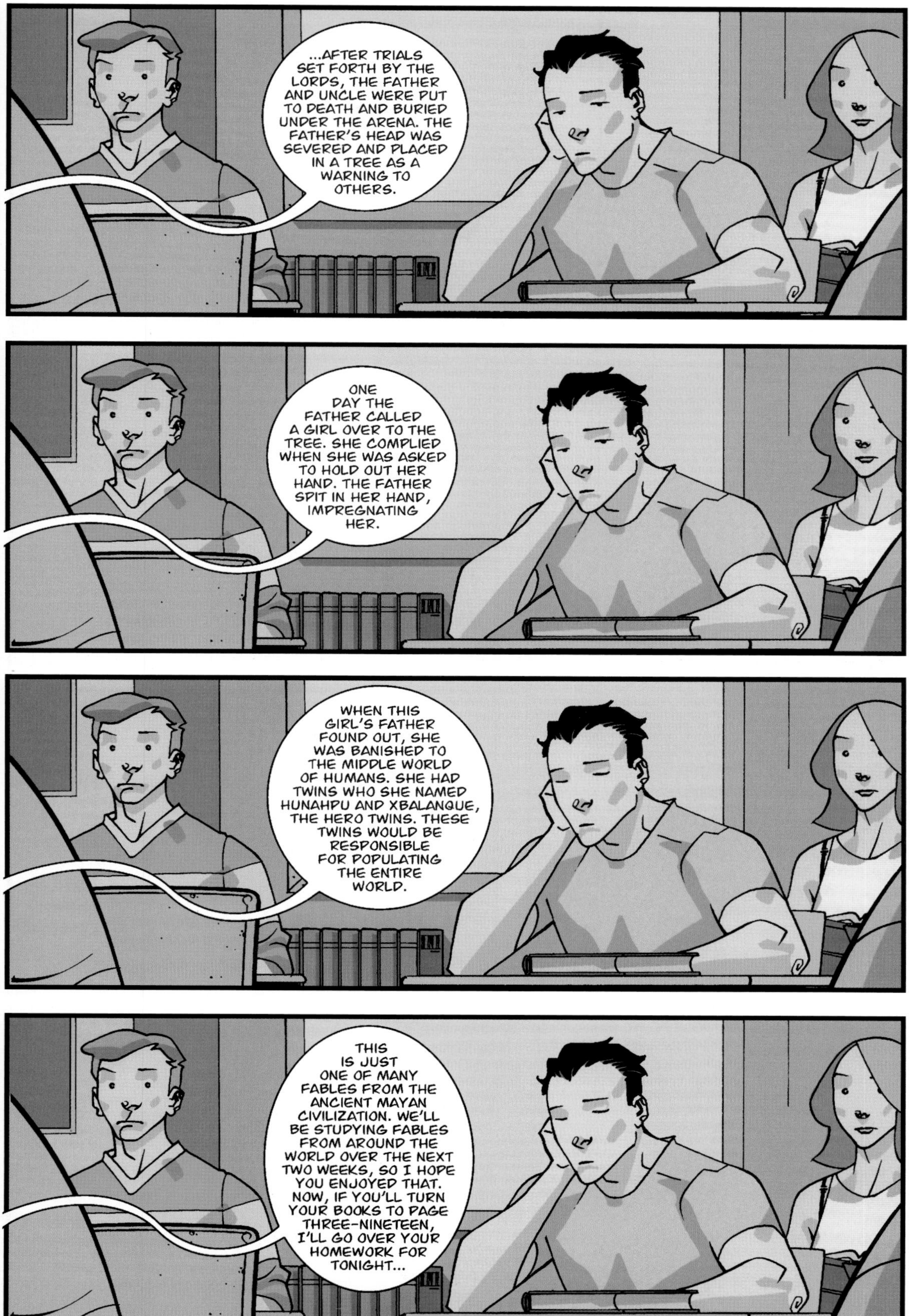
...AFTER TRIALS SET FORTH BY THE LORDS, THE FATHER AND UNCLE WERE PUT TO DEATH AND BURIED UNDER THE ARENA. THE FATHER'S HEAD WAS SEVERED AND PLACED IN A TREE AS A WARNING TO OTHERS.
ONE DAY THE FATHER CALLED A GIRL OVER TO THE TREE. SHE COMPLIED WHEN SHE WAS ASKED TO HOLD OUT HER HAND. THE FATHER SPIT IN HER HAND, IMPREGNATING HER.
WHEN THIS GIRL'S FATHER FOUND OUT, SHE WAS BANISHED TO THE MIDDLE WORLD OF HUMANS. SHE HAD TWINS WHO SHE NAMED HUNAHPU AND XBALANQUE, THE HERO TWINS. THESE TWINS WOULD BE RESPONSIBLE FOR POPULATING THE ENTIRE WORLD.
THIS IS JUST ONE OF MANY FABLES FROM THE ANCIENT MAYAN CIVILIZATION. WE'LL BE STUDYING FABLES FROM AROUND THE WORLD OVER THE NEXT TWO WEEKS, SO I HOPE YOU ENJOYED THAT. NOW, IF YOU'LL TURN YOUR BOOKS TO PAGE THREE-NINETEEN, I'LL GO OVER YOUR HOMEWORK FOR TONIGHT...

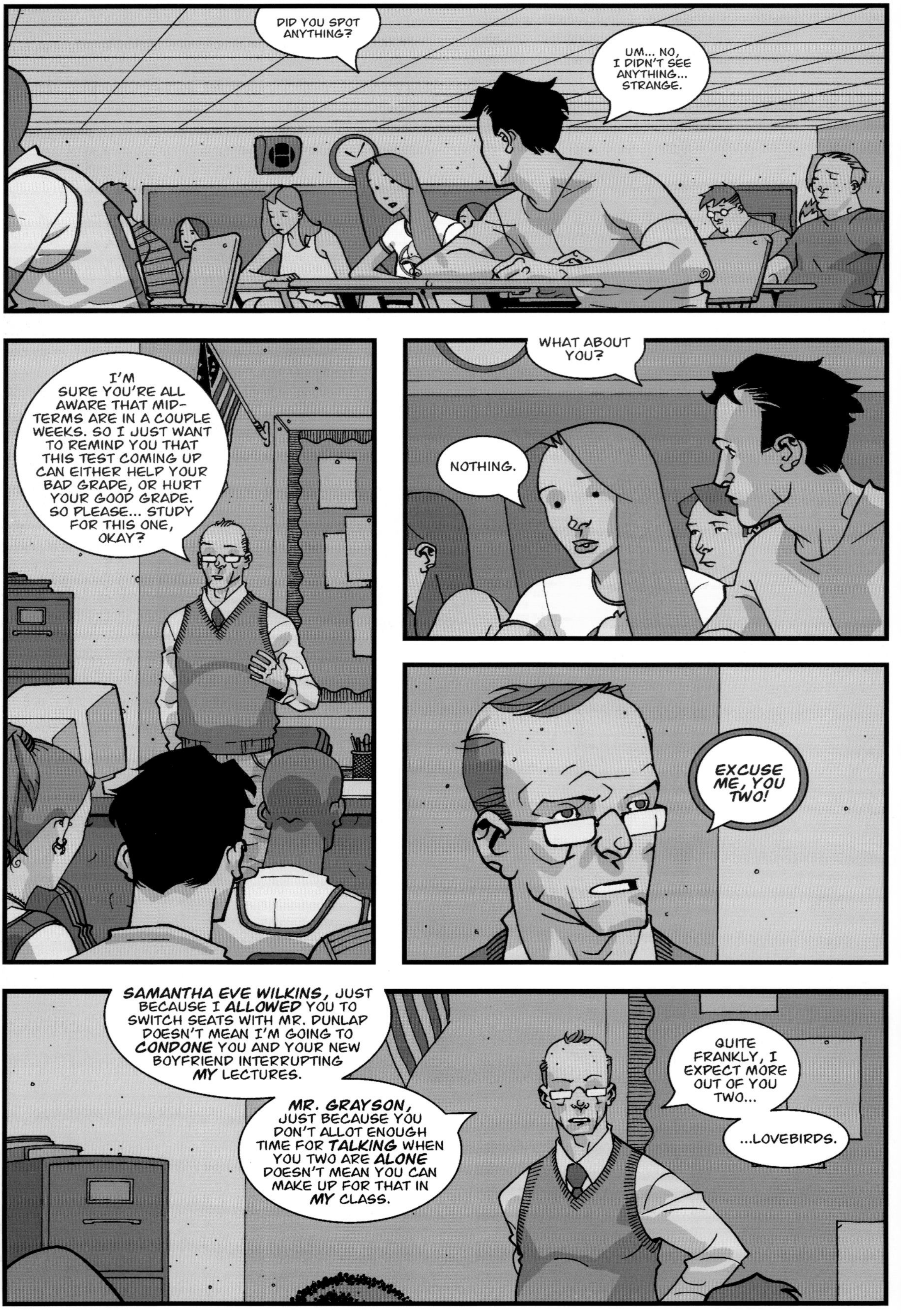
DID YOU SPOT ANYTHING?
UM... NO, I DIDN'T SEE ANYTHING... STRANGE.
I'M SURE YOU'RE ALL AWARE THAT MID-TERMS ARE IN A COUPLE WEEKS. SO I JUST WANT TO REMIND YOU THAT THIS TEST COMING UP CAN EITHER HELP YOUR BAD GRADE, OR HURT YOUR GOOD GRADE. SO PLEASE... STUDY FOR THIS ONE, OKAY?
WHAT ABOUT YOU?
NOTHING.
EXCUSE ME, YOU TWO!
SAMANTHA EVE WILKINS, JUST BECAUSE I ALLOWED YOU TO SWITCH SEATS WITH MR. DUNLAP DOESN'T MEAN I'M GOING TO CONDONE YOU AND YOUR NEW BOYFRIEND INTERRUPTING MY LECTURES.
MR. GRAYSON, JUST BECAUSE YOU DON'T ALLOT ENOUGH TIME FOR TALKING WHEN YOU TWO ARE ALONE DOESN'T MEAN YOU CAN MAKE UP FOR THAT IN MY CLASS.
QUITE FRANKLY, I EXPECT MORE OUT OF YOU TWO...
...LOVEBIRDS.

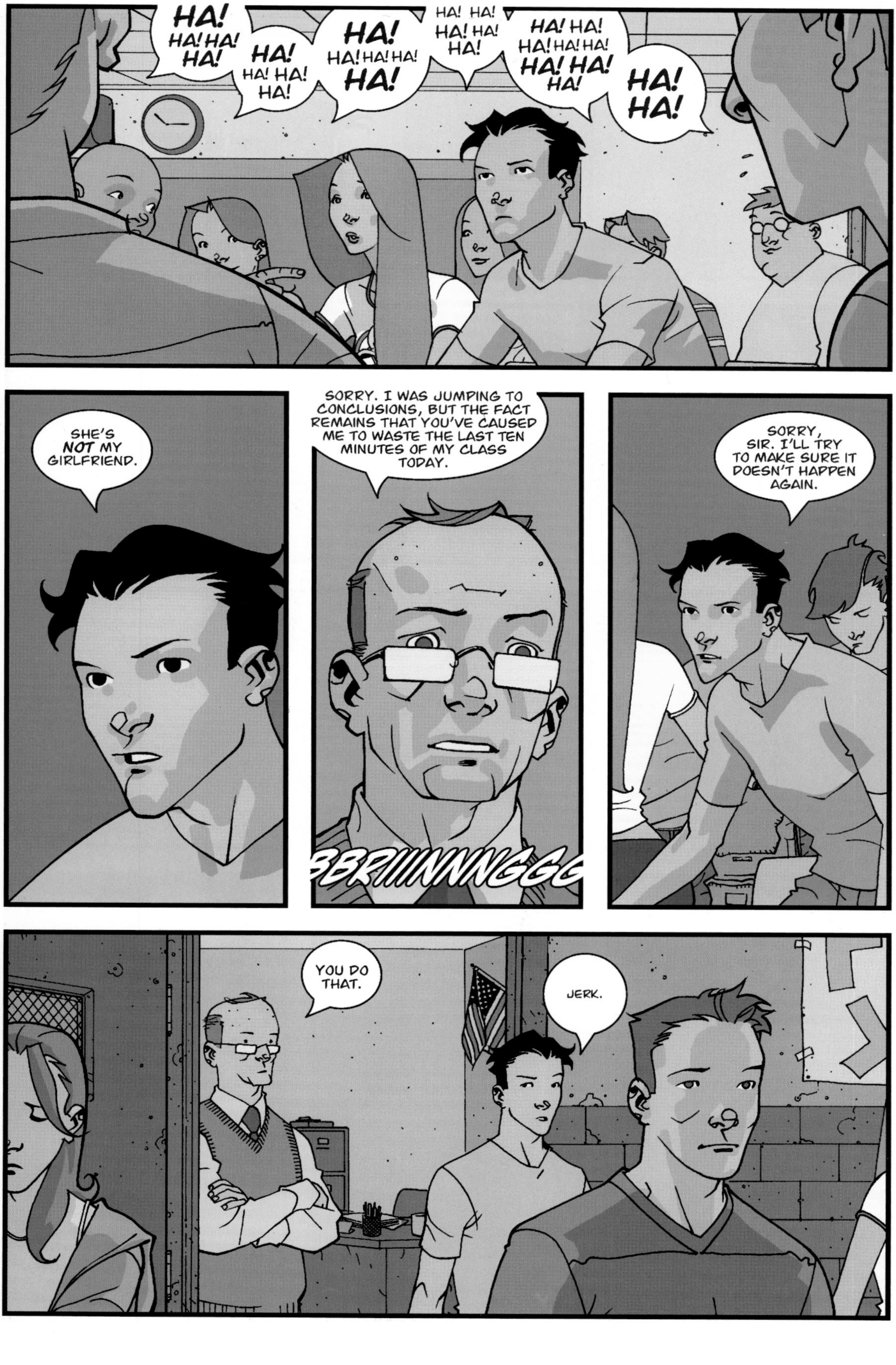
HA! HA! HA! HA!
HA! HA! HA! HA!
HA! HA! HA! HA! HA!
HA! HA! HA! HA!
HA! HA! HA! HA! HA! HA! HA! HA!
HA! HA!
SHE'S *NOT* MY GIRLFRIEND.
SORRY. I WAS JUMPING TO CONCLUSIONS, BUT THE FACT REMAINS THAT YOU'VE CAUSED ME TO WASTE THE LAST TEN MINUTES OF MY CLASS TODAY.
BBRIIINNNGGG
SORRY, SIR. I'LL TRY TO MAKE SURE IT DOESN'T HAPPEN AGAIN.
YOU DO THAT.
JERK.

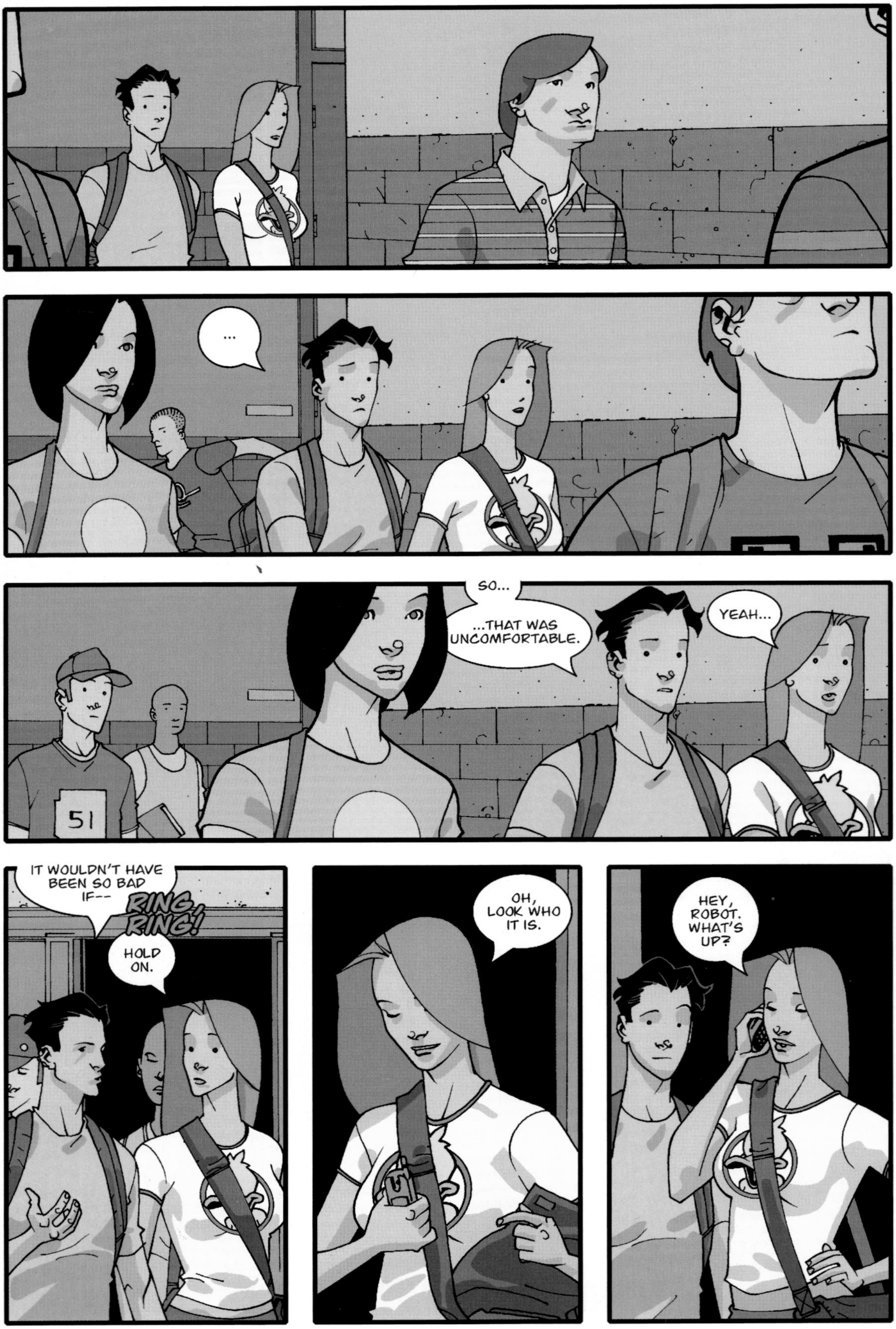
...
SO...
...THAT WAS UNCOMFORTABLE.
YEAH...
51
IT WOULDN'T HAVE BEEN SO BAD IF--
RING, RING!
HOLD ON.
OH, LOOK WHO IT IS.
HEY, ROBOT. WHAT'S UP?

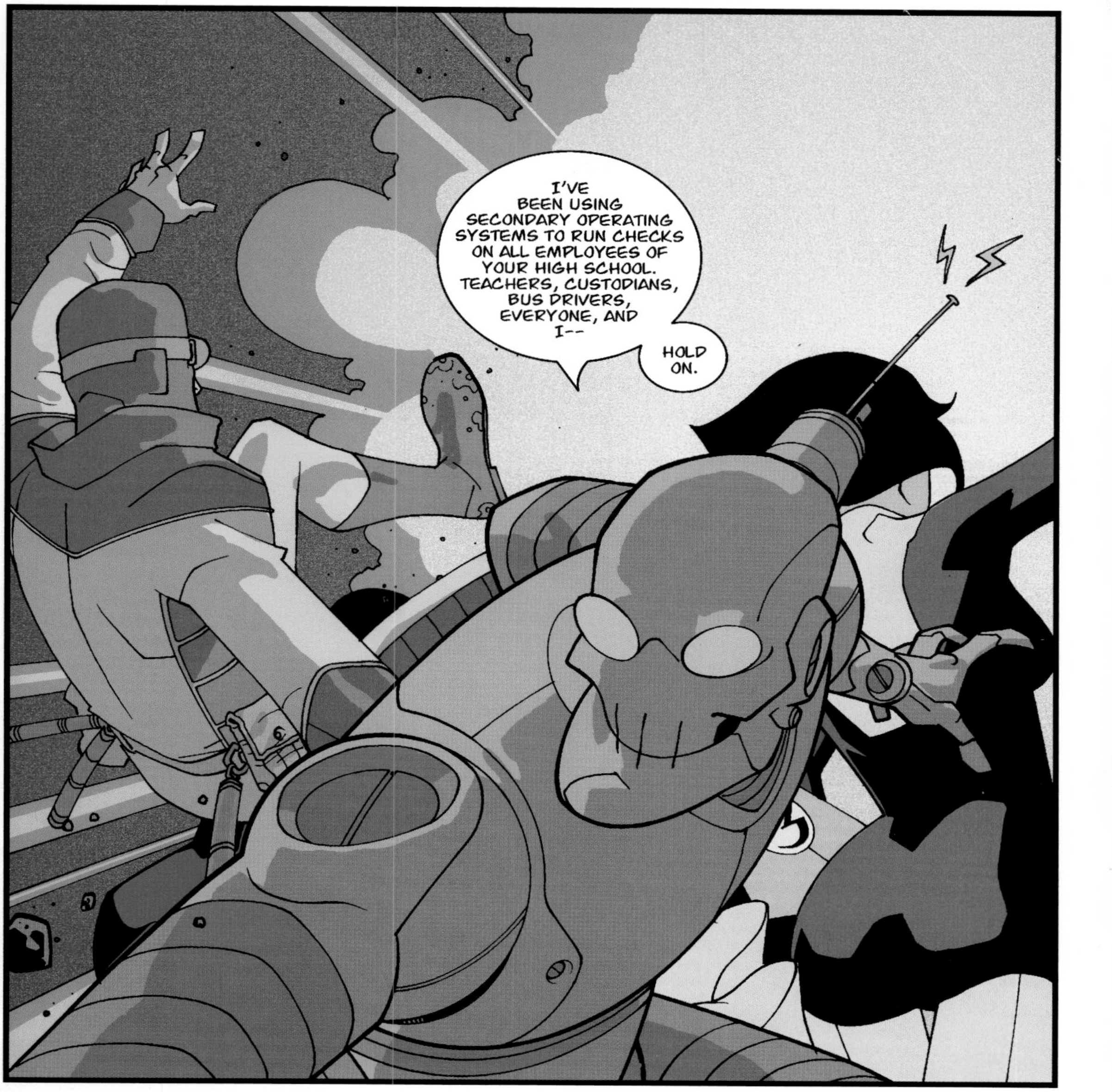
I'VE BEEN USING SECONDARY OPERATING SYSTEMS TO RUN CHECKS ON ALL EMPLOYEES OF YOUR HIGH SCHOOL. TEACHERS, CUSTODIANS, BUS DRIVERS, EVERYONE, AND I--
HOLD ON.

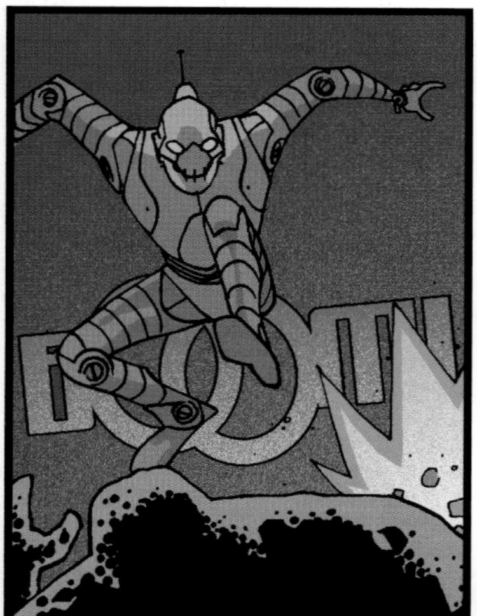

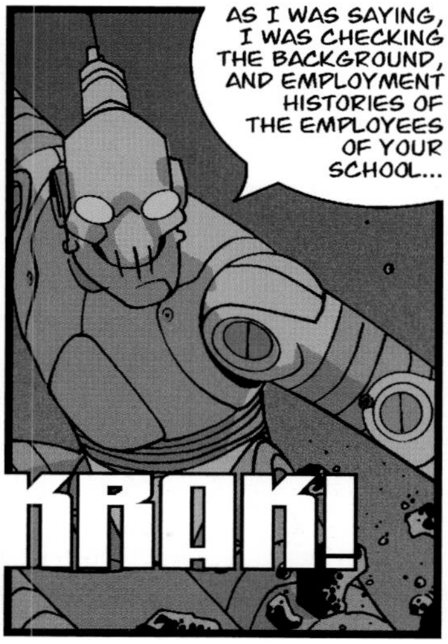
AS I WAS SAYING, I WAS CHECKING THE BACKGROUND, AND EMPLOYMENT HISTORIES OF THE EMPLOYEES OF YOUR SCHOOL...
KRAK!

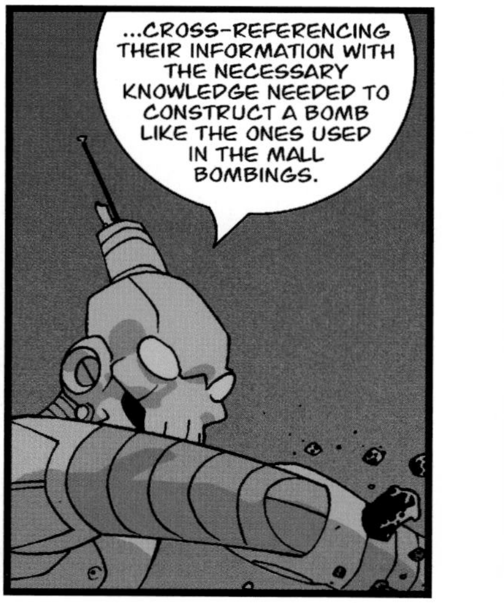
...CROSS-REFERENCING THEIR INFORMATION WITH THE NECESSARY KNOWLEDGE NEEDED TO CONSTRUCT A BOMB LIKE THE ONES USED IN THE MALL BOMBINGS.

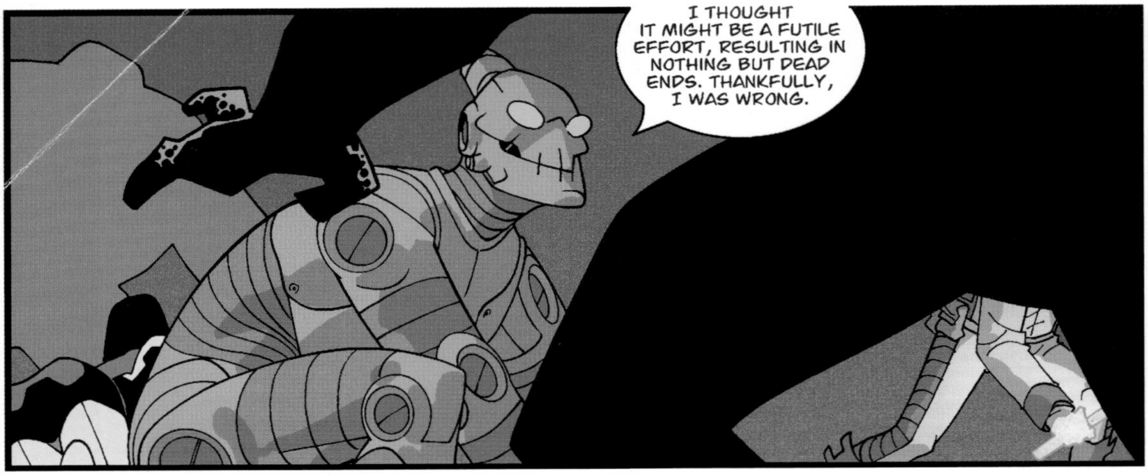
I THOUGHT IT MIGHT BE A FUTILE EFFORT, RESULTING IN NOTHING BUT DEAD ENDS. THANKFULLY, I WAS WRONG.
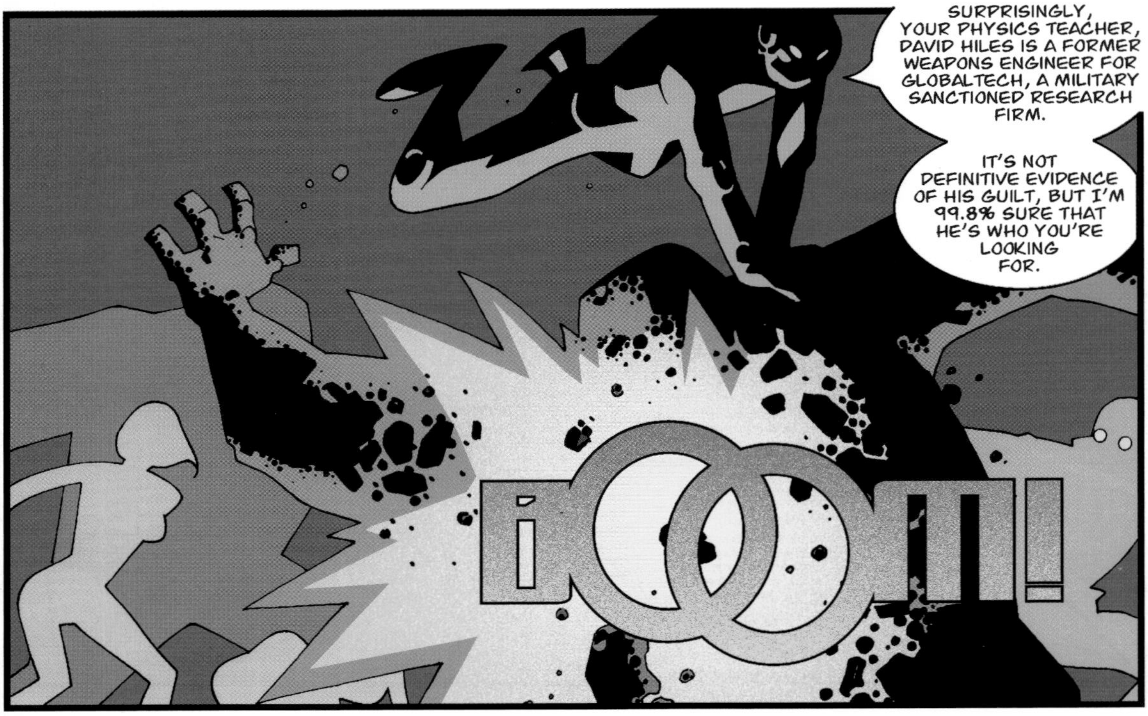
SURPRISINGLY, YOUR PHYSICS TEACHER, DAVID HILES IS A FORMER WEAPONS ENGINEER FOR GLOBALTECH, A MILITARY SANCTIONED RESEARCH FIRM.
IT'S NOT DEFINITIVE EVIDENCE OF HIS GUILT, BUT I'M 99.8% SURE THAT HE'S WHO YOU'RE LOOKING FOR.
BOOM!
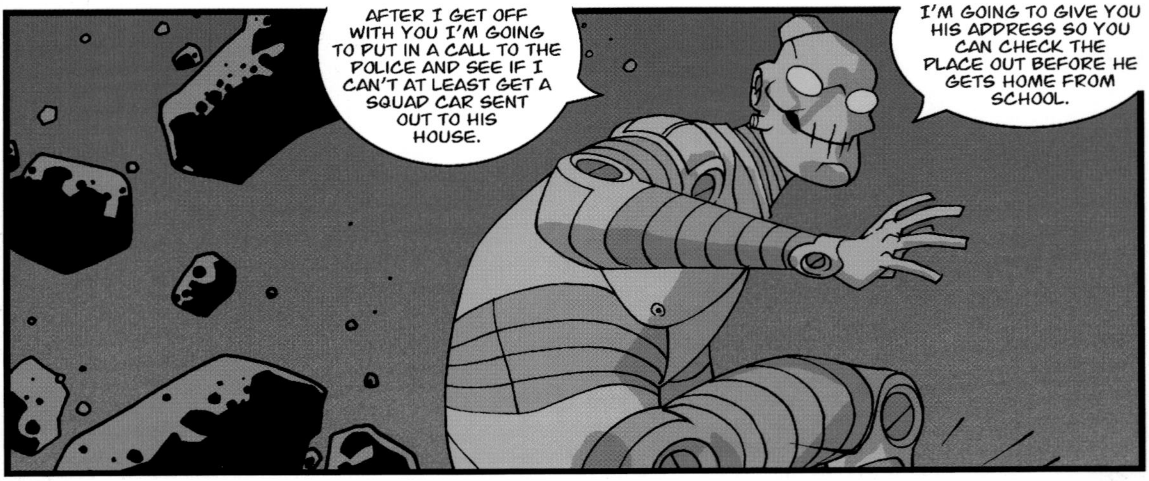
AFTER I GET OFF WITH YOU I'M GOING TO PUT IN A CALL TO THE POLICE AND SEE IF I CAN'T AT LEAST GET A SQUAD CAR SENT OUT TO HIS HOUSE.
I'M GOING TO GIVE YOU HIS ADDRESS SO YOU CAN CHECK THE PLACE OUT BEFORE HE GETS HOME FROM SCHOOL.

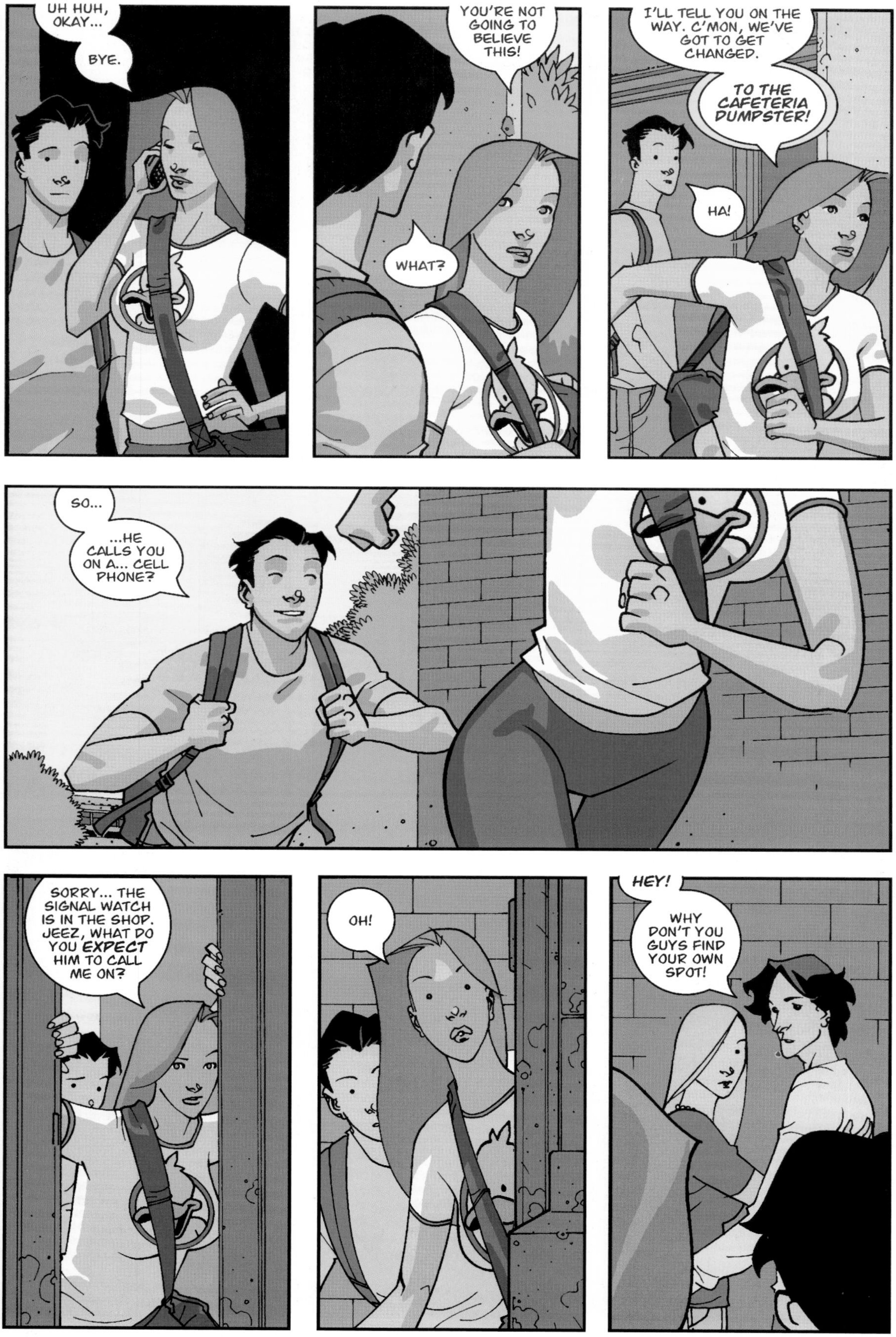
UH HUH, OKAY...
BYE.
YOU'RE NOT GOING TO BELIEVE THIS!
WHAT?
I'LL TELL YOU ON THE WAY. C'MON, WE'VE GOT TO GET CHANGED.
TO THE CAFETERIA DUMPSTER!
HA!
SO...
...HE CALLS YOU ON A... CELL PHONE?
SORRY... THE SIGNAL WATCH IS IN THE SHOP. JEEZ, WHAT DO YOU EXPECT HIM TO CALL ME ON?
OH!
HEY!
WHY DON'T YOU GUYS FIND YOUR OWN SPOT!

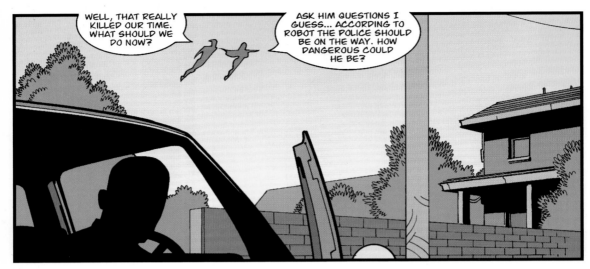

WELL, THAT REALLY KILLED OUR TIME. WHAT SHOULD WE DO NOW?

ASK HIM QUESTIONS I GUESS... ACCORDING TO ROBOT THE POLICE SHOULD BE ON THE WAY. HOW DANGEROUS COULD HE BE?

HOLD IT RIGHT THERE, SIR!

I DIDN'T EXPECT TO GET CAUGHT QUITE THIS EARLY, AND I CERTAINLY EXPECTED... MORE *CONVENTIONAL* AUTHORITIES WHEN THE TIME DID COME...

VERY WELL. MARK, SAMANTHA... PLEASE, DO COME INSIDE.

HOW DID YOU--?

ARE YOU KIDDING ME? YOU'RE NOT EVEN WEARING A MASK.

FOLLOW ME, I'LL SHOW YOU TO THE FOURTH MISSING STUDENT. I ASSURE YOU, I HAVE NO INTENTION OF RESISTING.

FOURTH?

YES. ONE OF THEM HASN'T BEEN REPORTED MISSING YET.

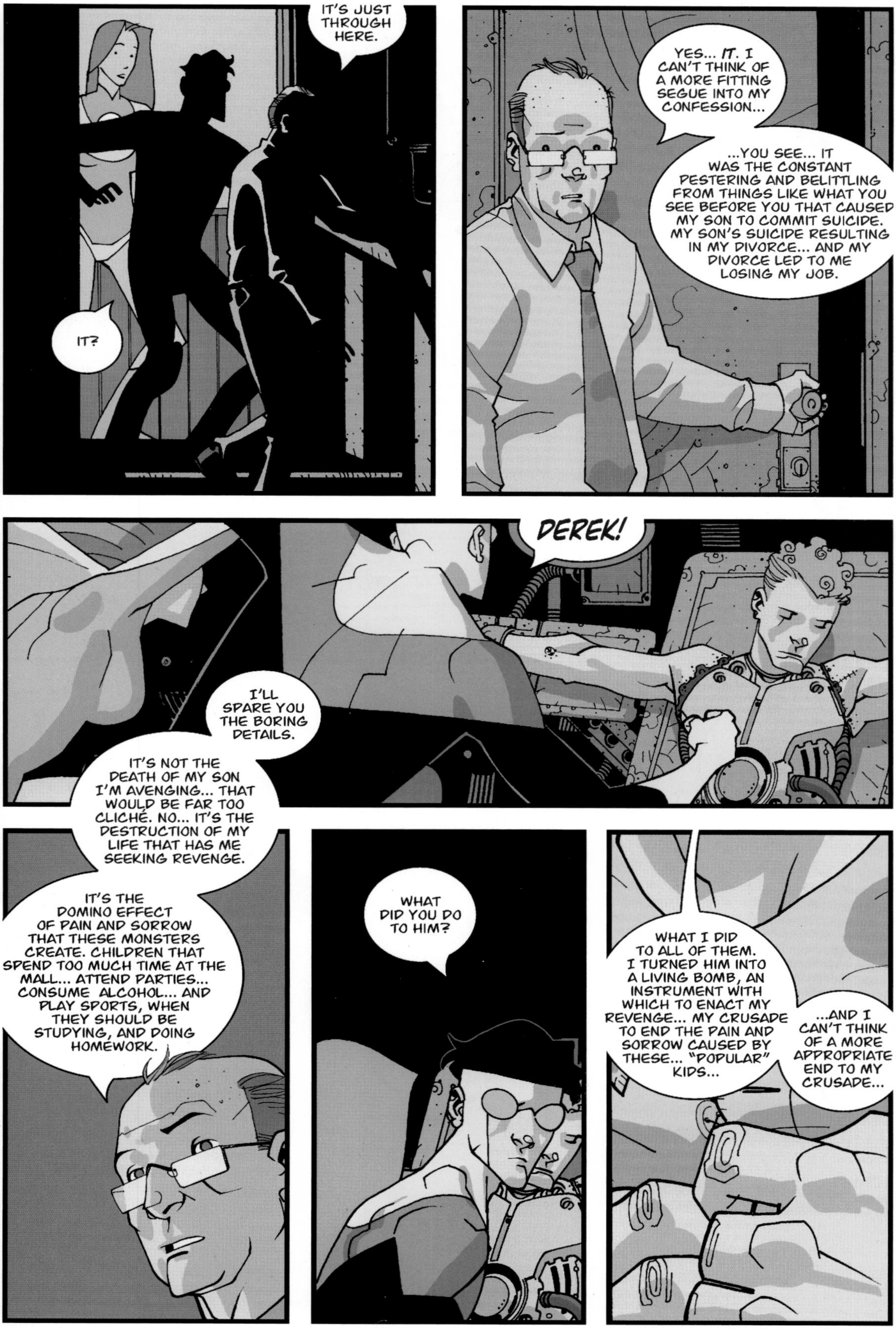

IT'S JUST THROUGH HERE.
IT?
YES... IT. I CAN'T THINK OF A MORE FITTING SEGUE INTO MY CONFESSION...
...YOU SEE... IT WAS THE CONSTANT PESTERING AND BELITTLING FROM THINGS LIKE WHAT YOU SEE BEFORE YOU THAT CAUSED MY SON TO COMMIT SUICIDE. MY SON'S SUICIDE RESULTING IN MY DIVORCE... AND MY DIVORCE LED TO ME LOSING MY JOB.
DEREK!
I'LL SPARE YOU THE BORING DETAILS.
IT'S NOT THE DEATH OF MY SON I'M AVENGING... THAT WOULD BE FAR TOO CLICHÉ. NO... IT'S THE DESTRUCTION OF MY LIFE THAT HAS ME SEEKING REVENGE.
IT'S THE DOMINO EFFECT OF PAIN AND SORROW THAT THESE MONSTERS CREATE. CHILDREN THAT SPEND TOO MUCH TIME AT THE MALL... ATTEND PARTIES... CONSUME ALCOHOL... AND PLAY SPORTS, WHEN THEY SHOULD BE STUDYING, AND DOING HOMEWORK.
WHAT DID YOU DO TO HIM?
WHAT I DID TO ALL OF THEM. I TURNED HIM INTO A LIVING BOMB, AN INSTRUMENT WITH WHICH TO ENACT MY REVENGE... MY CRUSADE TO END THE PAIN AND SORROW CAUSED BY THESE... "POPULAR" KIDS...
...AND I CAN'T THINK OF A MORE APPROPRIATE END TO MY CRUSADE...

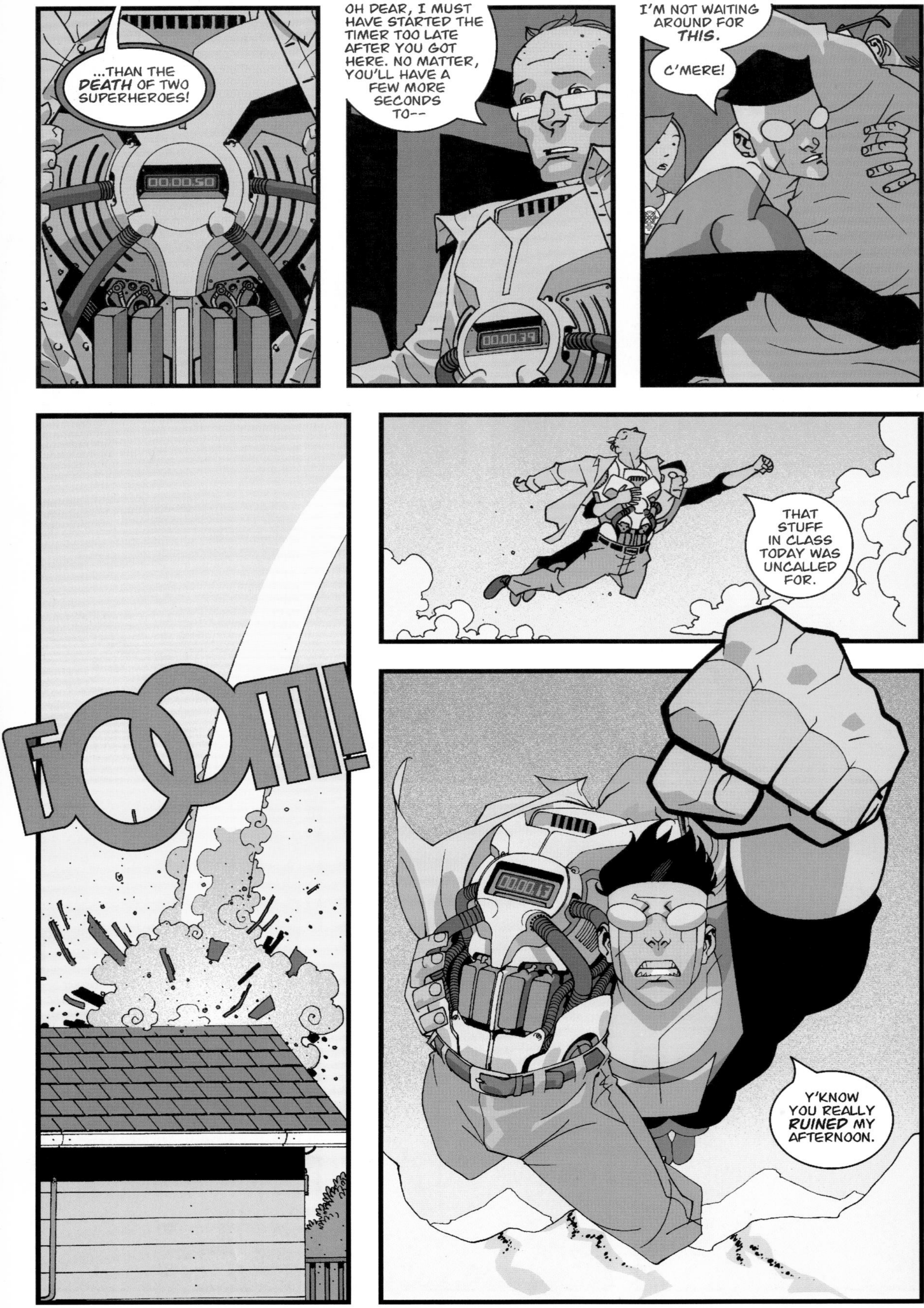
...THAN THE *DEATH* OF TWO SUPERHEROES!
00.00.50
OH DEAR, I MUST HAVE STARTED THE TIMER TOO LATE AFTER YOU GOT HERE. NO MATTER, YOU'LL HAVE A FEW MORE SECONDS TO--
00.00.39
I'M NOT WAITING AROUND FOR *THIS*.
C'MERE!
GOOM!
THAT STUFF IN CLASS TODAY WAS UNCALLED FOR.
00.00.13
Y'KNOW YOU REALLY *RUINED* MY AFTERNOON.

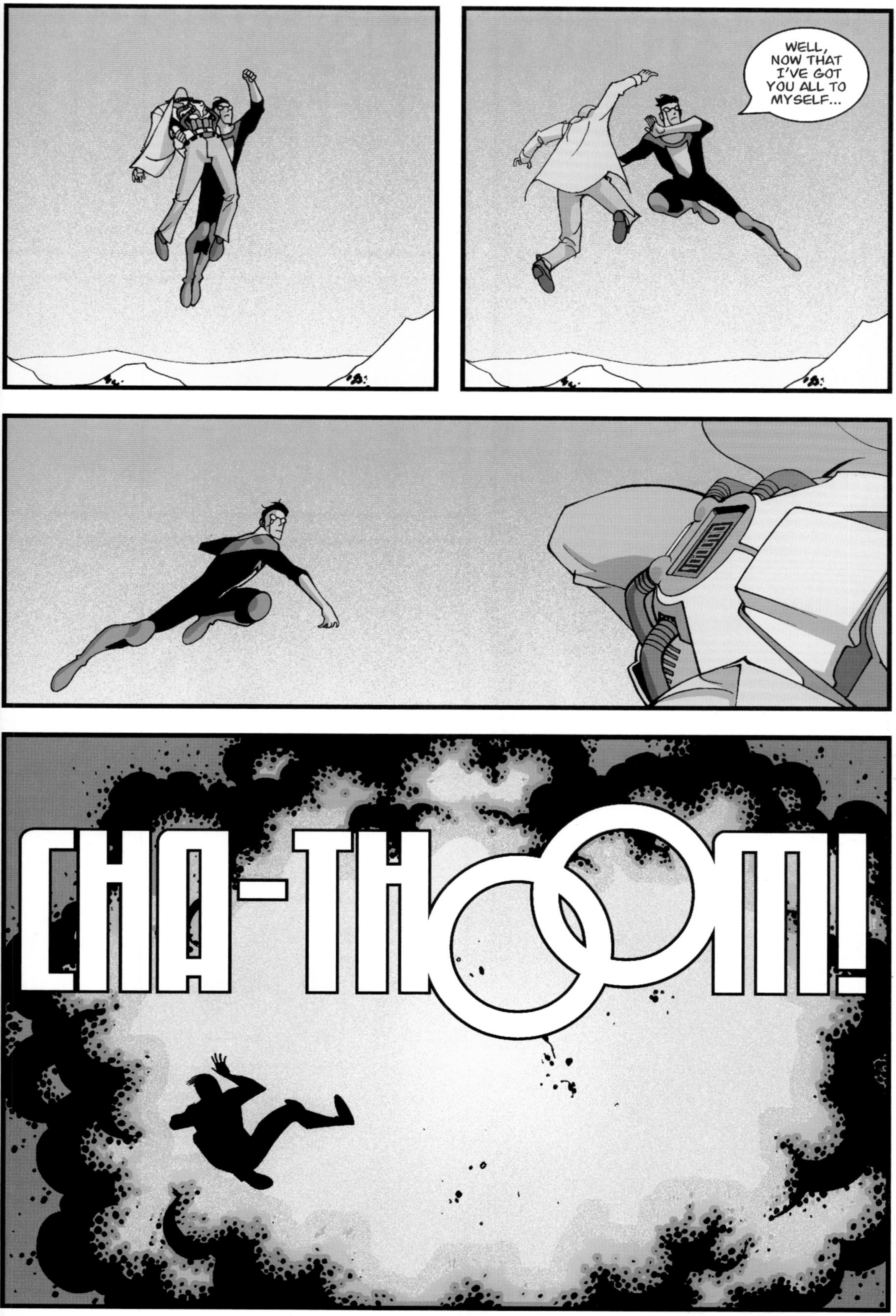
WELL, NOW THAT I'VE GOT YOU ALL TO MYSELF...
CHA-THOOM!

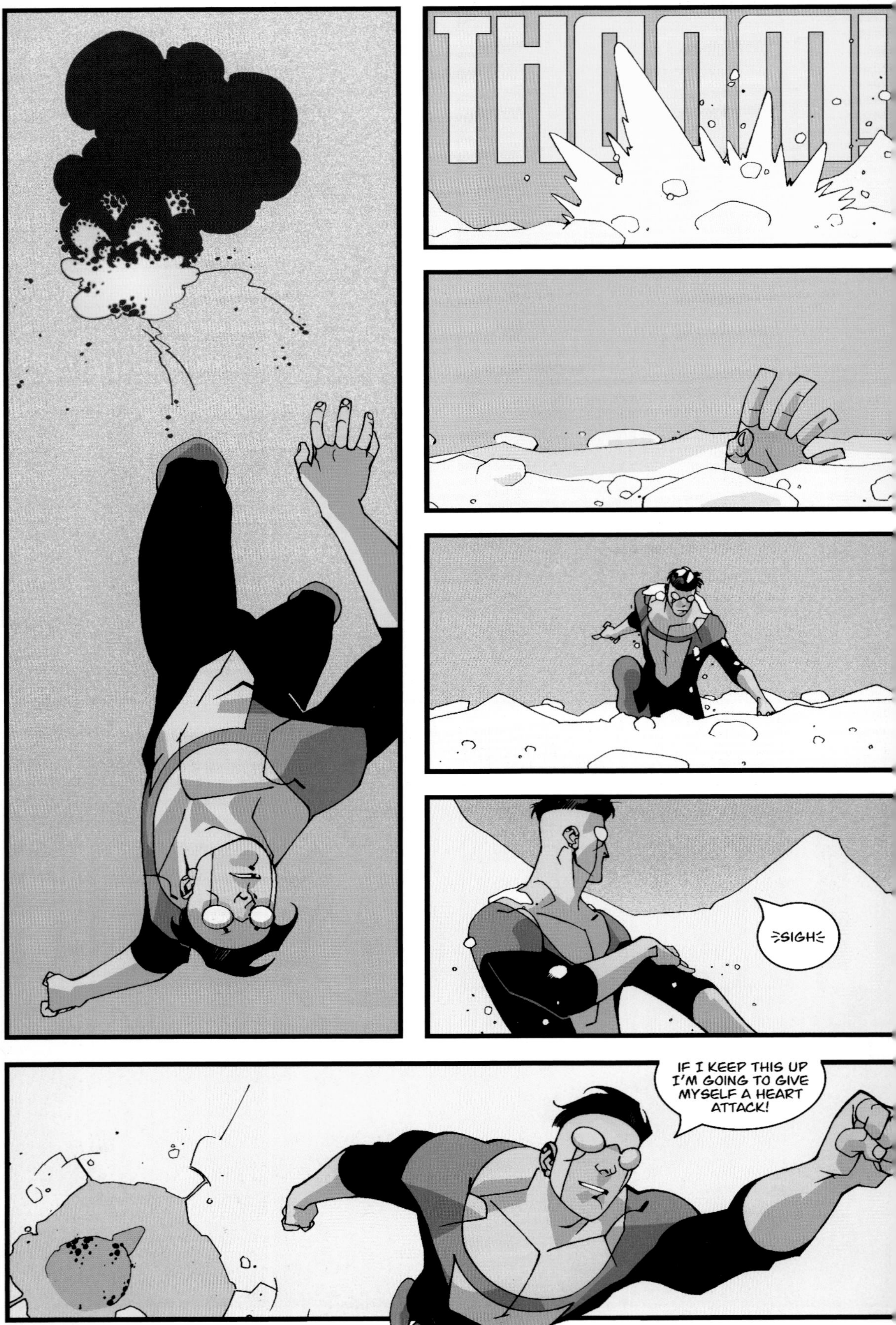
THOOM!
SIGH
IF I KEEP THIS UP I'M GOING TO GIVE MYSELF A HEART ATTACK!

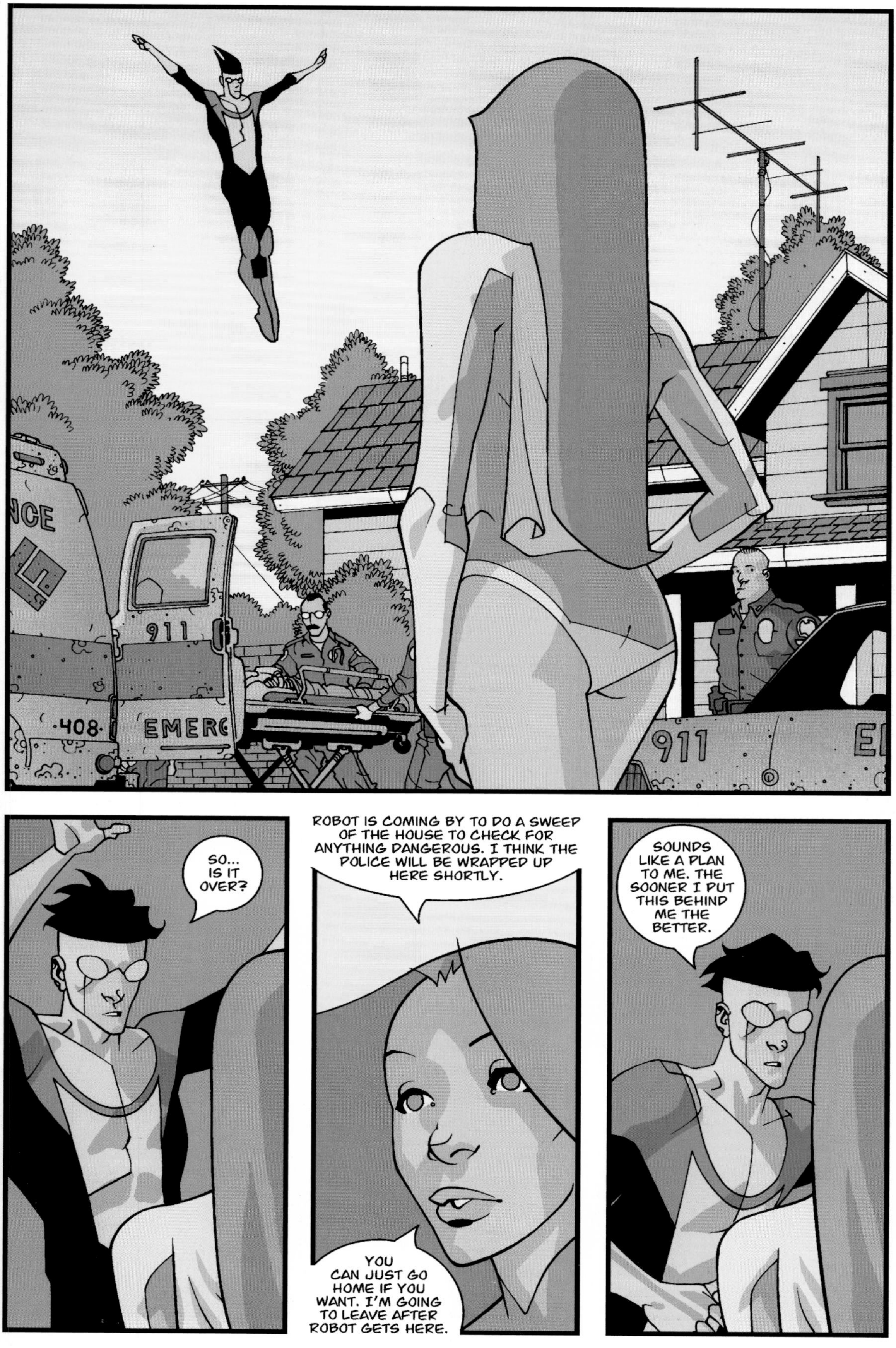
NCE
911
408
EMERG
911
E
SO... IS IT OVER?
ROBOT IS COMING BY TO DO A SWEEP OF THE HOUSE TO CHECK FOR ANYTHING DANGEROUS. I THINK THE POLICE WILL BE WRAPPED UP HERE SHORTLY.
YOU CAN JUST GO HOME IF YOU WANT. I'M GOING TO LEAVE AFTER ROBOT GETS HERE.
SOUNDS LIKE A PLAN TO ME. THE SOONER I PUT THIS BEHIND ME THE BETTER.

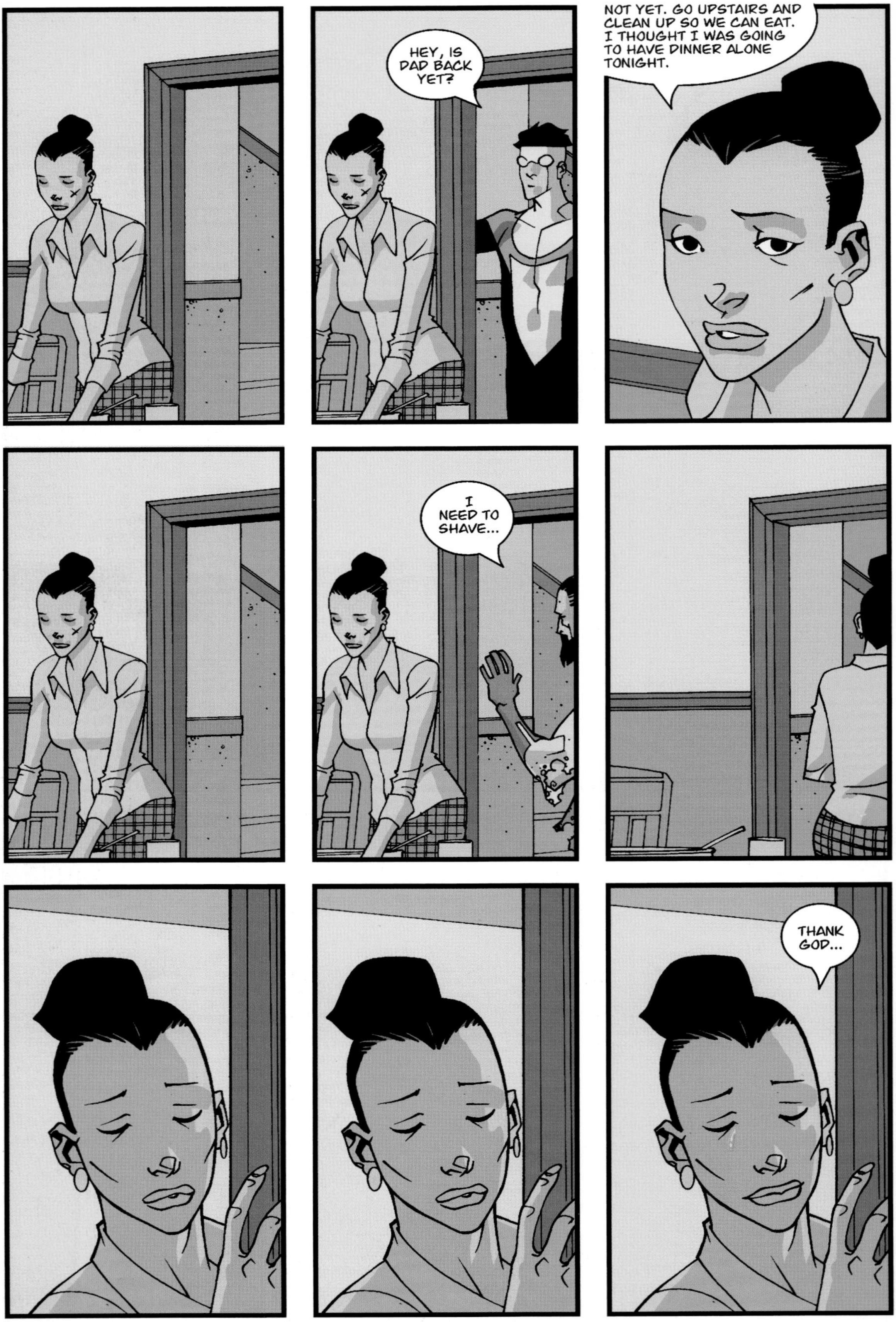
HEY, IS DAD BACK YET?
NOT YET. GO UPSTAIRS AND CLEAN UP SO WE CAN EAT. I THOUGHT I WAS GOING TO HAVE DINNER ALONE TONIGHT.
I NEED TO SHAVE...
THANK GOD...

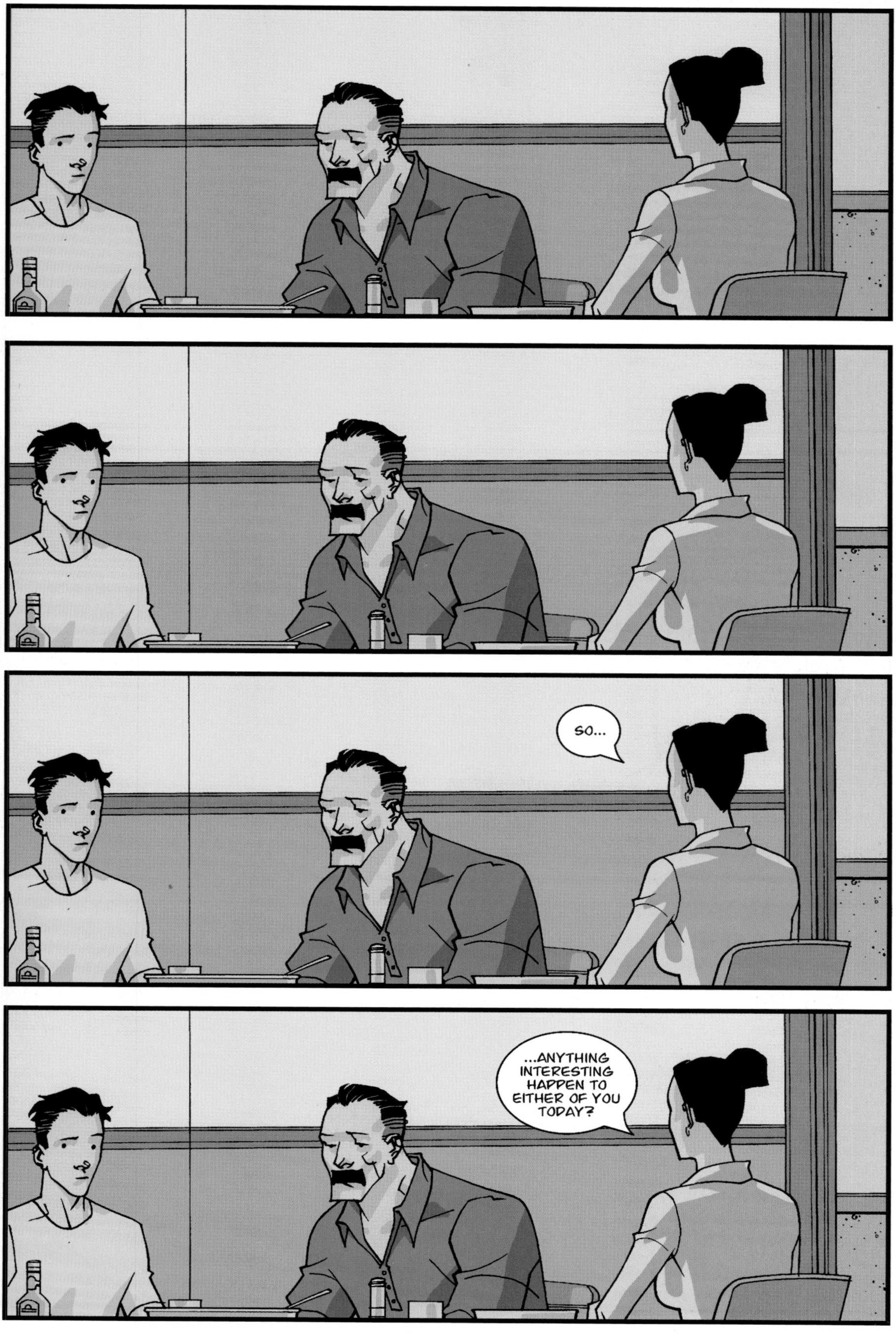
SO...
...ANYTHING INTERESTING HAPPEN TO EITHER OF YOU TODAY?

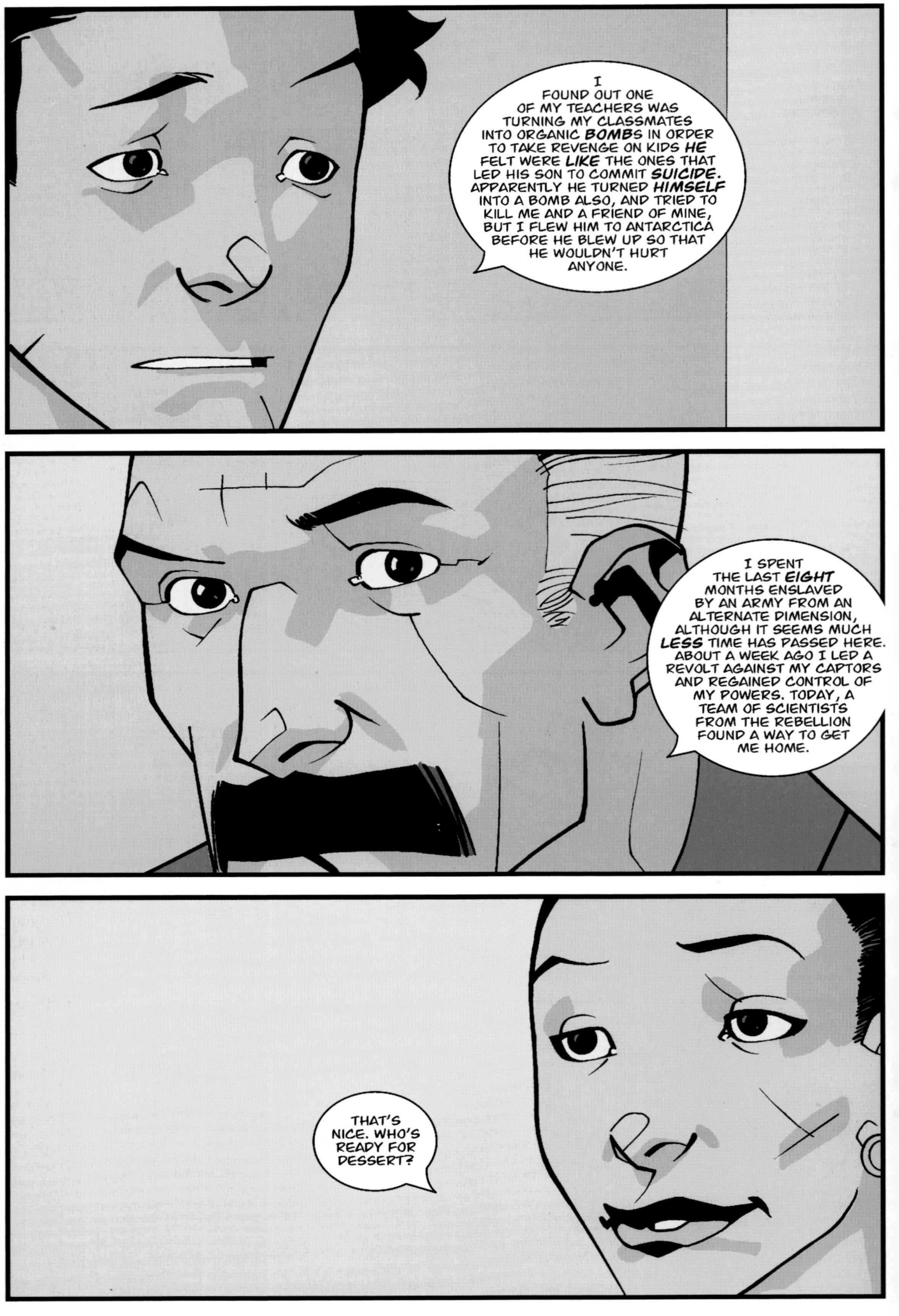
I FOUND OUT ONE OF MY TEACHERS WAS TURNING MY CLASSMATES INTO ORGANIC BOMBS IN ORDER TO TAKE REVENGE ON KIDS HE FELT WERE LIKE THE ONES THAT LED HIS SON TO COMMIT SUICIDE. APPARENTLY HE TURNED HIMSELF INTO A BOMB ALSO, AND TRIED TO KILL ME AND A FRIEND OF MINE, BUT I FLEW HIM TO ANTARCTICA BEFORE HE BLEW UP SO THAT HE WOULDN'T HURT ANYONE.
I SPENT THE LAST EIGHT MONTHS ENSLAVED BY AN ARMY FROM AN ALTERNATE DIMENSION, ALTHOUGH IT SEEMS MUCH LESS TIME HAS PASSED HERE. ABOUT A WEEK AGO I LED A REVOLT AGAINST MY CAPTORS AND REGAINED CONTROL OF MY POWERS. TODAY, A TEAM OF SCIENTISTS FROM THE REBELLION FOUND A WAY TO GET ME HOME.
THAT'S NICE. WHO'S READY FOR DESSERT?

# UNUSED COVERS

We went through a lot of versions of the first issue's cover. It all started out with a sketch I did of Mark flying up towards us with two bank robbers. Cory did the sketch below based on that, and it was pointed out that he'd look goofy if he smiled, and that he was flying from right to left. Since we read from left to right things flow better in comics if they MOVE in that direction too. Both of these problems were my fault. So Cory took over and came up with the second sketch you see... doesn't Mark look serious? The cover was finished up and sent to Val Staples to color, this was before Bill Crabtree came on board. Val did a hell of a job and I've always loved the way his stuff looks on Cory's work but there was a problem... the colors were WRONG!! And Jim Valentino said the overly blue background made him want to go to sleep... and this is the LAST thing we want to do to potential readers.

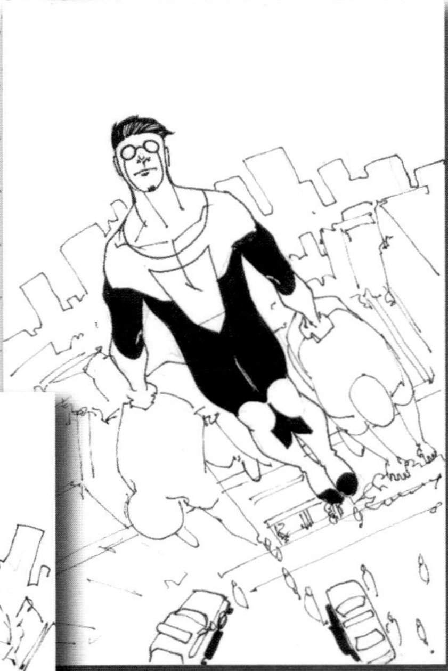

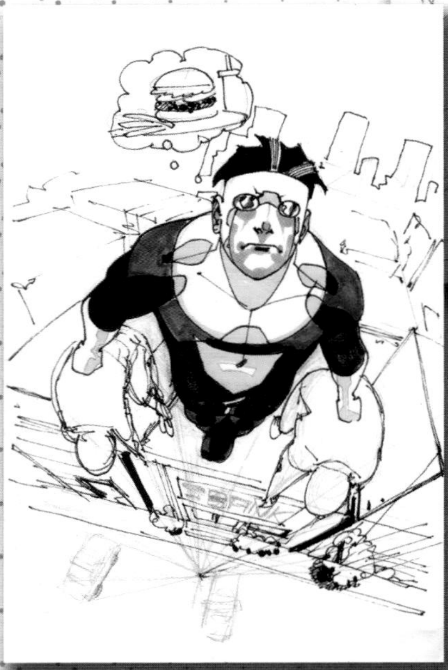

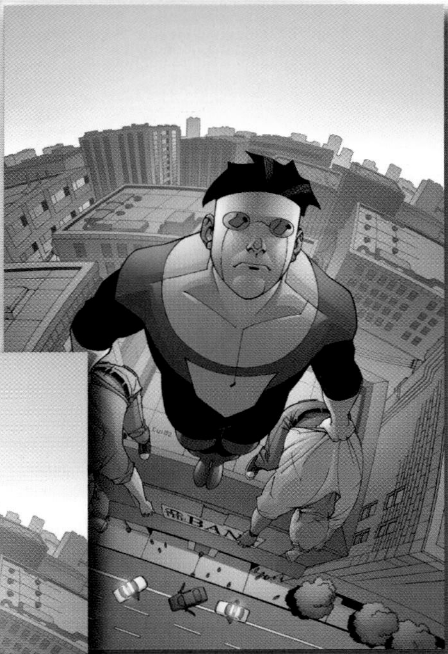

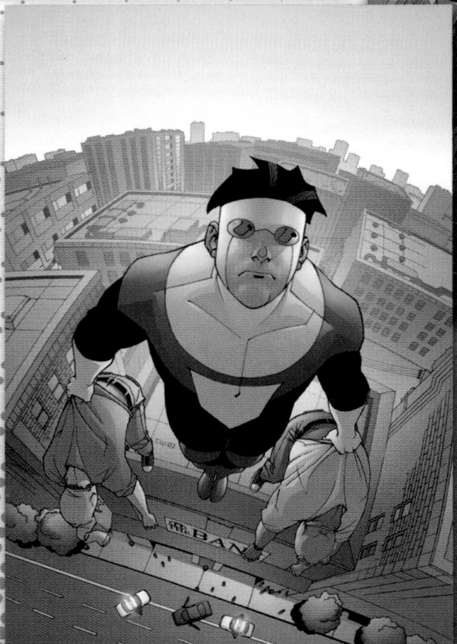

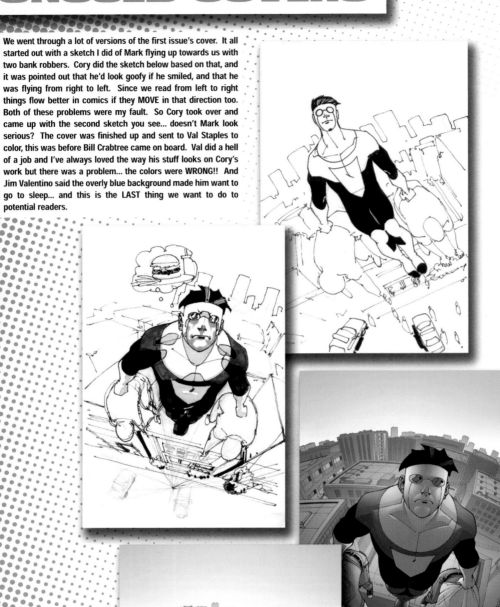

Val was swamped at this time, trying to launch that nifty *Masters of the Universe* comic so with his approval, Cory and I got our good pal Tony Moore to alter Val's version, changing the background and making the white on the costume yellow.

Later Cory and I decided that we weren't too keen on Mark's serious facial expression, so Cory altered the line art to make him smile just a little... and I requested some money be thrown in the air to play up the bank robbing angle. Around this time, young Bill Crabtree had come aboard. So he colored the version seen on the opposite page.

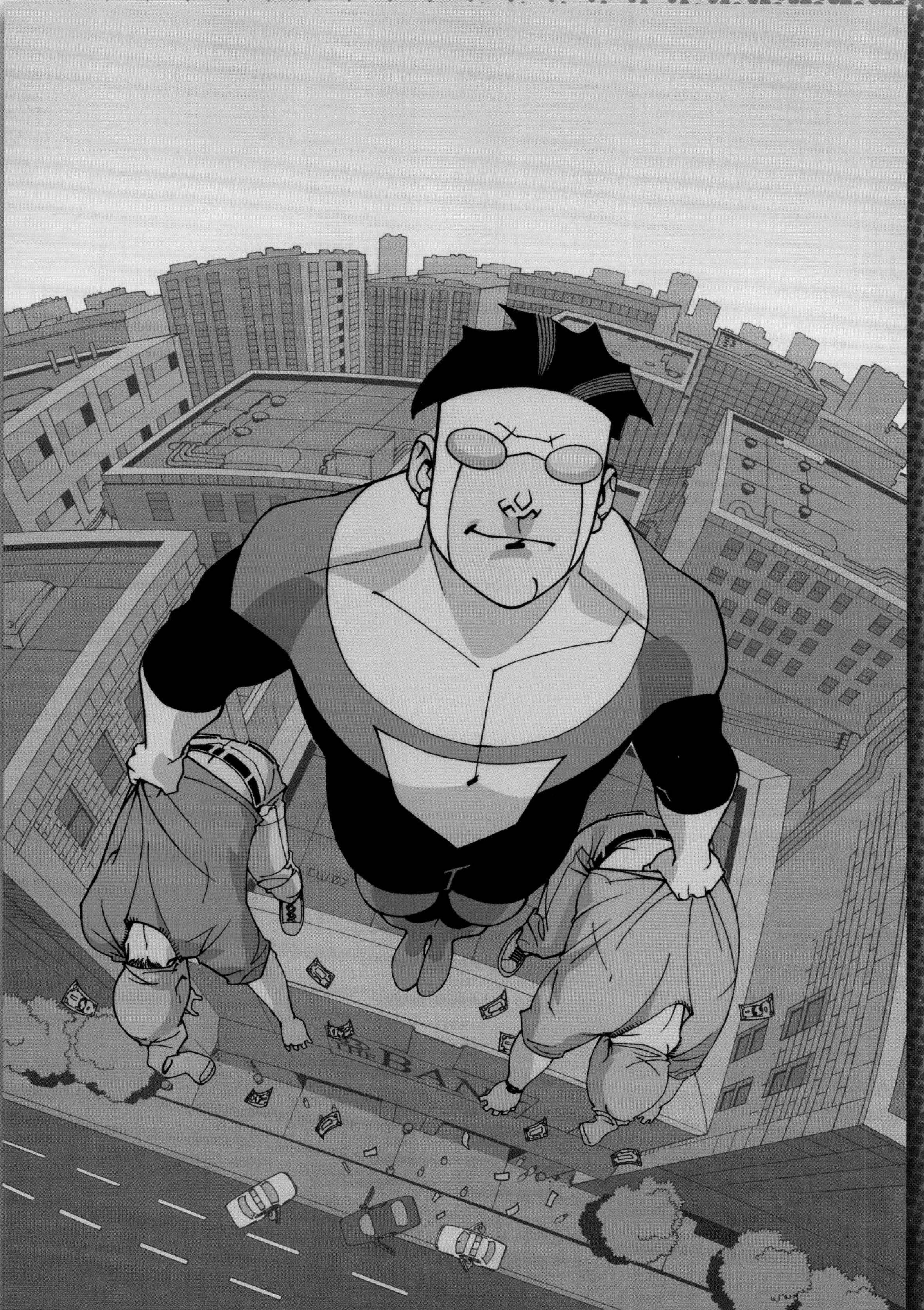

After all the initial promotion was out of the way... it was brought to our attention by Image that the original cover wasn't as strong as it could be and in their opinion would hurt our sales. That's not the smartest thing to do, so Cory immediately started burning the midnight oil trying to come up with something new. My pal Erik Larsen even threw his hat into the ring with the sketch below, and we were going to use it until Jim Valentino remembered a promo image Cory had done and thought it would make the perfect cover. Cory then took that image and came up with a new background for it. It was decided that reading the paper and washing dishes weren't very exciting, Jim suggested expanding the cracked wall panel that's behind Mark into the entire background... and thus, a cover was born.

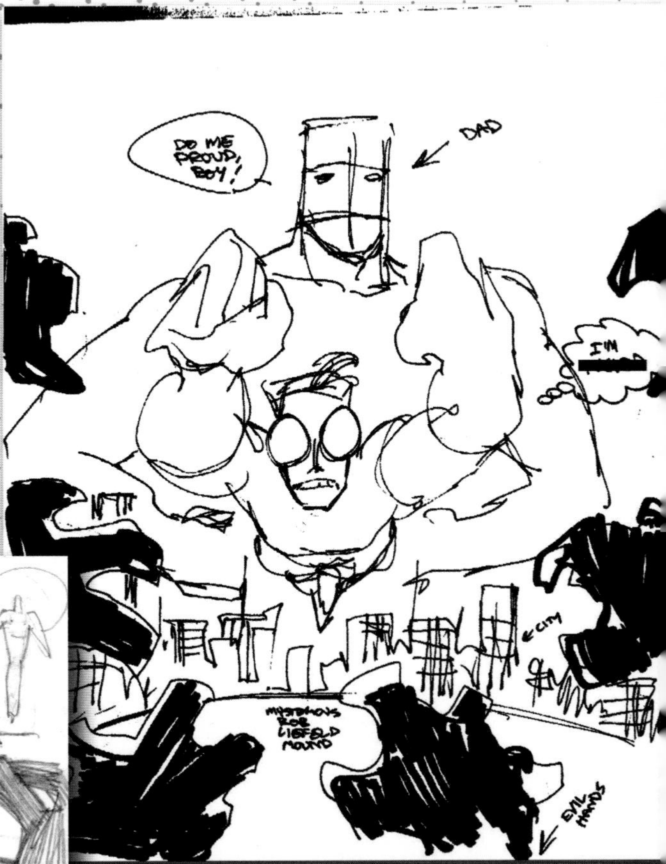
DO ME PROUD, BOY!
DAD
I'M [redacted]
CITY
MYSTERIOUS ROB LIEFELD MOUND
EVIL HANDS

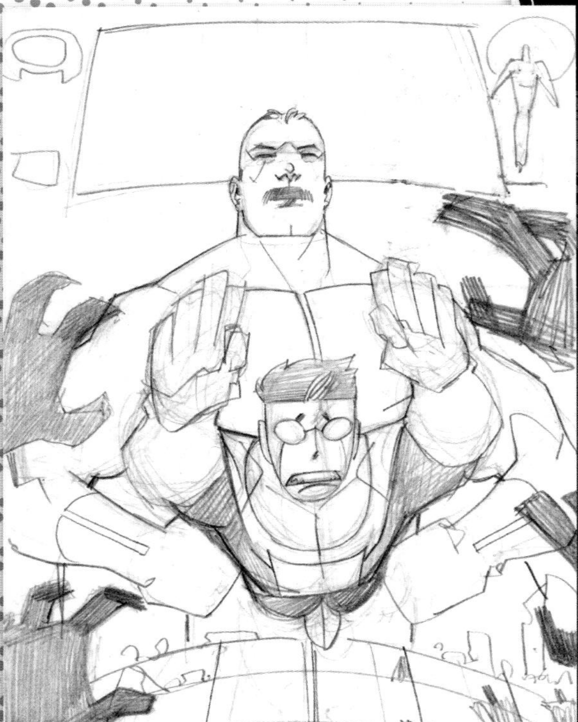

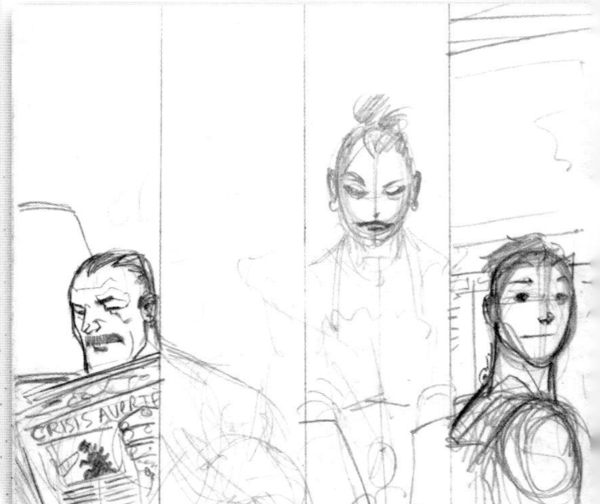
CRISIS AVERTE

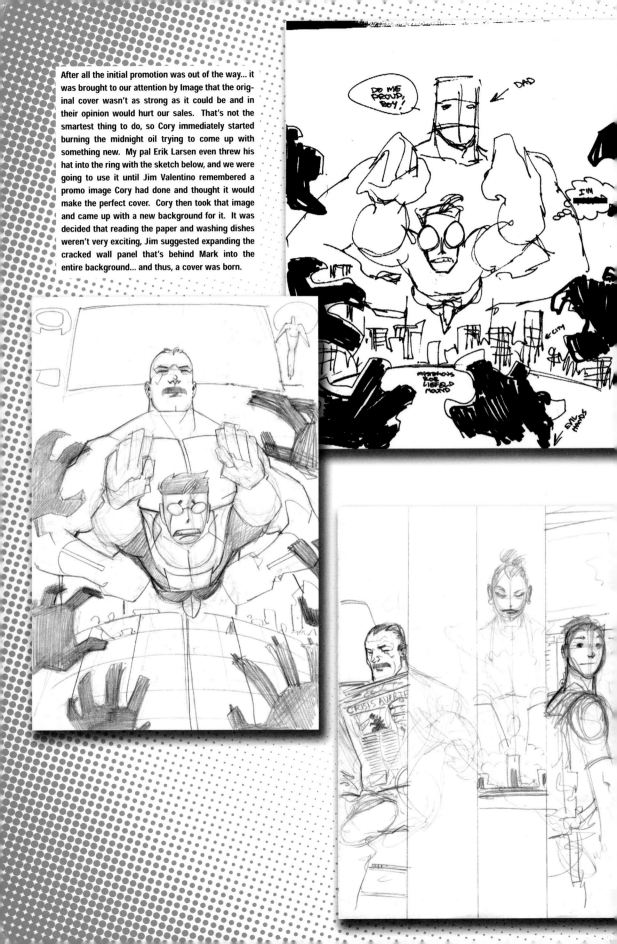

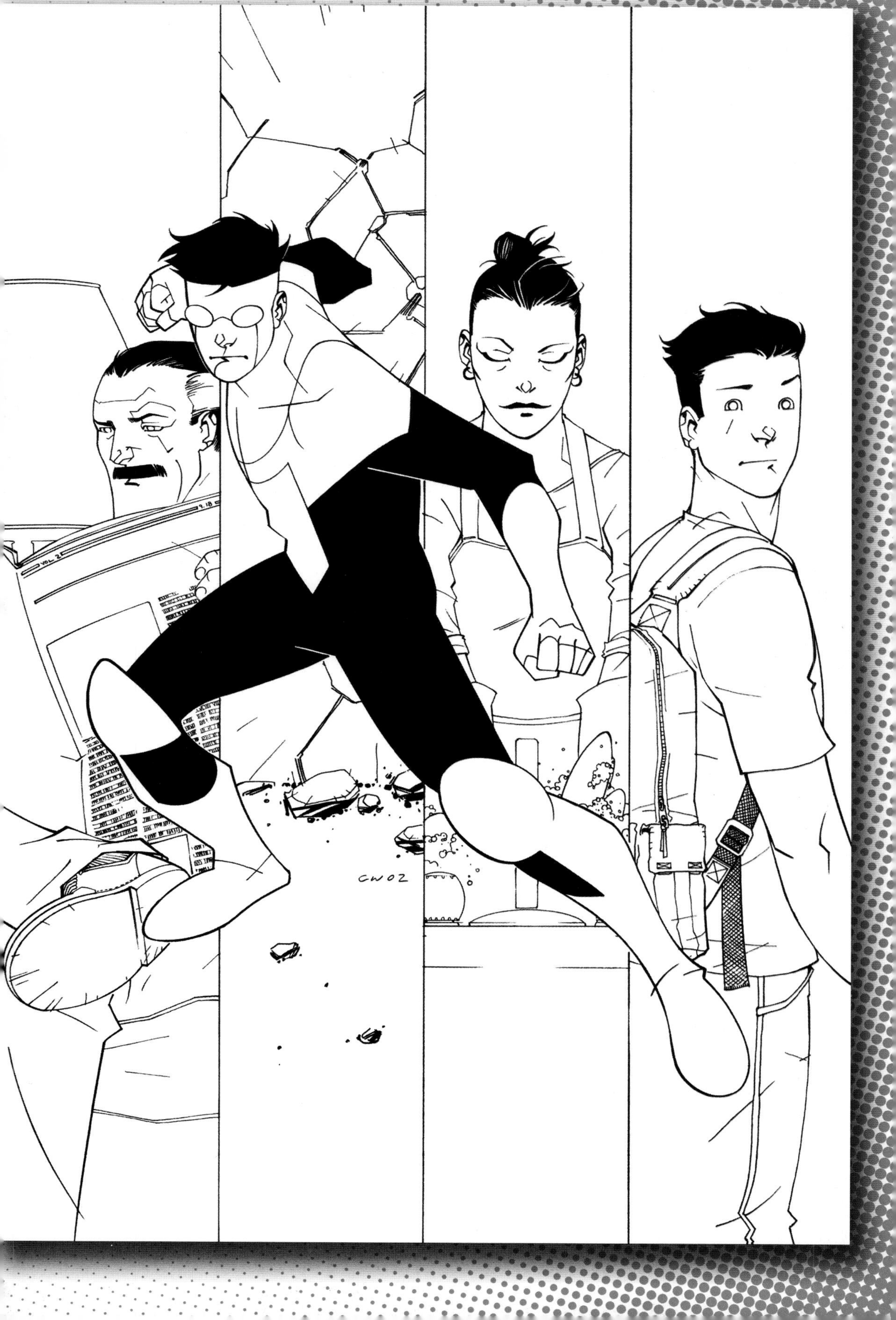

# PROMOTIONAL ART

Cory and I really wanted to have a Previews ad that was more than just a cover, so we did the page that you see on the opposite page, and all the illos seen below. Then Diamond stopped allowing Image enough space to do two-page solicitations for the first issues, and we didn't use any of it. Here's the image that became the cover for issue one, and Atom Eve's original costume. Actually most of the Teen Team is different in that picture below.

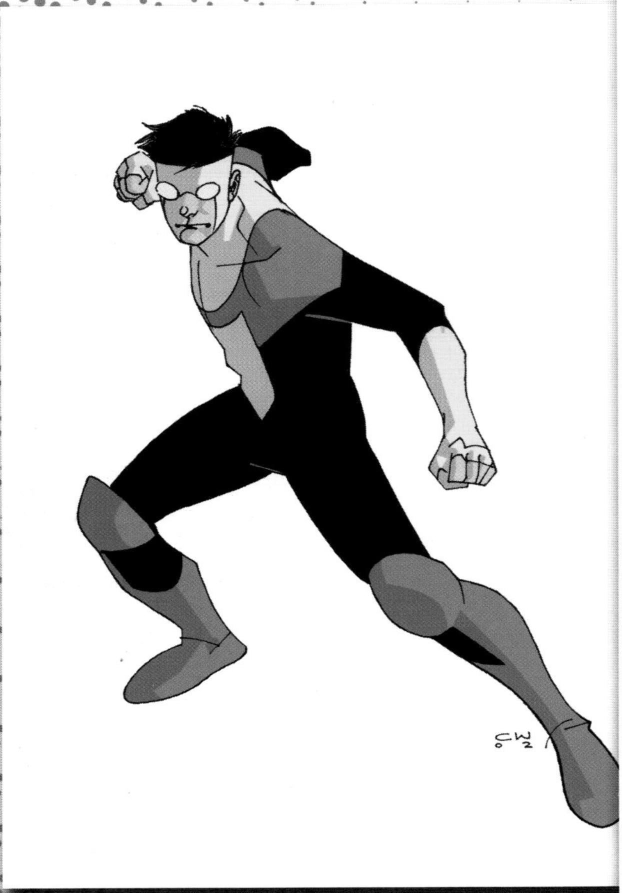

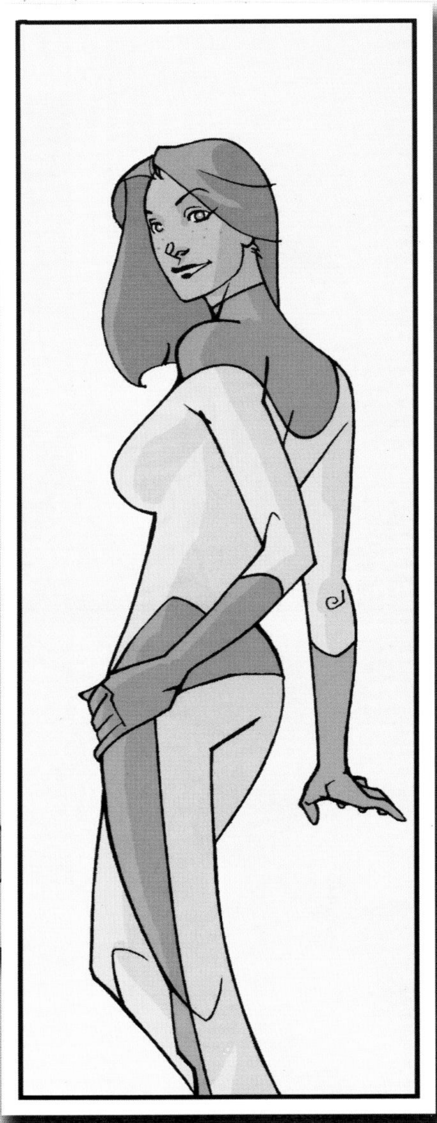

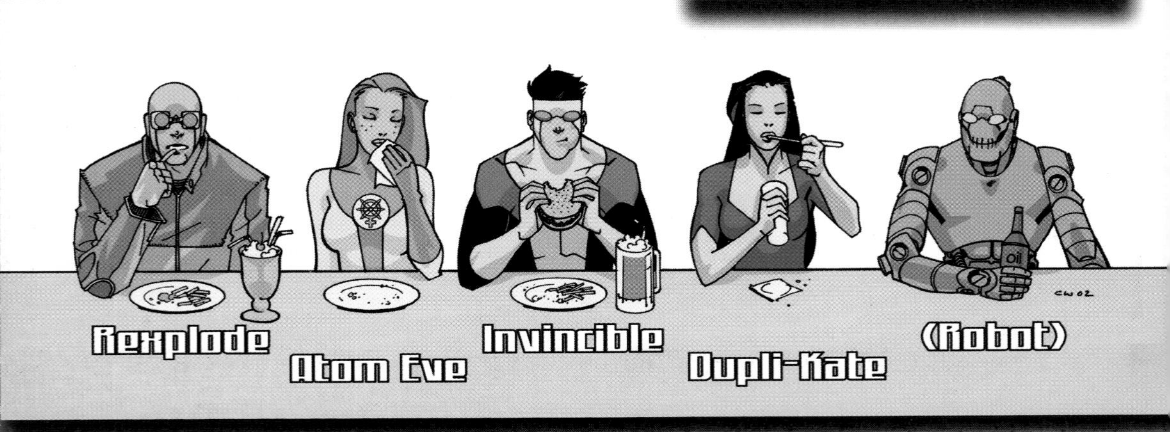
oil
Rexplode
Atom Eve
Invincible
Dupli-Kate
(Robot)

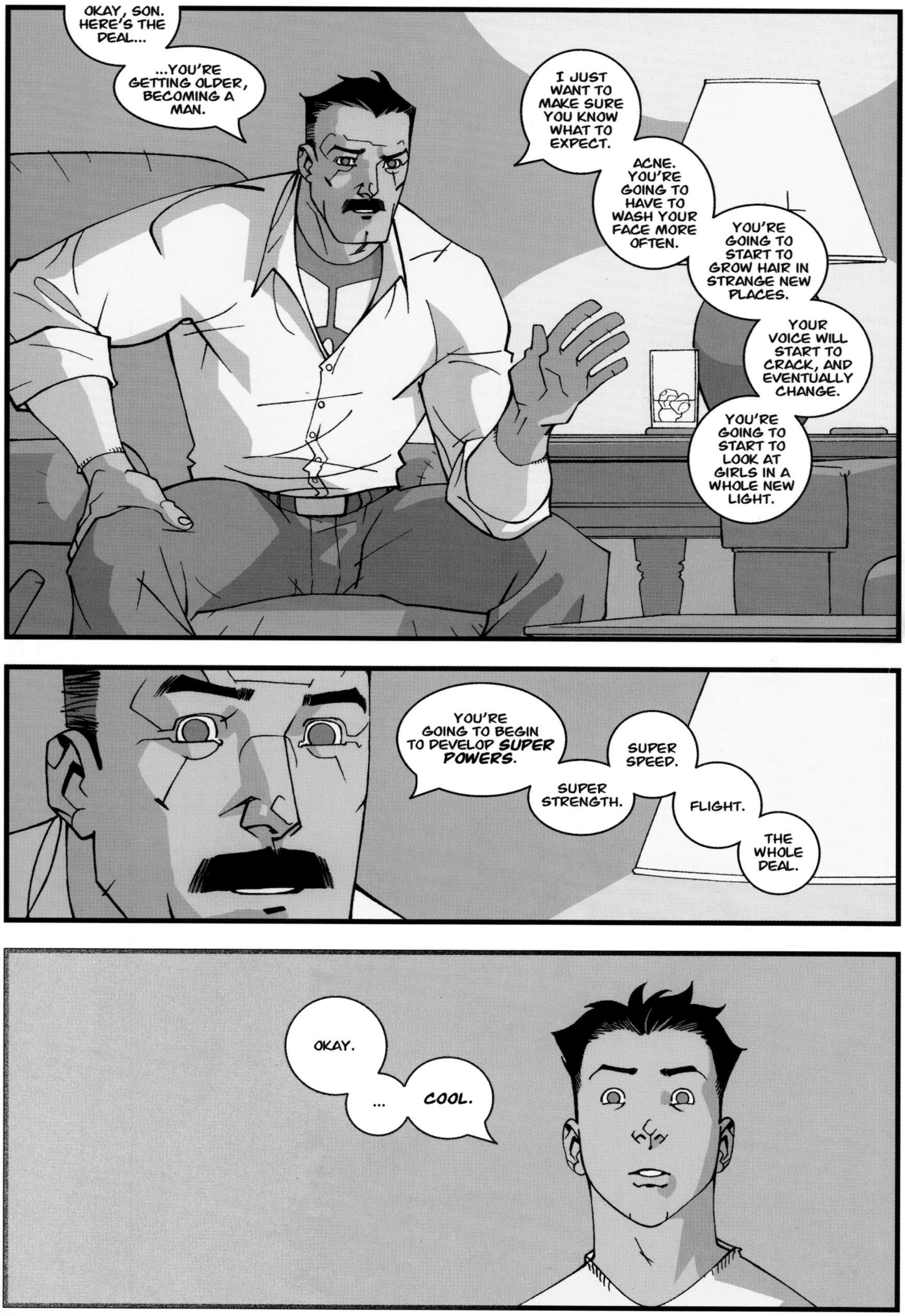
OKAY, SON. HERE'S THE DEAL...
...YOU'RE GETTING OLDER, BECOMING A MAN.
I JUST WANT TO MAKE SURE YOU KNOW WHAT TO EXPECT.
ACNE. YOU'RE GOING TO HAVE TO WASH YOUR FACE MORE OFTEN.
YOU'RE GOING TO START TO GROW HAIR IN STRANGE NEW PLACES.
YOUR VOICE WILL START TO CRACK, AND EVENTUALLY CHANGE.
YOU'RE GOING TO START TO LOOK AT GIRLS IN A WHOLE NEW LIGHT.
YOU'RE GOING TO BEGIN TO DEVELOP **SUPER POWERS**.
SUPER SPEED.
SUPER STRENGTH.
FLIGHT.
THE WHOLE DEAL.
OKAY.
...
COOL.

# PROPOSAL ART

It's a little known fact that Invincible was originally going to be called 'Bulletproof.' The name was changed because Image was publishing *Bulletproof Monk* and they thought it would conflict. Thank god for small miracles, huh? The first image below was going to be the cover of our proposal. This was the original Bulletproof costume. With the name changed, though... Cory and I wanted to somehow work in the letter 'I' to try and make the costume more iconic. Cory came up with the design that's used now and the proposal cover was changed at the last minute. And Yes, he was originally orange instead of blue, but the Bulletproof costume was yellow and blue... I guess we had it right the first time.

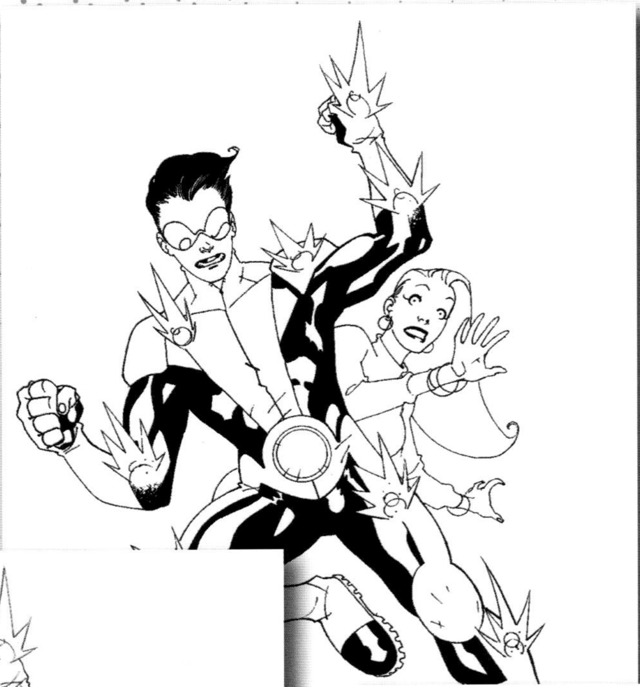

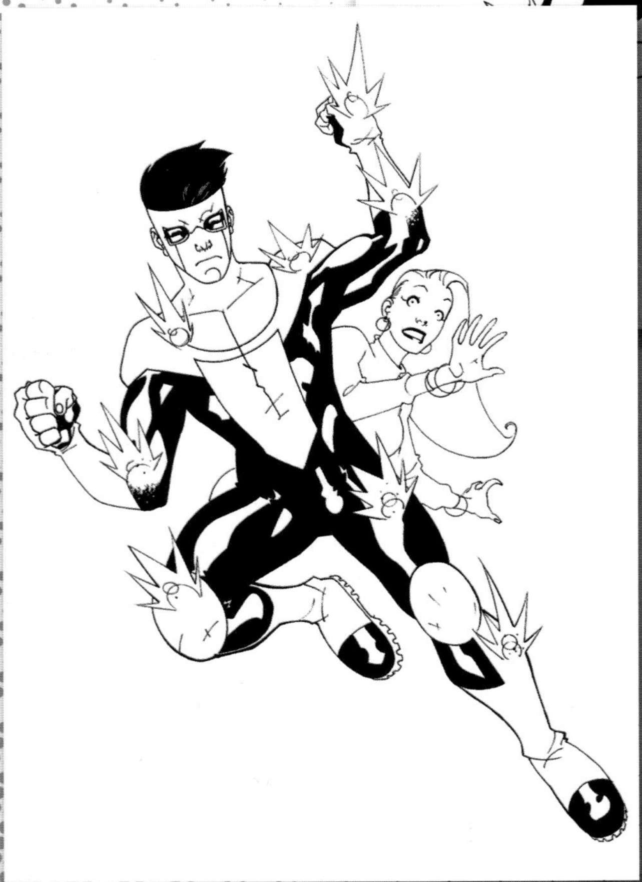

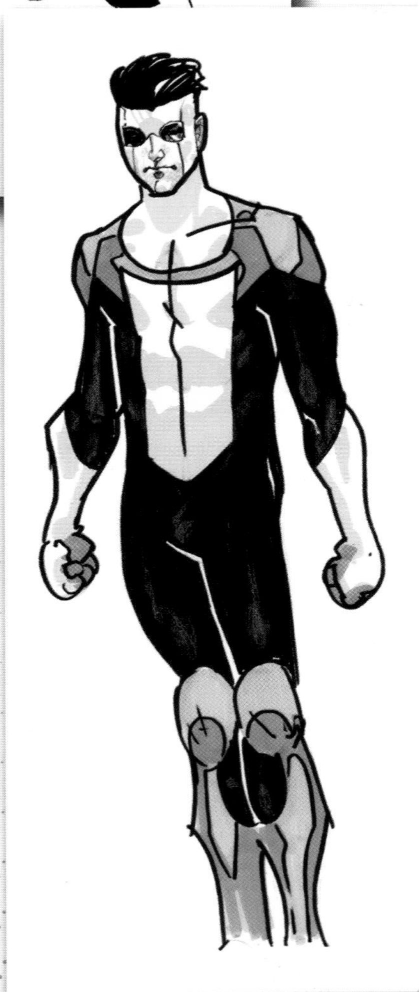

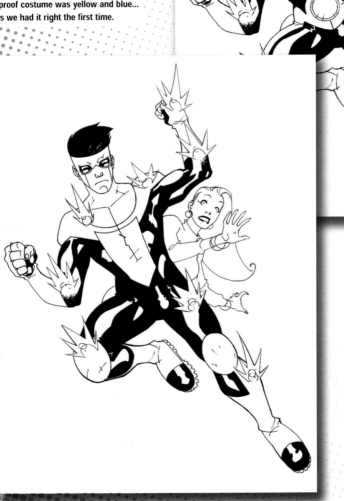

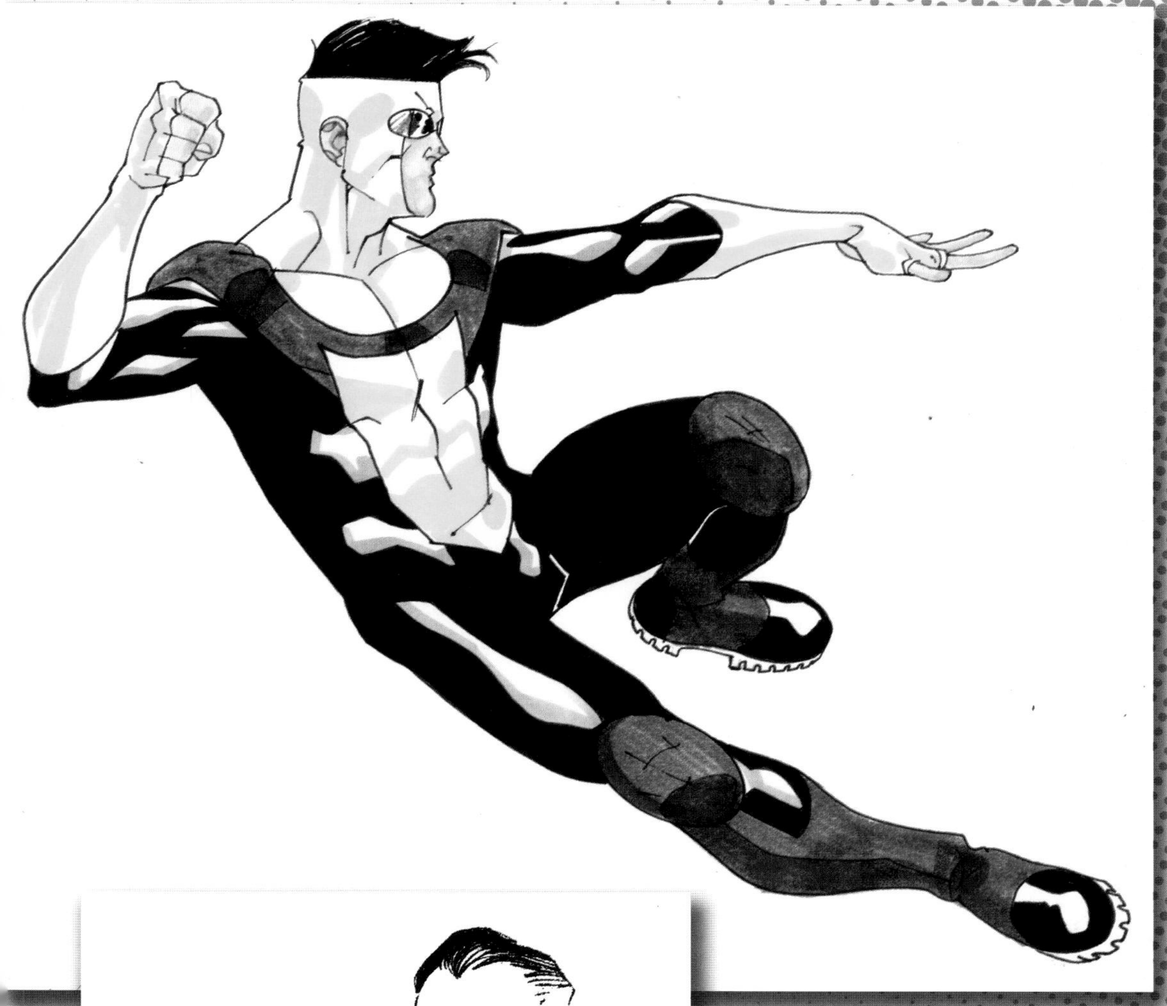

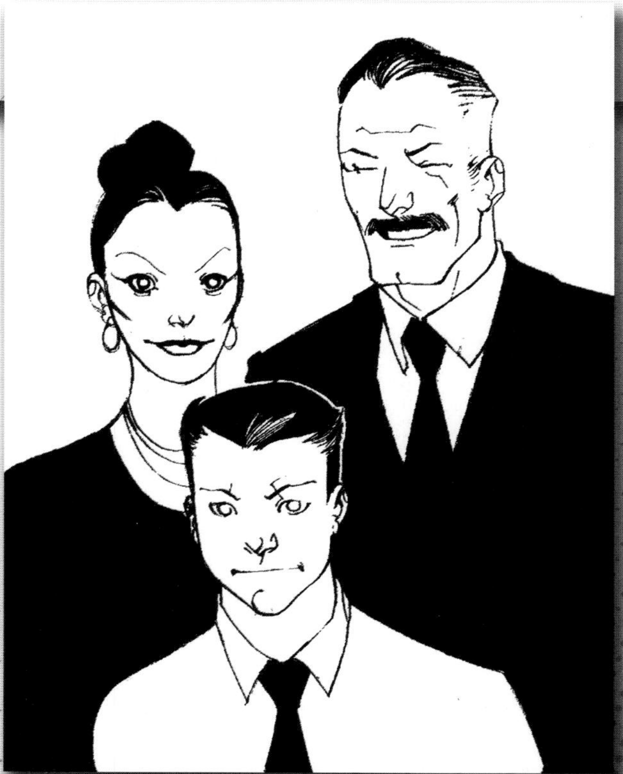

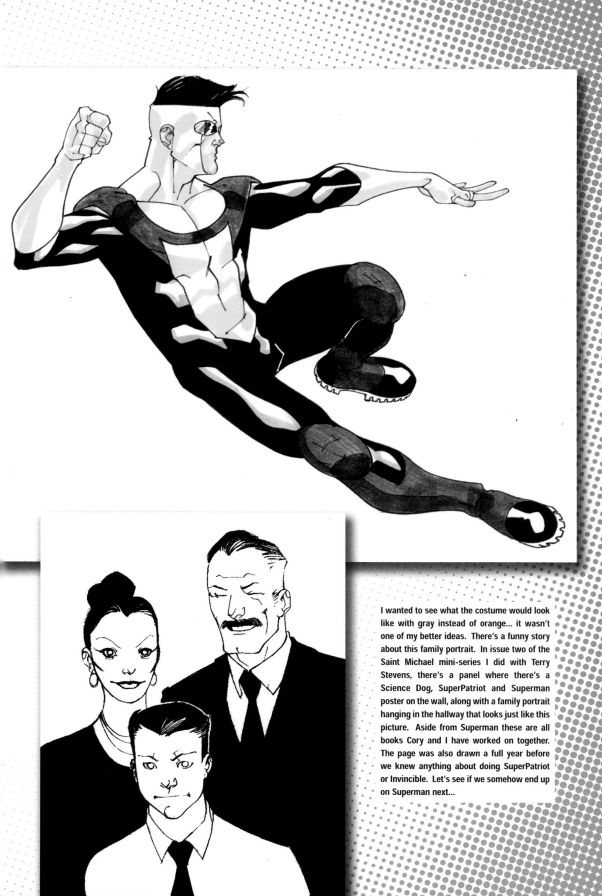

I wanted to see what the costume would look like with gray instead of orange... it wasn't one of my better ideas. There's a funny story about this family portrait. In issue two of the Saint Michael mini-series I did with Terry Stevens, there's a panel where there's a Science Dog, SuperPatriot and Superman poster on the wall, along with a family portrait hanging in the hallway that looks just like this picture. Aside from Superman these are all books Cory and I have worked on together. The page was also drawn a full year before we knew anything about doing SuperPatriot or Invincible. Let's see if we somehow end up on Superman next...

# SKETCHES

Below is the first ever drawing on Bulletproof/Invincible, as well as a couple other drawings from when he was called Bulletproof. Originally... Mark's powers were going to be solar power-based, and the disks were going to be designed by Robot to store solar energy in case of an emergency. Then he was going to have an invisible aura around him that altered the density of stuff to make him able to fly... and super strong... and stuff... but then I found out that's what Jay Faerber and Jamal Igle's guy, Venture did. Now... well... where's the fun if it's explained.

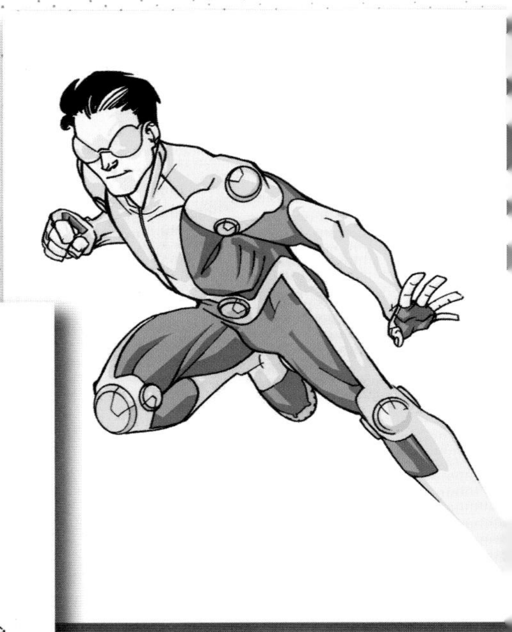

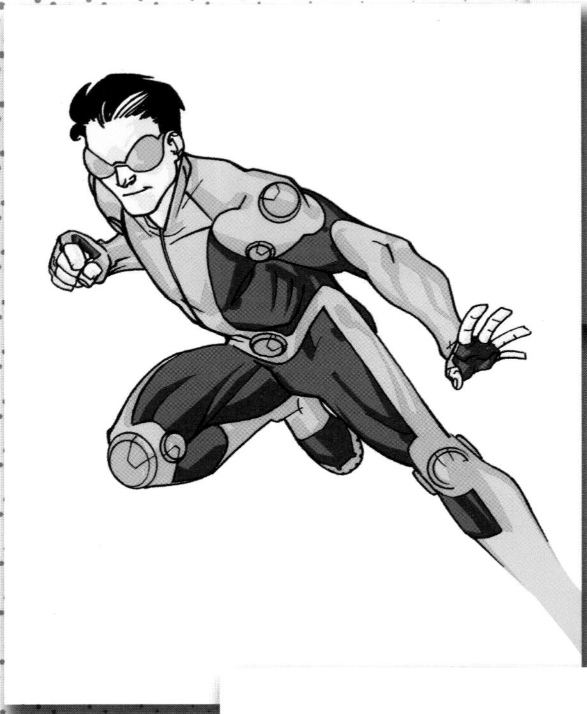

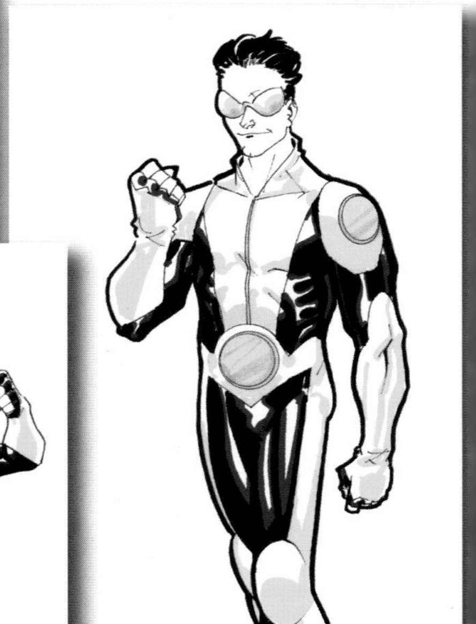

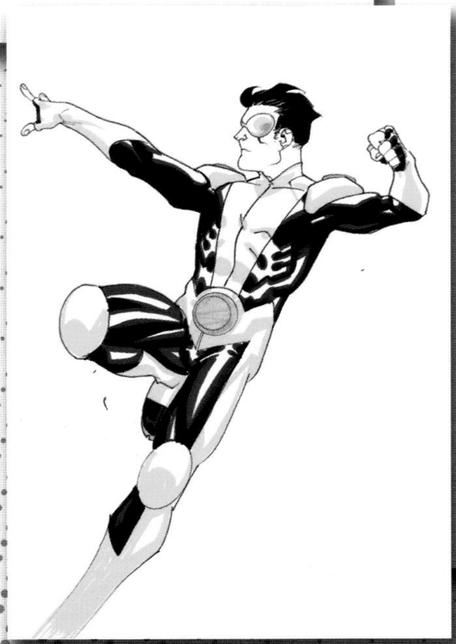

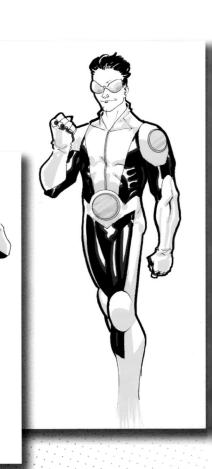

Below are some sketches by me, I'm sure you'll have no trouble picking them out. One was an attempt at putting an 'I' on the Bulletproof costume before Cory came up with the new design that we went with. Another little known fact is that when Invincible was called Bulletproof, Omni-Man was called Supra-Man. Image made us change it fearing that DC might not enjoy us using a name that when pronounced out loud is almost impossible to distinguish from their beloved trademark character. I really liked the undies that Supra-Man wore. When Cory remembered that Nolan came to earth in the '80s and wouldn't really have a classic looking costume, we scrapped this look and went with a more modern one.

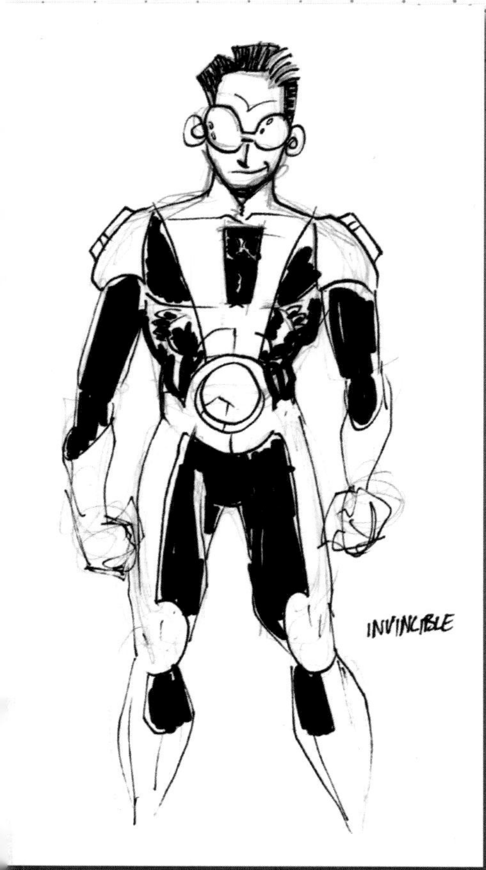
INVINCIBLE

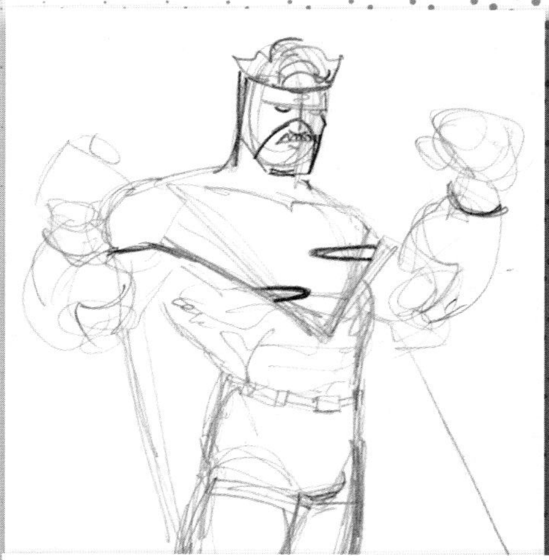

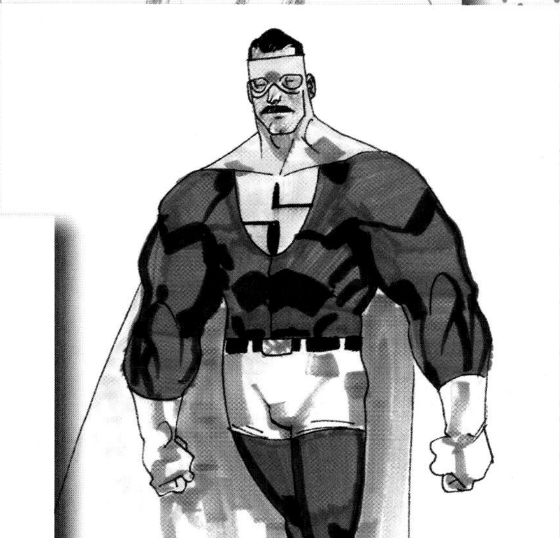
SUPRAMAN

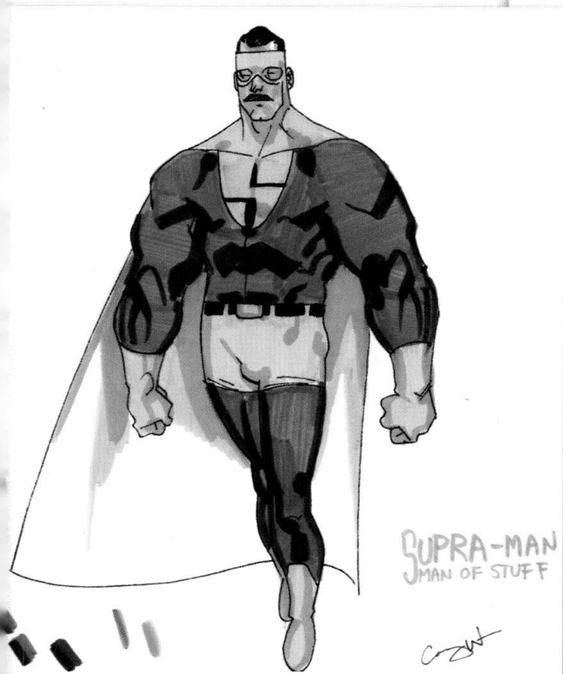
SUPRA-MAN
MAN OF STUFF

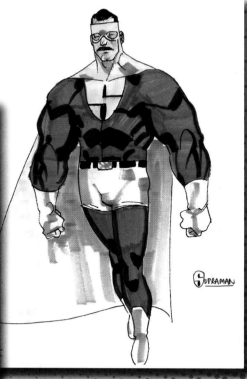

Here are some early designs for the Teen Team, and the first drawing of the more 'modern' costume for Supra-Man/Omni-Man. Robot was all Cory's idea... I really just came up with the know-it-all personality to go with the design. Cory also came up with the BRILLIANT name Atom Eve... but Rex Splode and Dupli-Kate are all me. Some people think the Teen Team's names are a little funky... I prefer to think of them as awesome.

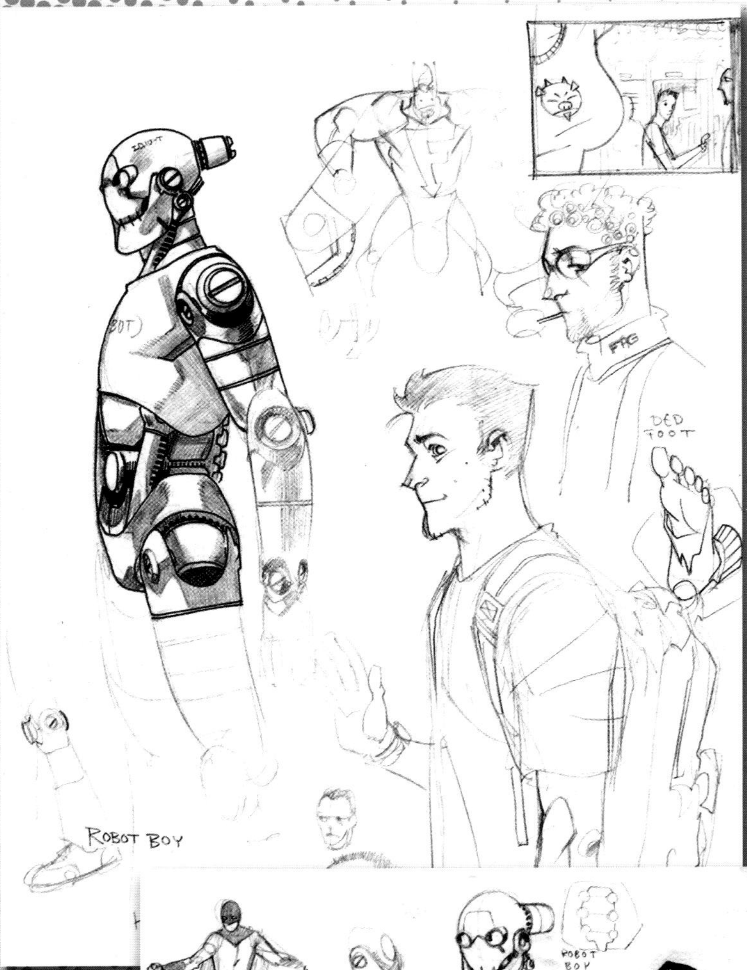
DED FOOT
ROBOT BOY

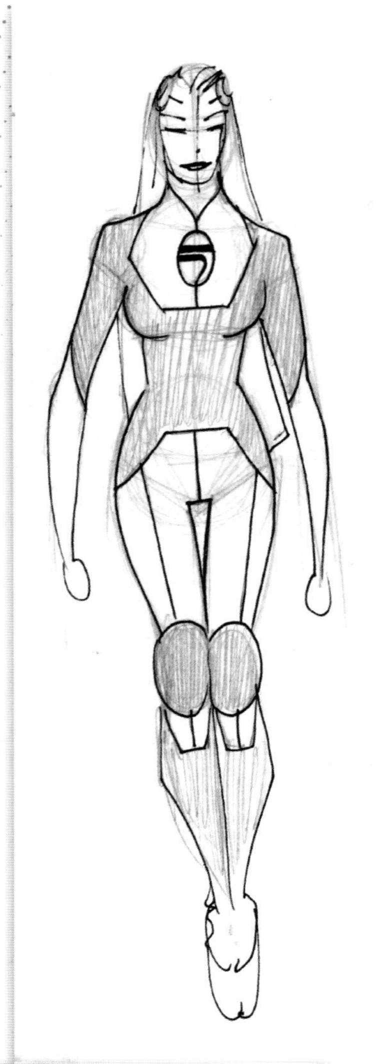

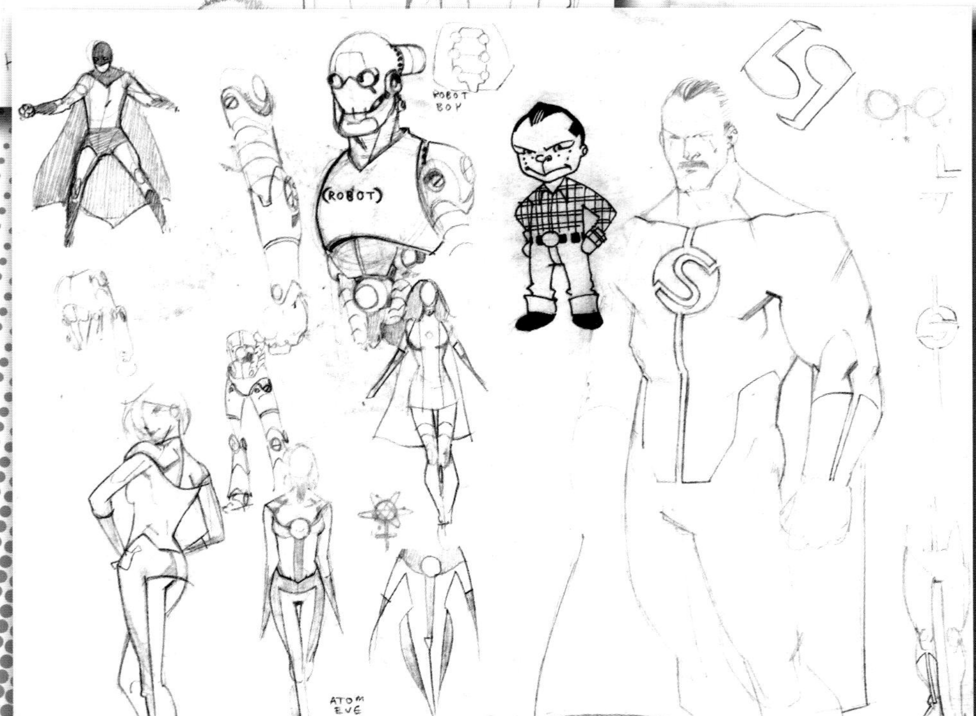
ROBOT BOY
(ROBOT)
ATOM EVE

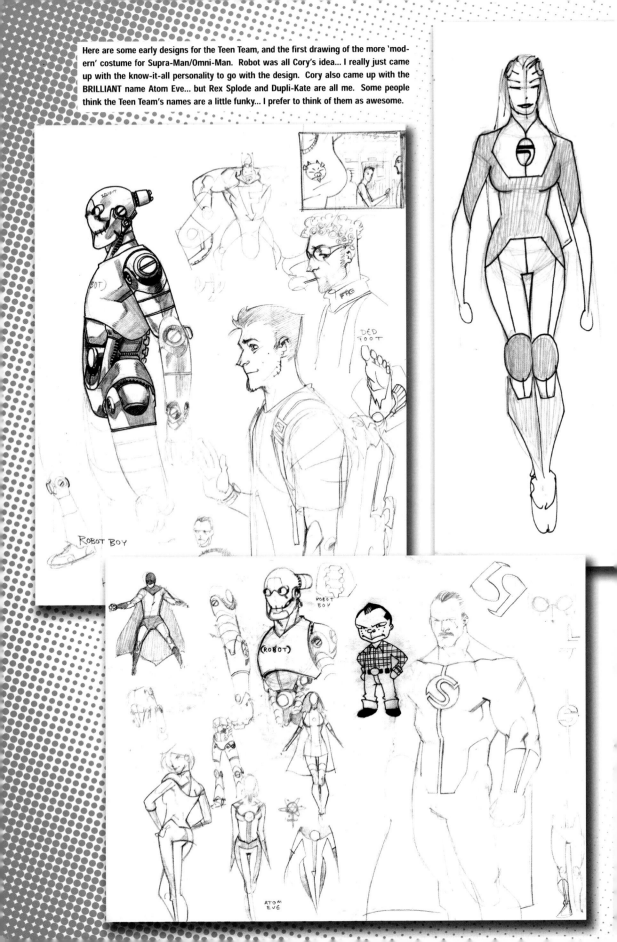

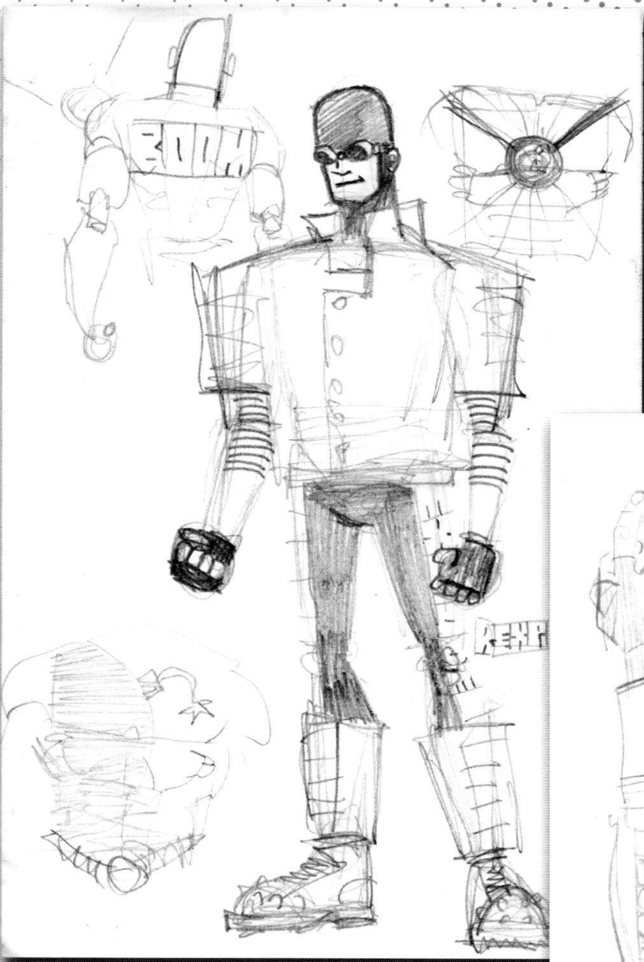

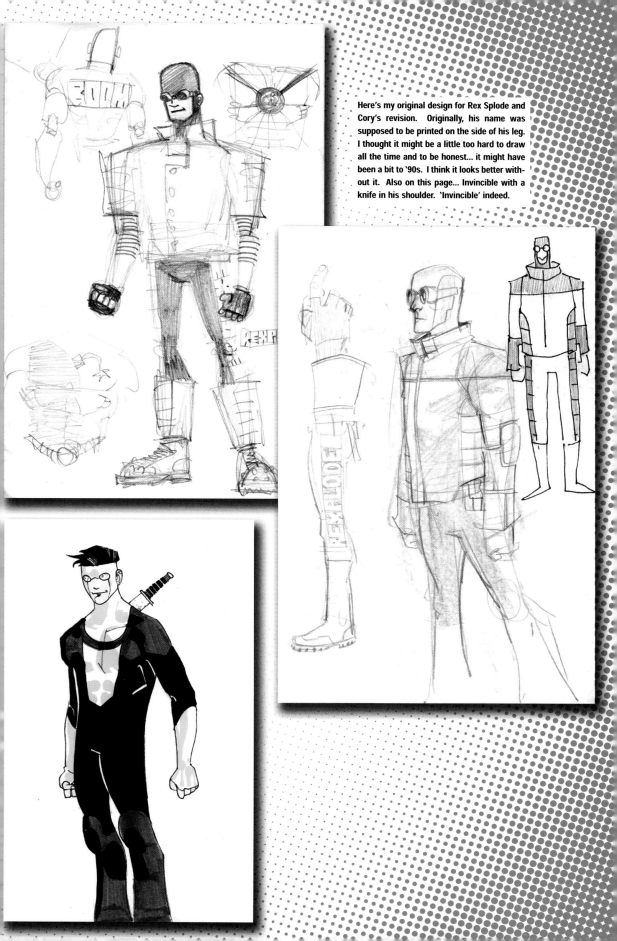

Here's my original design for Rex Splode and Cory's revision. Originally, his name was supposed to be printed on the side of his leg. I thought it might be a little too hard to draw all the time and to be honest... it might have been a bit to '90s. I think it looks better without it. Also on this page... Invincible with a knife in his shoulder. 'Invincible' indeed.

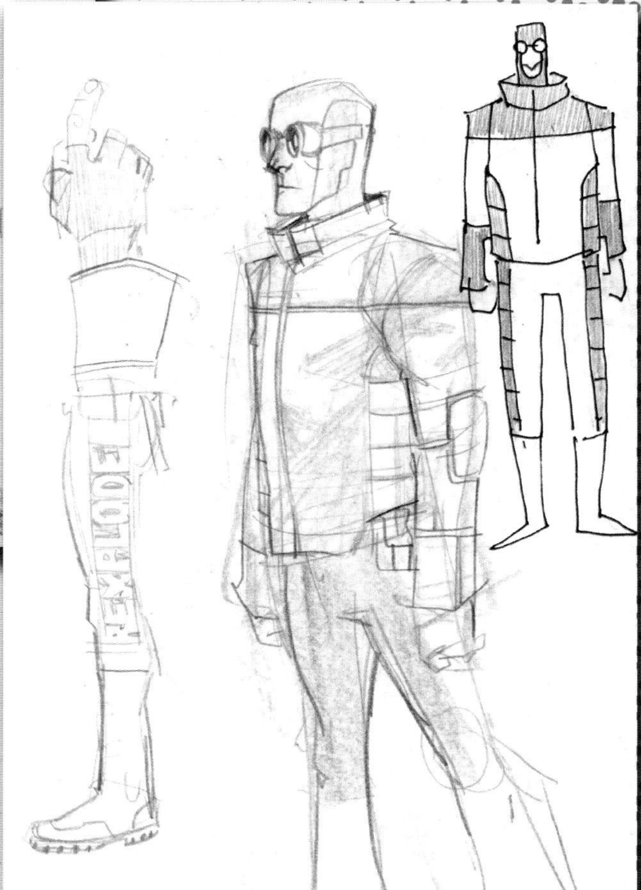

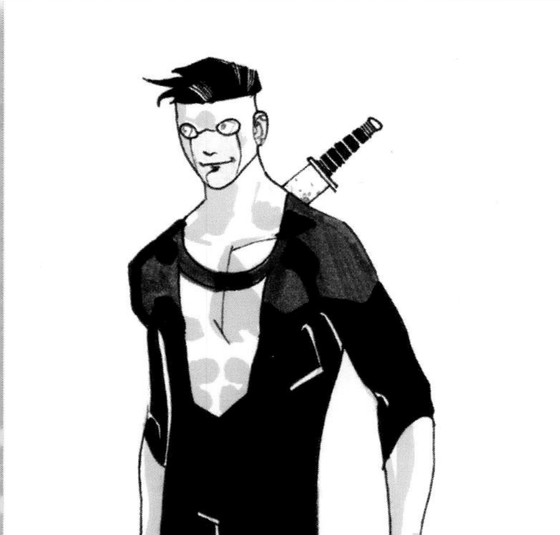

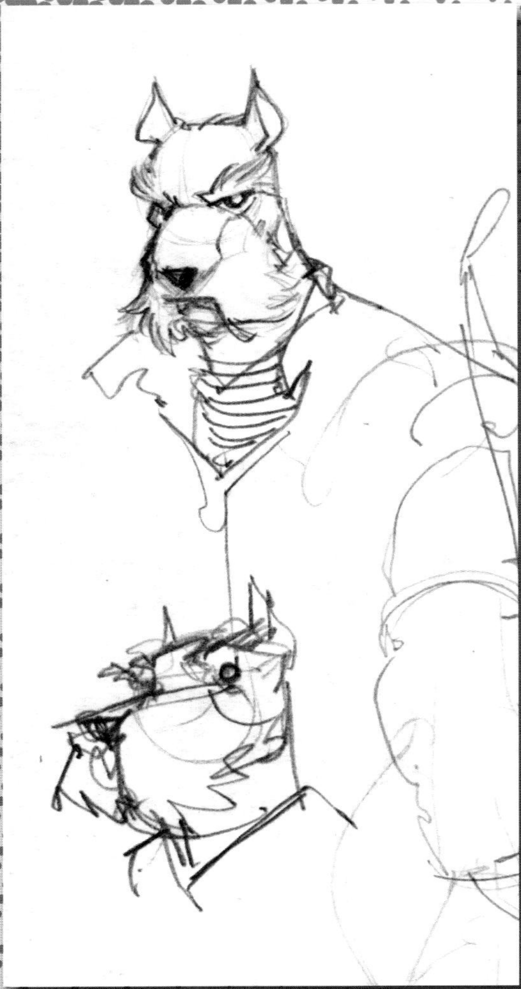

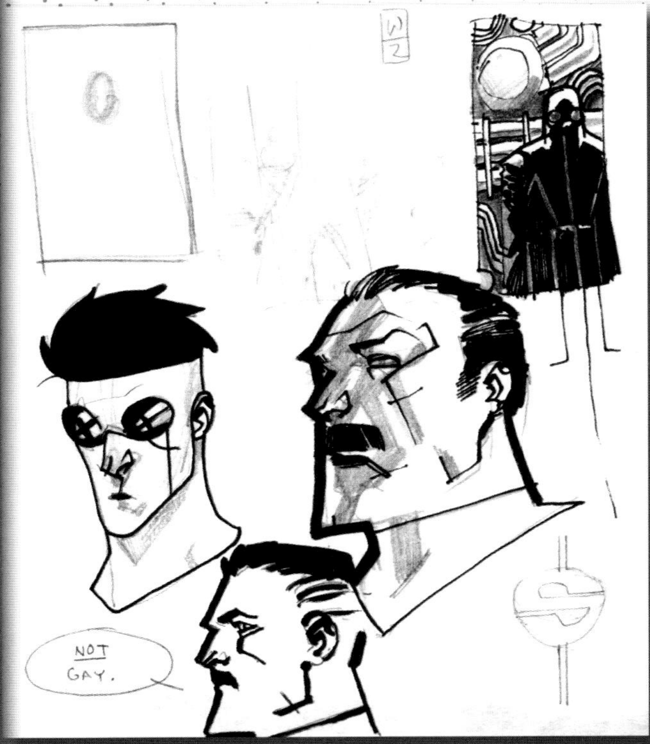
NOT GAY.

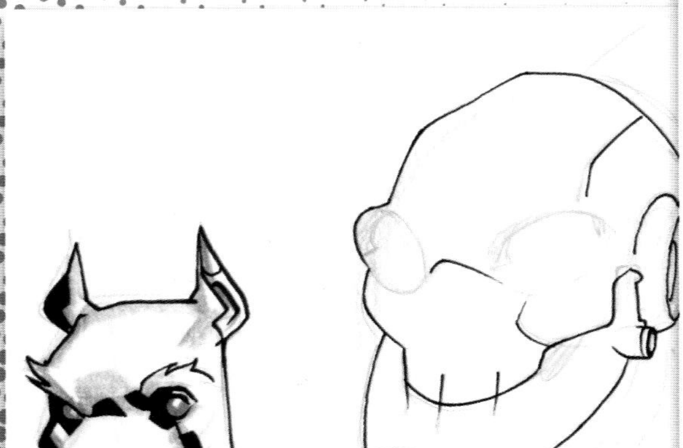

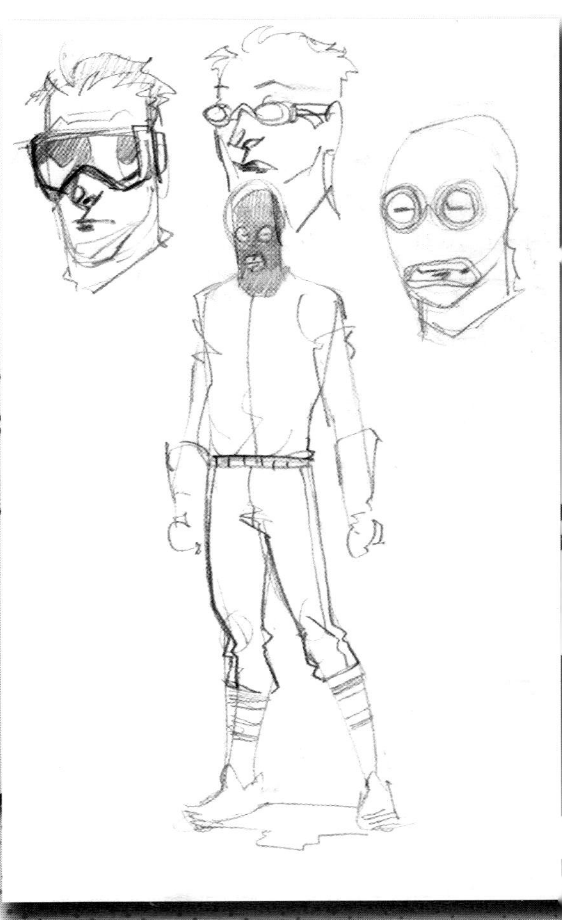

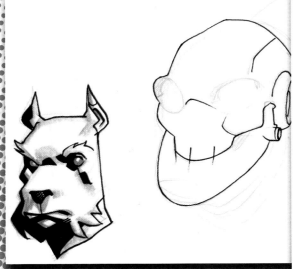

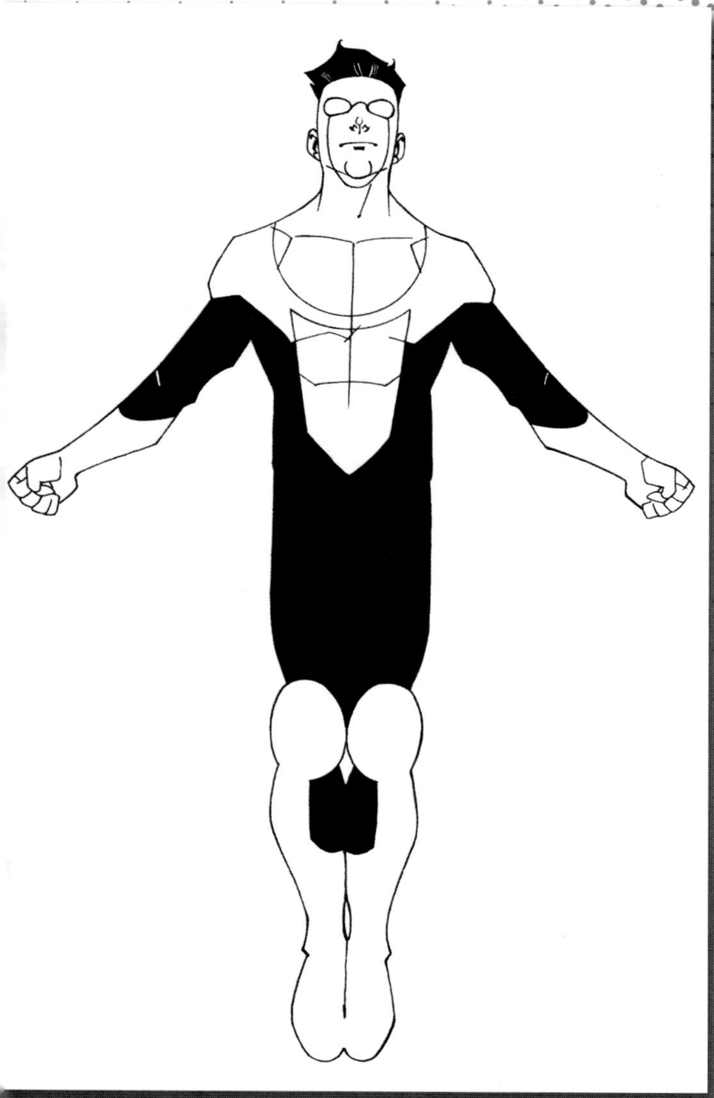

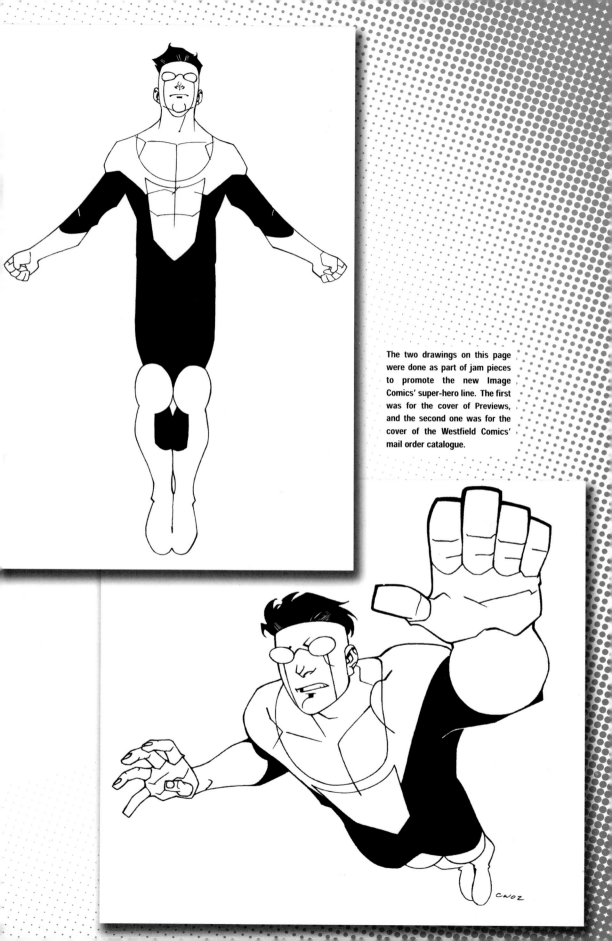

The two drawings on this page were done as part of jam pieces to promote the new Image Comics' super-hero line. The first was for the cover of Previews, and the second one was for the cover of the Westfield Comics' mail order catalogue.

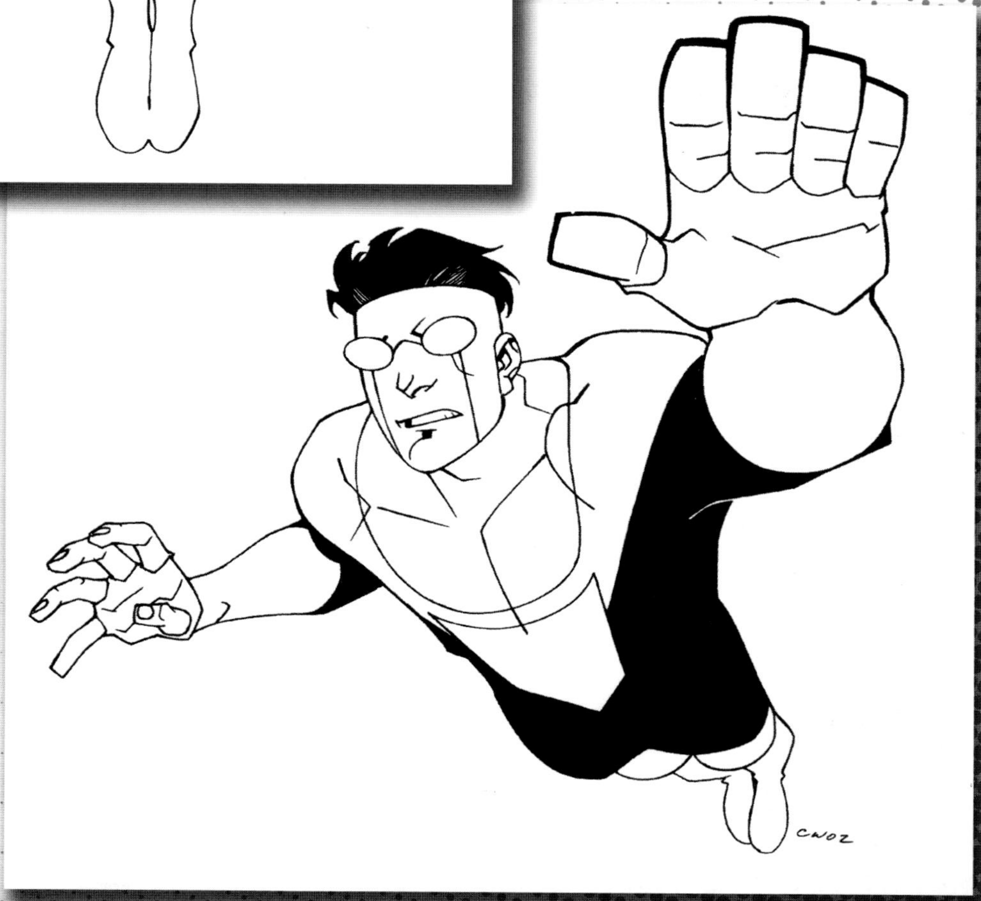
CWOZ

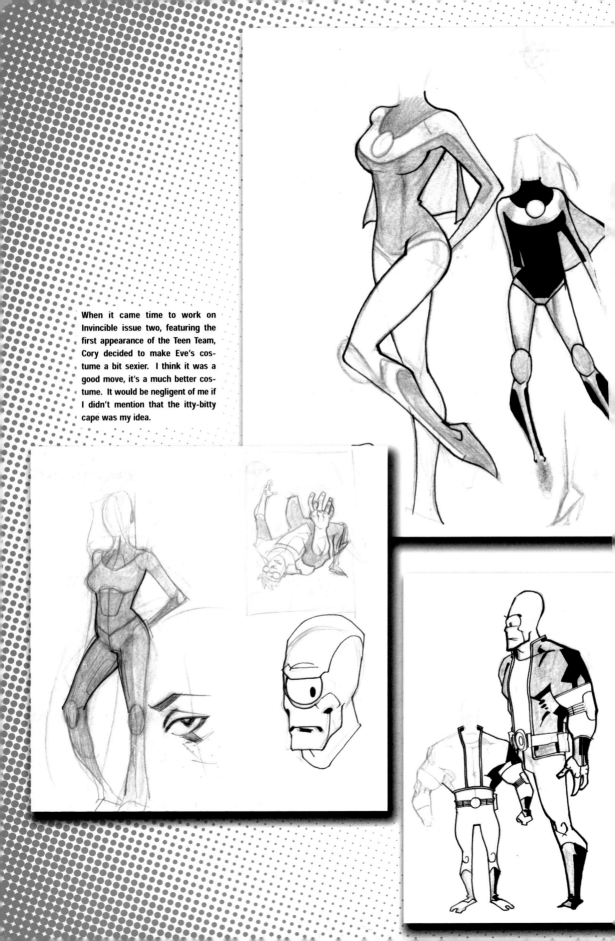

When it came time to work on Invincible issue two, featuring the first appearance of the Teen Team, Cory decided to make Eve's costume a bit sexier. I think it was a good move, it's a much better costume. It would be negligent of me if I didn't mention that the itty-bitty cape was my idea.

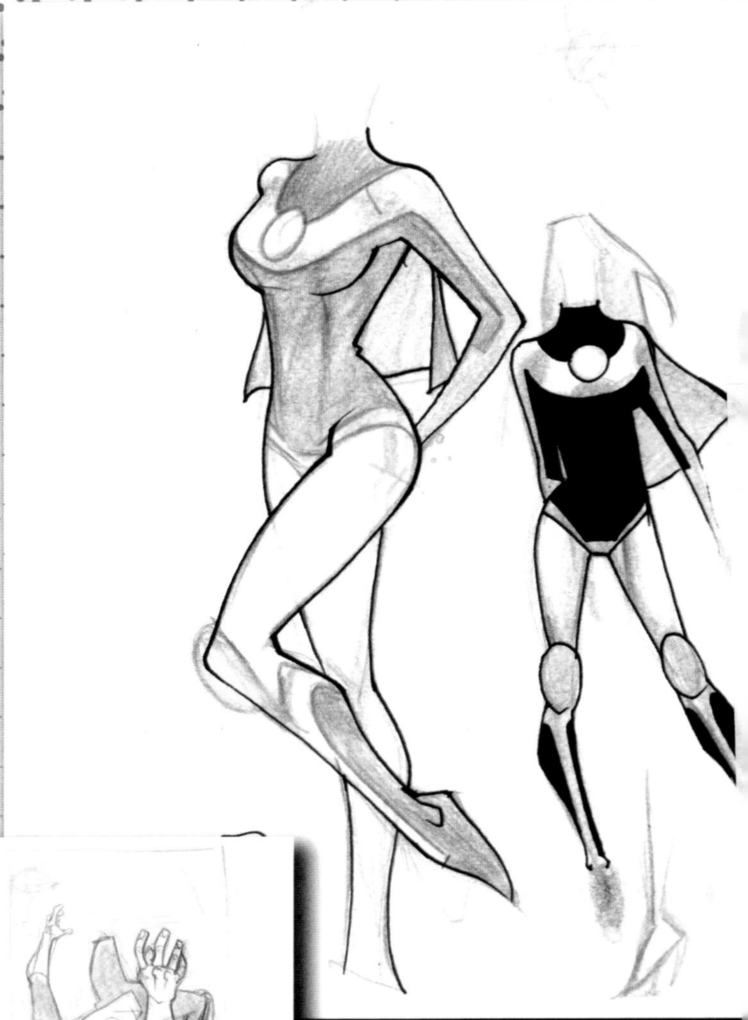

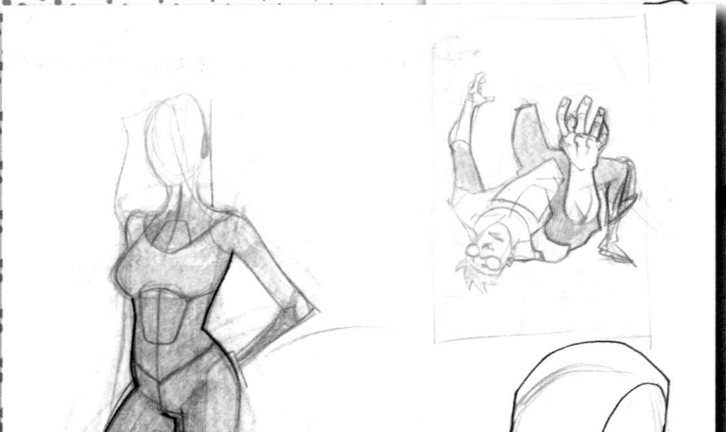

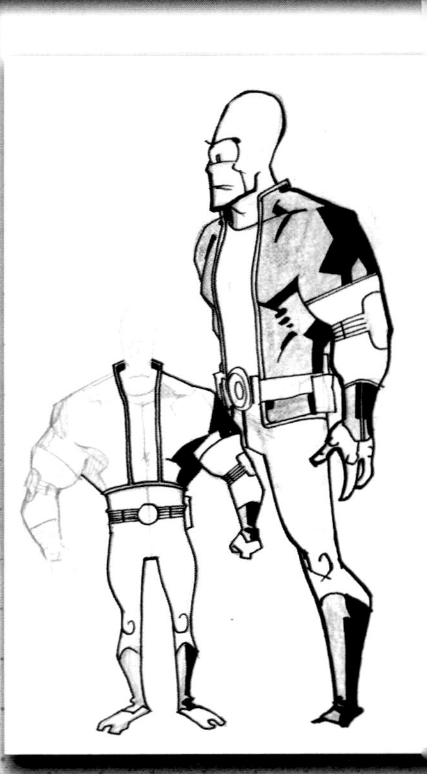

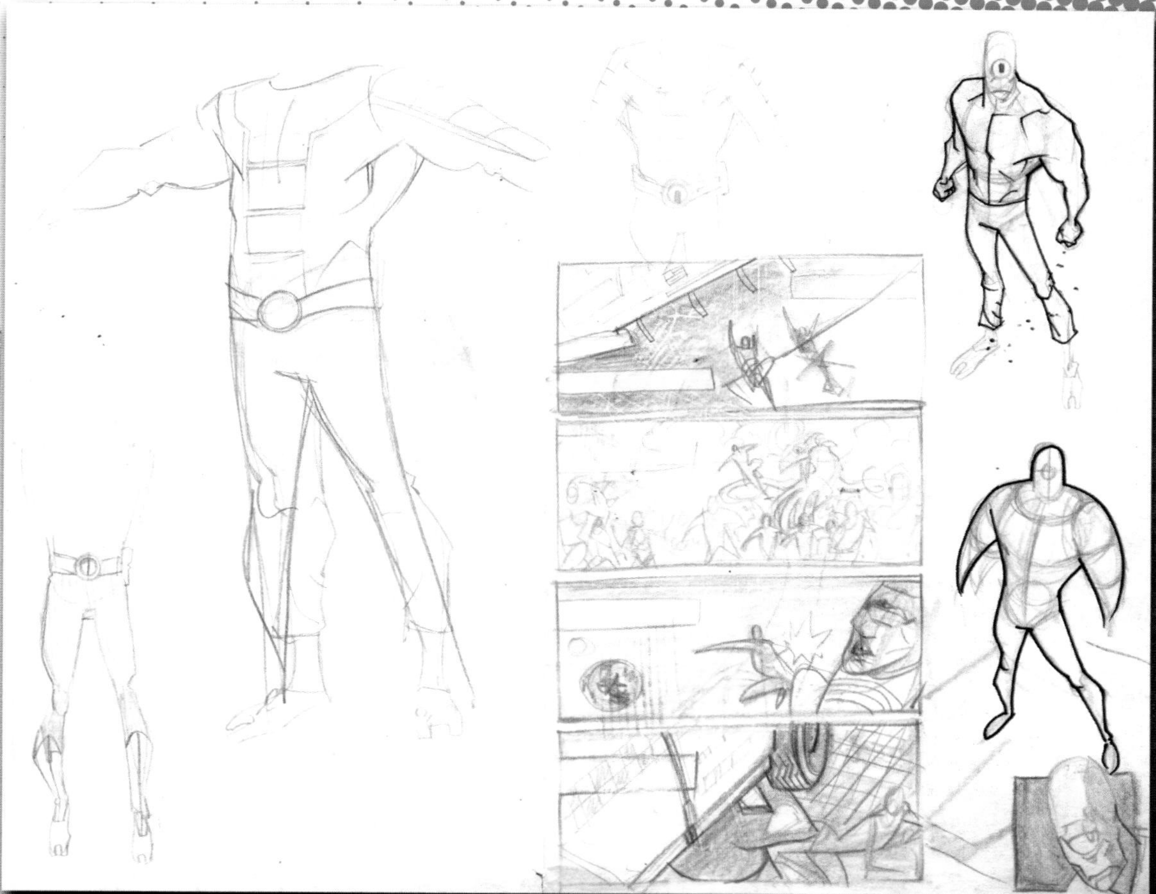

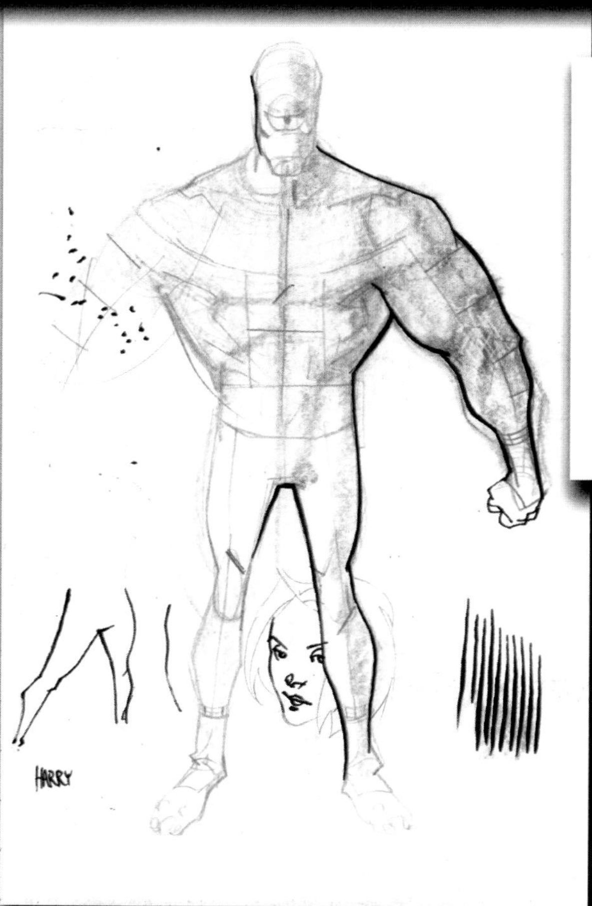

HARRY

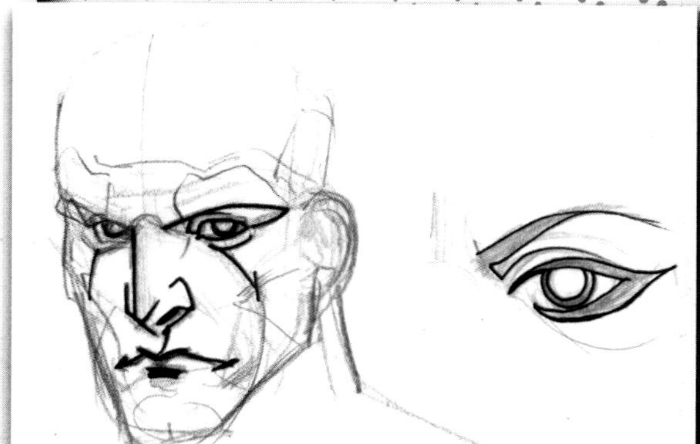

Also making his first appearance in issue two, in one measly panel, is Allen the Alien. His first full appearance is in issue five, but Cory had to get him nailed down while working on issue two.

On this page we see some designs for Mauler, as well as the supporting character William. When we started working on issue one I told Bill Crabtree that I'd try to get Cory to throw him in the book. I think that's always fun to do, and people seem to enjoy it. When I decided which character to make Bill, it was just one of Mark's friends from high school... no big deal. At the time I had forgotten that I had big plans for the guy... so now Bill Crabtree himself is a major supporting character in one of the books he colors.

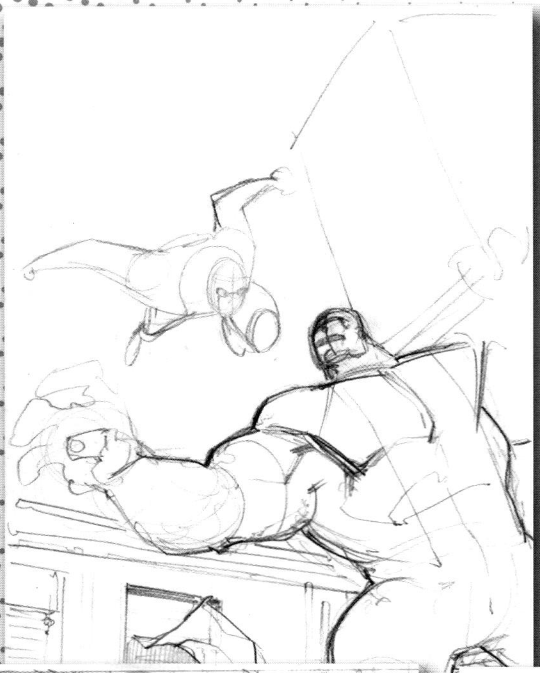

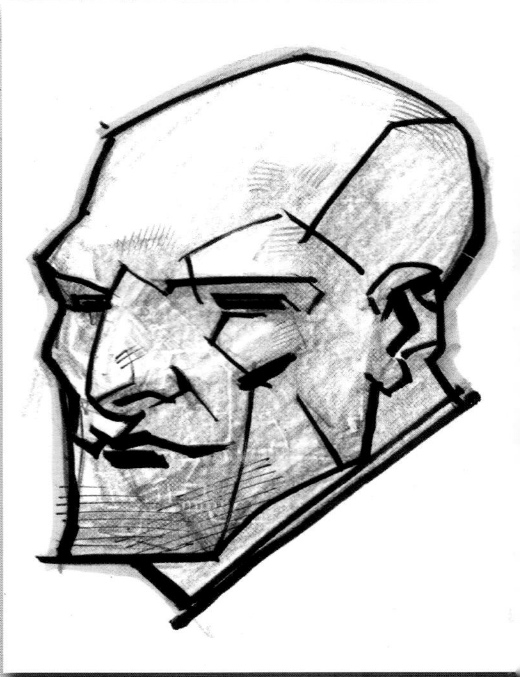

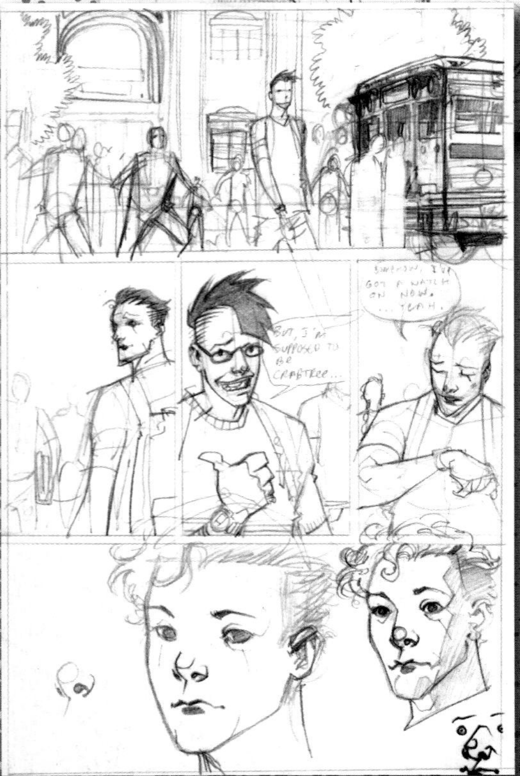
BUT, I'M SUPPOSED TO BE CRABTREE...
GOT A WATCH ON NOW. ...YEAH.

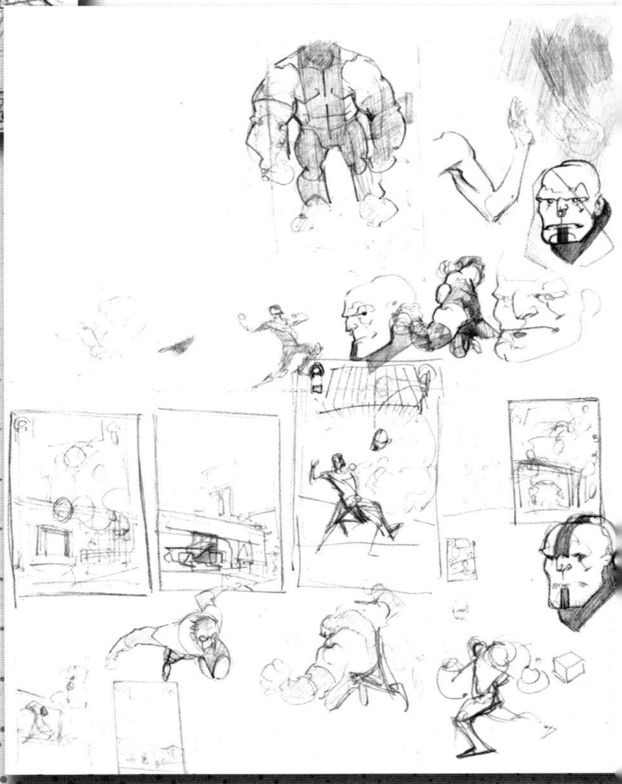

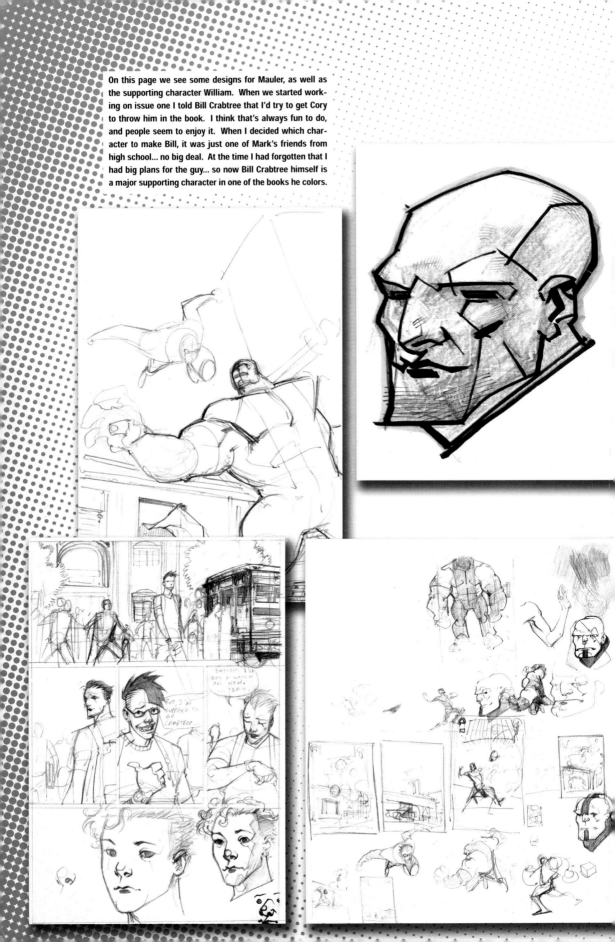

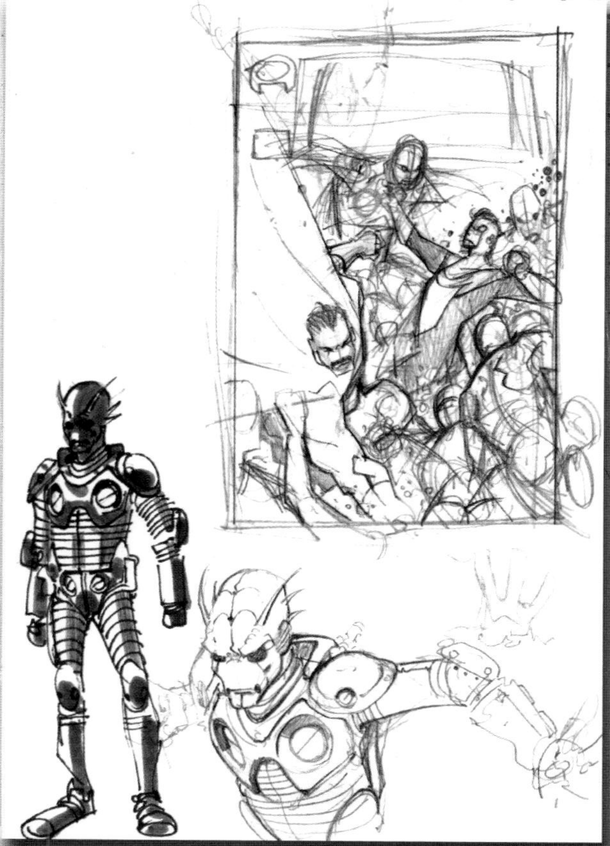

Here we see some designs for the aliens in issue 3... still no name for those guys. Also seen here, the cover sketch for the cover of this very trade. It's based on a suggestion Kurt Busiek had for the cover of issue 2. He didn't seem too keen on most of the covers we did in this arc so I asked him to tell me what he would have done to try and get a feel for what he thought was a good cover. When he suggested this one I thought it would be perfect for the trade. Cory and Bill really hit this one out of the park... I just love how the cover for this book turned out.

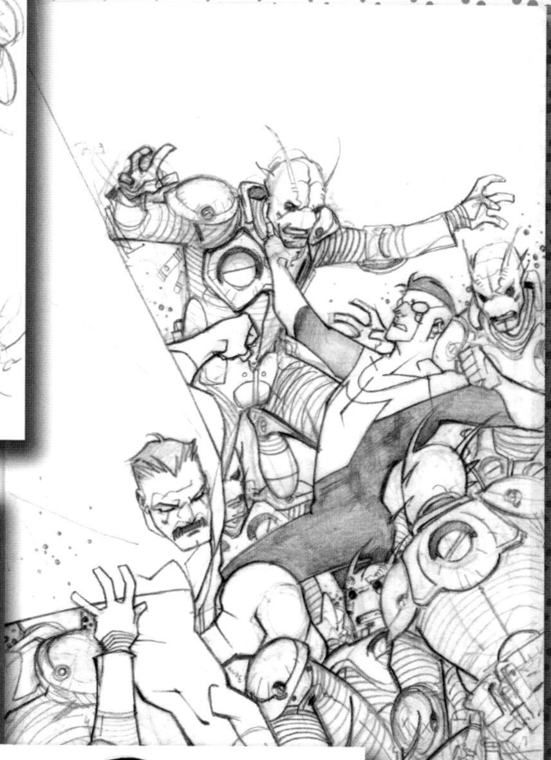

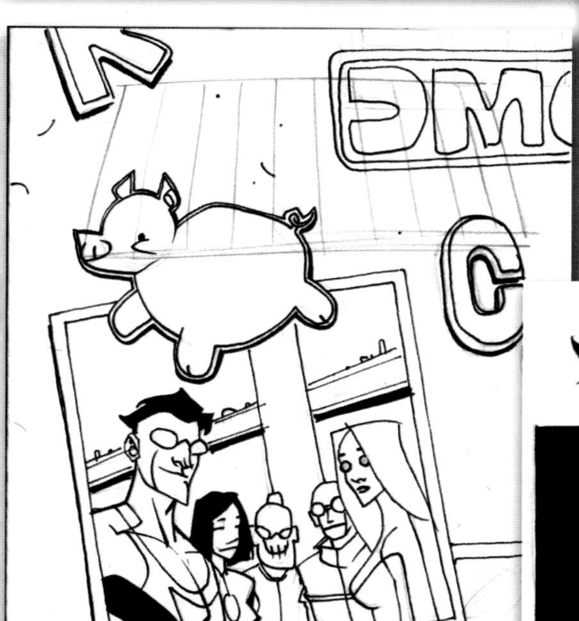
Mark's 1st Team-Up
PING LIST
GGS
ILK
KE MIX

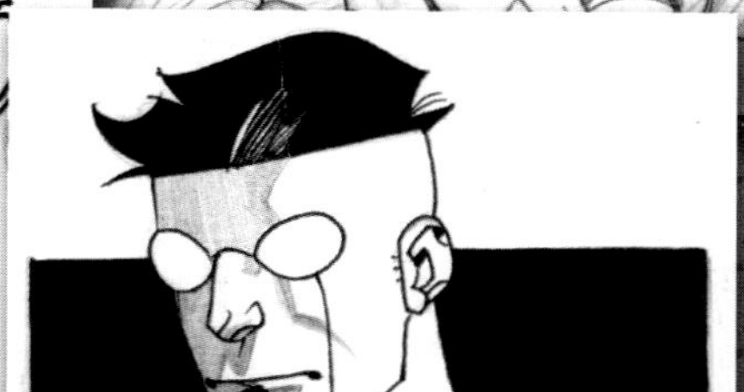
CW 02

# MORE GREAT TITLES FROM IMAGE

**image COMICS**

## BACKLIST

**A DISTANT SOIL VOL I**
**THE GATHERING**
ISBN: 1-887259-51-2
STAR07382

**AGE OF BRONZE VOL I**
**A THOUSAND SHIPS**
ISBN: 1-58240-2000
STAR13458

**ARIA VOL I**
**THE MAGIC OF ARIA**
ISBN: 1-58240-139-X
STAR11559

**AVIGON**
ISBN: 1-58240-182-9
STAR11946

**BLUNTMAN AND CHRONIC**
1-58240-208-6
STAR13070

**BULLETPROOF MONK**
ISBN: 1-58240-244-2
STAR16331

**CHASING DOGMA**
ISBN: 1-58240-206-X
STAR13071

**CLERKS**
THE COMIC BOOKS
ISBN: 1-58240-209-4
STAR13071

**DARKNESS VOL I**
**COMING OF AGE**
ISBN: 1-58240-032-6
STAR08526

**DAWN VOL II**
**RETURN OF THE GODDESS**
ISBN: 1-58240-242-6
STAR15771

**DELICATE CREATURES**
ISBN: 1-58240-225-6
STAR14906

**E.V.E. PROTOMECHA VOL I**
**SINS OF THE DAUGHTER**
ISBN: 1-58240-214-0
STAR13075

**FATHOM VOL I**
ISBN: 1-58240-210-8
STAR15804

**G.I. JOE VOL I**
**REINSTATED**
ISBN: 1-58240-252-3
STAR16642

**GOLDFISH**
**THE DEFINITIVE COLLECTION**
ISBN: 1-58240-195-0
STAR13576

**JINX**
**THE DEFINITIVE COLLECTION**
ISBN: 1-58240-179-9
STAR13039

**KABUKI VOL I**
**CIRCLE OF BLOOD**
ISBN: 1-88727-9-806
STAR12480

**KIN VOL I**
**DESCENT OF MAN**
**ISBN: 1-58240-224-8**
**STAR15032**

**LAZARUS CHURCHYARD**
**THE FINAL CUT**
ISBN: 1-58240-180-2
STAR12720

**LEAVE IT TO CHANCE VOL I**
**SHAMAN'S RAIN**
ISBN: 1-58240-253-1
STAR16641

**LIBERTY MEADOWS VOL I**
**EDEN**
ISBN: 1-58240-260-4
STAR16143

**MAGDALENA VOL I**
**BLOOD DIVINE**
ISBN: 1-58240-215-9
STAR15519

**MAGE:**
**THE HERO DEFINED VOL I**
ISBN: 1-58240-012-1
STAR08160

**NOWHERESVILLE**
ISBN: 1-58240-241-8
STAR15904

**OBERGEIST VOL I**
**THE DIRECTOR'S CUT**
ISBN: 1-58240-243-4
STAR15853

**POWERS VOL I**
**WHO KILLED RETRO GIRL?**
ISBN: 1-58240-223-X
STAR12482

**RISING STARS VOL I**
**BORN IN FIRE**
ISBN: 1-58240-172-1
STAR12207

**SAVAGE DRAGON VOL I**
**BAPTISM OF FIRE**
ISBN: 1-58240-165-9
STAR13080

**TELLOS VOL I**
**RELUCTANT HEROES**
ISBN: 1-58240-186-1
STAR12831

**TOMB RAIDER VOL I**
**SAGA OF THE MEDUSA MASK**
ISBN: 1-58240-164-0
STAR03000

**TORSO**
**THE DEFINITIVE COLLECTION**
ISBN: 1-58240-174-8
STAR12688

**VIOLENT MESSIAHS VOL I**
**THE BOOK OF JOB**
ISBN: 1-58240-236-1
STAR160053

**WITCHBLADE VOL I**
**ORIGINS**
ISBN: 1-887279-65-2
STAR07991

**ZORRO**
**THE COMPLETE ALEX TOTH**
ISBN: 1-58240-090-3
STAR14527

For The Comic Shop
Near You Carrying
Comics And
Collections From
Image Comics,
Please Call Toll
Free
1-888-Comic Book.